Growing Up NASCAR

Racing's Most Outrageous
Promoter Tells All

Humpy Wheeler and
Peter Golenbock

First published in 2010 by MBI Publishing Company LLC and Motorbooks, an imprint of
MBI Publishing Company, 400 First Avenue North, Suite 300, Minneapolis, MN, 55401 USA

The information in this book is true and complete to the best of our knowledge. All
recommendations are made without any guarantee on the part of the author or Publisher, who
also disclaim any liability incurred in connection with the use of this data or specific details.

We recognize, further, that some words, model names, and designations mentioned herein
are the property of the trademark holder. We use them for identification purposes only.
This is not an official publication.

MBI Publishing Company titles are also available at discounts in bulk quantity for
industrial or sales-promotional use. For details write to Special Sales Manager at MBI
Publishing Company, 400 First Avenue North, Suite 300, Minneapolis, MN, 55401 USA

To find out more about our books, visit us online at www.motorbooks.com.

ISBN-13: 978-0-7603-3775-2

Library of Congress Cataloging-in-Publication Data

Wheeler, Humpy.
  Growing up NASCAR : racing's most outrageous promoter tells all / Humpy Wheeler,
Peter Golenbock.
    p. cm.
  ISBN 978-0-7603-3775-2 (hb w/ jkt)
  1. Stock car racing--United States. 2. NASCAR (Association). 3. Racetracks (Automobile
racing)--United States. 4. Wheeler, Humpy. 5. Promoters--United States--Biography. I.
Golenbock, Peter, 1946- II. Title.
  GV1029.9.S74W48 2010
  796.720973--dc22
                                    2009049814

Editor: Darwin Holmstrom
Design Manager: Brenda C. Canales
Layout: Diana Boger
Cover designer: John Barnett
Front cover illustration: Deb Hoeffner
Back cover photo: Nancy Pierce/Time Life Pictures/Getty Images.

Printed in the United States of America

Contents

CHAPTER 1

We Watched the Race Cars Go By

I WAS BORN HOWARD WHEELER IN 1938, but everyone except my mother, brother, and sister called me Humpy. Actually, I am Humpy Jr. My father, Howard Wheeler Sr., played on the Red Grange, Illinois, football team. Bob Zuppke, the famous coach, caught my dad smoking Camel cigarettes his sophomore year. After that, before every practice, Zuppke made Dad run around the field for thirty minutes. From the Camel cigarettes logo, his teammates began calling him Humpy. He later became a coach, and you can't get rid of a nickname in sports. So, when I was born, I became Little Humpy. Then I got into sports, and I have always remained Humpy.

I grew up in Belmont, North Carolina, about seven miles from the old Charlotte Speedway. By the time I was nine years old, there were 5,000 people and 26 cotton mills and absolutely nothing to do.

During World War II, I lived with my grandparents in Bessemer City. My grandfather, Nathan Dobbins, was a carpenter who built houses. This was back in the days when you built a house from start to finish. You framed it, wired it, walled it, roofed it, and painted it. My grandfather could do all of that. My grandfather would let me go out to the woodworking shop with him, and he'd run the lathe and let me learn how to do it.

My grandfather rolled his own cigarettes. He smoked Bugler tobacco, which he carried in a pouch. He had two acres of land on which he grew vegetables, and he had half an acre of chickens. By the time I was five years old, I had learned to wring a chicken's neck and chop off its head. My grandmother also was self-sufficient. We didn't go to the grocery store a whole lot. She bought meat. My grandfather would go down to the flour mill and buy corn and biscuit flour, and my grandmother would can preserves from fruit they grew for the winter. She cooked on a wood stove with no dials or gauges.

THERE WAS VERY LITTLE entertainment. It was gaunt living. Simple pleasures were appreciated. Most people were living hand to mouth, because, generally, they had four or five kids.

There was no TV. Well, there was TV, but no one had one. After we moved to Belmont, the big decision on Saturday afternoons was where to go to the movies. There was always at least one movie theater in a mill town, and it was always set apart from downtown. We would go to the Iris Theater, named after the owner's wife. The other theater was in the East End—as though the town was big enough to have an East End—but the film had to be damn good for my brother and me to go there, because, if you went, you knew you would have to fight your way back home. It was like being in Baghdad. You had to fight block to block to get home.

The railroad tracks were a block from our house. We lived across the tracks in the wealthier area, though it was a territorial thing more than a class thing. The East End started at the tracks. To the kids from the East End, I was a stranger, and they didn't like strangers coming into their territory. They especially didn't want the so-called "uptown kids" around their neighborhood.

I was eleven, and my brother was eight. We'd go to the movies down there, and then we'd quietly leave, and trouble usually started a block or two later with a rock. Or taunting: "We're going to whip your ass." As we got older, it got worse. Those teenage fights could become really vicious. Not only was there territorial warfare, but intercity as well. Mount Holly was two miles away, and if those boys came to Belmont, there was a fight. If we went over there, there was a fight. No question about it. It was so bad that there wasn't a high school football game without a fight in the stands or somewhere else after the game.

Three of the meanest towns were Belmont, Gaffney, and Lincolnton. Fortunately, there was a rigid code of conduct, so there were no knives or blackjacks or guns. Anyone who pulled a knife was a chicken, a blackjack was totally unfair, and a gun was taboo.

There was a meanness in the Scotch-Irish culture that didn't exist in other cultures. This was because of the poverty—a dour existence—and the lack of ability to laugh and have fun like the Italians do. It also had to do with very strict religious codes that left no place to vent your temper. Some of the fundamentalist religions would not even permit women to wear makeup. They had to wear long dresses, and the lack of access to women added to everyone's irritability.

Alcohol laws also contributed to the meanness and violence that were part of the South's culture. You couldn't legally buy alcohol in a lot of counties in North Carolina. So, instead of having a drink every night, on Friday night you might drink a whole bottle, and that led to trouble. The Scotch-Irish didn't have the tolerance for alcohol that the French or the Italians or even the regular Irish did. After the Scotch-Irish drank, they lost their tempers very quickly.

There was something the Scots called "the red." At the point when someone goes "red," that's the point when you don't want to be around them. You'd say, "Uh-oh, Johnny's going to go red on us." You didn't want to fool around with Johnny when that happened.

And they tended to gang up. There would be groups of boys who would gang up and pick on you. When I was thirteen, I delivered papers. I was probably two miles from my home one afternoon when a gang of six boys I knew pulled up in a car beside me and pushed me off a bank, sending my papers flying into a ditch. A mailman, who had been a Marine in World War II, saw what was going on, and he came to my rescue and stopped it. I told myself, *I'm going to get every damn one of them back individually, one by one.*

After I learned how to fight, and before I was sixteen, I did just that. I would walk up to each one and say, "Do you remember the time you pushed me into that ditch?" And then—whap!

Growing up Catholic in a Scotch-Irish universe, I spent most of my childhood mad. One outlet I embraced to channel my anger was the sport of boxing. Boxing, not basketball, was the big winter sport. Boxing was popular because the older men recognized that if they could get the kids in the boxing ring, they could eliminate a lot of the street fighting. Once a kid started boxing, he felt it was stupid to hit someone with bare knuckles. I would think, *I don't want to break my knuckles on his stupid head*. From the time I was eleven through my teenage years, the number of fights I was involved in was unbelievable.

Boxing is a relatively cheap sport, and our boxing club in Belmont was in the basement underneath the jail. The ring was stuck back in the corner of the room, so the ropes on three sides were right against concrete blocks. If you got hit in the chin against the ropes, the back of your head would hit the concrete. As a result, no Belmont boxer ever got caught against the ropes. Belmont had some great boxing teams. All the mill towns had boxing teams. The roughest kids ended up on the boxing teams. I ended up befriending the kids I used to get in fights with because I started boxing with them.

You could go down there when you were ten or eleven, but you didn't start fighting out of town until you were sixteen. A lot of pro boxers came out of Belmont, though most of the kids didn't go on to college but went into the service and ended up on the elite service boxing teams at Camp Lejeune, Norfolk Navy, and the San Diego Marines.

My father was the coach and athletic director at Belmont Abbey College, and he made me go to the prep school attached to the college when it was time for me to go to high school. I didn't like that one bit because they didn't play football. Unable to play football, I became serious about boxing. At the same time, it was a very good school. We had to study Latin and Greek but in a really interesting environment. In the mornings I'd be with the Benedictine monks learning Latin, and in the afternoons I'd be up to my elbows in grease with the good old boys.

After I joined the Belmont Boxing Club, I did very well. I was in tournaments fighting guys from the service. I'd go to Charlotte to box with the pros all the time. I was a light-heavyweight, and I ended up with a record of forty wins and two losses. I won the Carolina Golden Gloves a few times. One year I beat a guy by the name of Lionel Benton from Florence, South Carolina. He was real good, and I wasn't supposed to beat him. There were 400 fighters in the tournament, and the night I fought him in the Charlotte Coliseum there were 11,000 people in the stands.

The following summer my mother came to see me fight for the first time. My opponent was a big muscular guy with a big right hook. In the first round he hit me in the side of the head with that hook and really jarred me. It ticked me off, and I threw a right and caught him on the button and knocked him out cold. My mother never came to another one of my fights.

When I beat him, I was sure this was going to be my way of getting out of Belmont. It was my junior year in high school, and I was looking for a college scholarship.

One time I fought an opponent who was black. It may well have been one of the early integrated fights, because, during the days of Jim Crow, whites and blacks boxed separately. The blacks boxed in places like barns, and the white guys fought in respectable places like armories and ballparks. Ordinarily you didn't mix, though we did spar. The fight against the black guy was a pretty good one. He was really tough, and it was maybe a draw at best, but I won a by unanimous decision because the judges were white and gave me the fight. I thought, *This ain't right.* For him to win, he would have had to knock me out.

My most memorable fight came the following year. I fought Graydean Laughter (pronounced *Lowder*). He was from Rutherfordton, and he was being touted for the Olympics. There was a boxer from Louisville by the name of Cassius Clay, and everyone said Graydean could beat him. I fought Laughter in Mount Holly, and from the time the bell rang until the time the fight was over, I never backed away from him. I won by unanimous decision.

I was going to go to Michigan State on a boxing scholarship. What cured me of all this was Al McGuire. He was the basketball coach at Belmont Abbey back then. He invited me on a recruiting trip to New York. We went down to the Lower East Side of Manhattan to this bar where a bunch of broken-down boxers were sitting, guys with cauliflower ears who weren't talking right. I went home thinking, *That isn't a very good way to end up.* I guarantee you this had been set up by my father, who did things like that, and by Al, who also did things like that. They never said a word. But that took the wind out of my sails as far as me looking at boxing as a career.

I was going to go to Michigan State on a boxing scholarship. But then during my senior year in high school a boxer from the University of Wisconsin was killed in the ring, and the NCAA banned boxing from college athletics. That left football. I loved the contact. I relished hitting people. I transferred to Charlotte Catholic High School my senior year, developed quite a reputation, and ended up getting a football scholarship to the University of South Carolina (USC).

§

BELMONT HAD A TYPICAL southern downtown with the buildings flush against each other. We had a grocery, a pharmacy (the doctor lived over the pharmacy), a jewelry store, and always a five-and-dime store. We also had a BF Goodrich auto store and a shoe shop. That was about it. No extraneous stores. What was interesting about living in that particular town was what I learned from the people who owned the stores. Most of the shop owners were veterans of World War II, and a number of them were injured in the war and handicapped. The jeweler, for example, was crippled, injured in the South Pacific.

We also had a store that sold nuts and bolts. That's all they sold because the mills bought so much of that stuff. Mr. Ford owned the nuts-and-bolts shop, and if I needed a part, I would go down there to talk to him. The store was long and narrow, like a bowling alley, and against the walls he had all these different nuts and bolts in wooden cabinets. He had a library-like ladder on a roller so you could climb up to the ceiling. The top of the climb was about fourteen feet high.

He always wore a green eyeshade and a green apron. I'd go in there, and he would teach me about different threads, carriage bolts, and cotter pins. Every once in a while I'd help him clean up, and about once a week he'd have me go up the ladder and get the bolts at the top—usually the biggest bolts that were least needed—so he could fill an order. It was a valuable education.

One day I went in there, and Mr. Ford was totally distressed and frustrated. He said, "The world is coming to an end." He had gotten some bolts from a company in Rockford, Illinois, that had Japanese equipment, and their nuts and bolts were metric. One of the mills had bought a machine that was metric—the entrance of the metric system in Belmont—and he said, "This will ruin the country. It's a Communist plot." Even though the Russian Revolution had nothing to do with the metric system. He figured nobody's tools were going to fit anymore, so the world was coming to an end. Then he showed me what the difference was, and talked about millimeters and centimeters. Of course, none of that was taught in the schools.

But if I had any kind of nuts-and-bolts problem, I'd go down there and show Mr. Ford what I had. He'd always have a solution and he knew how to tell me what to do. He wouldn't do it for me. He'd tell me what to do, and he'd always have me bring it back after I fixed it and show him what I did. He wanted to make sure I had done it right.

It was the same way with the men working at the two car dealerships. I knew all the mechanics down there, and I could walk into the service area anytime. Some of them were ten years older than me, but they would always help me no matter what my problem was. And there were times when one of the mechanics would call me on the phone and say, "Listen, I'm changing a ring gear and pinion on this truck. Would you like to watch me do it?" I'd go down and watch him, and then I'd know what to do. It was a good place to learn.

As was the shoe shop, which was owned by Mr. McCorkle. What I learned from him was how to treat customers. Mr. McCorkle had shoes everywhere. This was back in the days when people would repair what they owned until it fell apart. I'd take some shoes there, and he'd let me go in the back. I was just fascinated by all the things he did, how he put on half soles, heels, and full soles, and how he stitched leather. But what he did best was handle people.

Say a woman came in and said she wanted a pair of shoes fixed for her husband, and she wanted to know when she could get them back. Some people didn't have but two pairs of shoes, Sunday shoes and work shoes, so she might need them fairly quick. Mr. McCorkle would be sitting there with 300 pairs of shoes to fix, so he couldn't always do it right away. But he always acted like he could. He'd say, "I'm going to get right to 'em, Mrs. Smith. I'm going to take care of them, because I know Frank wants them back." Well, it might be three days before he got them back, but he always acted like she was the only person he was dealing with. He had that knack, and I never forgot him.

I also remember the man who ran the mercantile store in Bessemer City. He had a huge, long beard; he said that because the South lost the Civil War, he would never shave. His specialty was taking off warts. If you had a wart, any kind of wart, he could take it off. I don't know how he did it. The people who ran those stores were wonderful and particularly wonderful to kids.

Saturday night Grandmother would bake biscuits, which would be piled high and served with molasses in real country butter. You poured the molasses on your plate, and you put the butter on top of the molasses, and you took a fork and squished it all in so you had this mixture of butter and molasses. Then you got these hot biscuits, and you sopped them in there, and that's what you ate for supper on Saturday night. Sunday you went to church, and after church you had a big meal—it was the meal of the week. Usually Grandmother cooked a couple of baked chickens, and you had corn bread—you always had corn bread—and peas and beans, corn on the cob, squash, onions sometimes, and then potatoes—usually mashed potatoes and gravy. And there was always a pie or cake for dessert.

Then everyone would wobble to the front porch and sit, because this was back in the strict days when people didn't do anything on Sunday. So you'd sit on the front porch, and neighbors would walk by, and they'd stop and talk. It was a day of socializing, because people worked six days a week, and everyone was glad to have the day off. And this brought about the enduring Sunday visit, which was such a part of the southern culture, and something I absolutely hated as a kid because inevitably your relatives or some neighbor would come over to visit on Sunday, and if the weather wasn't right you would have to go into the living room and listen to the adults talk about dull, boring things like what was ailing Aunt Millie. Even worse was going to visit someone else and having to sit there like a prisoner watching the dust mites.

Then there was the thing called the Sunday drive. People in the mill villages didn't drive during the week, so if they had a car, which a lot of them didn't, they'd go out on Sunday and see things.

We boys could escape all this dull mongering if they let us go out and play. On Sunday it was Little Rascals' time. A bunch of us would go out to Highway 29, the main thoroughfare, and we'd watch the cars go down the highway. It was a chance to see the new 1947 models, something you didn't see in Belmont because we only had two new-car dealerships, Ford and Chevy, and they only had a couple of cars in their showrooms. As a result you didn't get to see Cadillacs or Oldsmobiles, much less anything like an MG. That would have floored everybody.

The highway was also where I saw my first race cars. I saw cars with numbers on them go by, and I was fascinated because I knew they were going to the speedway.

I knew the names of the drivers: Buck Baker, Speedy Thompson, Fireball Roberts, Banjo Matthews, and Cotton Owens. If you lived in that area you just knew them, so I developed an interest in stock car racing.

We would thumb rides to the track. Back then you could do that. People were always willing to give a kid a ride. It would take two seconds for someone to come along and take us. The track let kids get in free if they were accompanied by an adult, so all you had to do was go up to some guy and say, "Can I go in with you?" He'd say, "Sure," and you got in for free.

Charlotte Motor Speedway was a typical old-timey track, three-quarters of a mile of dirt. The surface was red clay. It had a weathered board fence all the way around it. It had a guardrail in the third and fourth turns, but it didn't have one around the first or second. It was a big track for those days. The grandstands were gum lumber.

I remember the first time I went there. They were running Modifieds that day, the most popular cars. They were old Fords—'37 and '39 coupes—and they ran flathead engines with multiple carburetors and pickup truck rear ends. Everything was out of a junkyard. The place was crowded. For most of the time, I stood at the end of the grandstand watching the cars go into the first turn. It got pretty dusty after a while, and there were lots of wrecks. From that point on, I was smitten.

My father didn't approve. He was a Northerner, and he didn't like racing at all. He was strictly football, basketball, and baseball. He wanted me to make something of myself. He didn't want me to become a car mechanic, and he didn't want me to have anything to do with racing, because there was no money in it and also because socially it was not the thing to do. It was a very, very rough sport back in those days.

My mother, who was Scotch-Irish, saw racing as something I had developed a passion for, and she encouraged my interest, which was unusual because the parents of the rest of the kids in our social circle didn't feel that way.

This was right after World War II. The middle class of the South was beginning to form, thanks to the war and the Veterans Affairs (VA) program. Up until then there literally had been no middle class. Parents like mine wanted their kids to have a better life than they had, because most had come from pretty hard times. For those striving to escape poverty and enter the middle class, there were three things you just didn't do back in those days. You didn't live in a log house, you didn't listen to hillbilly music, and you didn't go to stock car races. Now the lower class, the mill workers, they listened to hillbilly music and Hank Snow, and they liked Fireball Roberts and Speedy Thompson. And they went to stock car races as I did.

By the time I was thirteen, I was going to every stock car race I could. I attended the very first National Association for Stock Car Auto Racing (NASCAR) Grand National Cup race, which was held at the Charlotte Speedway in 1949. Glenn Dunaway won, and after the race he was disqualified for using bootlegger's springs.

What I remember most about the race was that I didn't like it. Bill France came up with the idea of racing new cars because it was a chance to get the car companies to sponsor his governing body, NASCAR, and his races. Before that most of the stock cars were Modifieds—cars with a lot of horsepower. The new cars had a lot less horsepower, and during a hundred-mile race the cars tended to get strung out, and the racing wasn't very good. I wasn't enthralled with it, and I don't think a lot of other race fans were either. There wasn't enough horsepower, and there wasn't enough fire-in-the-belly kind of racing.

Big Bill France started NASCAR. I was aware of him because he did a lot of promoting around where I lived. France was from Daytona Beach, but he spent a lot of time in the Carolinas, and Charlotte in particular. In those days there were two types of racing: NASCAR racing and what France referred to as Outlaw Racing, which meant anything that wasn't NASCAR. I liked the way he coined that.

France ran the old Charlotte Speedway, and he promoted quite a few races in the Carolinas. When I was thirteen there were a hundred dirt tracks in the two Carolinas because it was so cheap to race. Around Belmont there were several—Robinwood Speedway, Charlotte Speedway, the Charlotte Fairgrounds, the Belmont midget track, and the South Carolina Fairgrounds in Rock Hill.

I always said there was nothing more dangerous than a race fan with grading equipment because he'd probably build a racetrack. And that's what inevitably happened. Even little Belmont had a racetrack. It was only an eighth of a mile, and we ran what they called micro-midgets on it—cheap little midget race cars with motor-scooter engines. This was before go-karts. They were pretty fast and ran up to sixty miles an hour. People would pay admission and watch. Twenty-five cars would be entered, and it was pretty interesting. When I was thirteen I actually owned one. My mother acted like it wasn't there and my father didn't want to believe it was there.

I entered my micro-midget in exactly one race. It was a chain-driven scooter engine, and soon after the race began the chain fell off, and I was done. I never could make that thing work right. I didn't like that kind of racing anyway. The car eventually burned up.

Like everyone else, I didn't have any extra money, so when I was eleven I delivered papers and mowed grass. I wasn't satisfied with the money I was making doing that, so when I was thirteen I started looking around, figuring I could do something to fill a need. You couldn't get a real job until you were sixteen, and so after looking around I saw there wasn't a single bicycle shop in Belmont, and I decided to open one. I asked my mother if I could use the garage for my business, and she said I could have half of it.

My grandfather had taught me something about fixing things, and I always liked to work on bicycles. I could take one apart and put it back together again, and I had some tools. Mom let me put up a sign in front of the house that said "Wheeler's Bicycle Shop." I put an ad in the *Belmont Banner*, a weekly paper. My first customer was my scoutmaster. He was doing it to help me out, though I didn't realize it then. It was the most complicated job I could have gotten because it was a three-speed English bike, and I had never seen one before. It wasn't shifting right. It took me a week to figure it out, but I finally did, and I fixed it. I charged him a dollar.

Business started coming in, but not fast enough to suit me. I decided I had to do something, so I started promoting bicycle races. The Great Belmont Bicycle Race of 1951 was the first race I ever promoted. I was thirteen.

I held the race on the football field at Belmont Abbey. My dad was athletic director, so he let me use the field. This was back in the days of balloon tires, so the race didn't wreck the grass. I bought a trophy. Six boys entered, and Jimmy Abernathy won it. Many years later when I was running the Charlotte Motor Speedway, he came in one day and he said, "I want to give you this trophy back." I still have it.

After that race I decided to hold weekly races. Belmont had a community center almost across the street from my house. It had a big yard, and I started holding races there every Saturday at ten o'clock. There was no entry fee. I figured the bike riders would tear up their bicycles racing them, and I'd fix them up. I had rules. You had to have fenders. You couldn't take them off. I wanted them bending their fenders so I could fix them.

Every Saturday between thirty and forty bicyclists would show up, and they'd race. I raced, too, every once in a while, but usually I was the flagman. The riders would smash and bash and crash, and every once in a while there'd be a fight, but it was a lot of fun.

I never asked permission to hold the races at the town community center. I figured if they had objections, they'd stop me, but they never did. The town fathers never said a word to me. There were two trees at either end of the center, and we wore out a path around those trees. The track was probably a sixteenth of a mile, and we'd run five laps. The wear and tear on those bikes helped pick up my bicycle business.

With the money I made, I was able to buy a regular road car. You weren't supposed to drive until you were sixteen, but there were only two policemen in Belmont, and one of them was Chief Hoover, a friend of my dad's. One time when I was thirteen, he saw me driving my car, and he said, "What are you doing?"

"Delivering bicycles," I said. He figured that was all right as long as I was doing something fruitful.

"I don't want you going out at night," he said.

ONE REPAIR I WAS UNABLE to make was truing wheels. They'd warp, and straightening them out involved a pretty complicated procedure that I just could not master. I tried, but they never came out right.

I called the Norris Bicycle Shop, which was three miles away in Cramerton, and an old woman with a gravelly voice answered. I told her who I was—she said she knew my shop—and I asked if they trued wheels. She said they did. I said I had four wheels for her shop to fix.

The house, which was backed up against the woods and the hills, was kind of a scary place. It looked like the Munster's House with a tower behind it and a six-foot stockade fence all around the yard. The old lady took the wheels, and a couple days later I went back to get them, and they were perfect. They charged me fifty cents a wheel, and I charged my customers seventy-five cents.

The old woman would not let me meet the man who did the actual work, but after six weeks I got a call from Mr. Norris. He had a funny-sounding voice. He wanted to know if I would paint some of his bicycle frames for his customers in exchange for him truing wheels for mine. I said yes, but even after painting some frames for him, I still hadn't met him.

One night Mr. Norris called to say one of the frames that I had painted had a run and needed to be fixed. I apologized and took it back—it wasn't much of a run, but I fixed it anyway. I brought it back to his shop about six o'clock. I said, "Mrs. Norris, I really want to speak with him." And I was insistent. She said, "We've been talking about this. I guess we'll let you do it." She told me where Mr. Norris' shop was located.

I went through the house, which was dark. It was November, and night fell early. I went out the back door where there was a rope that stretched about

fifty feet to the garage where Mr. Norris was working on his bikes. There were
no lights on. I walked along the rope until I got to the door of the garage. I
opened it. It was pitch-black inside. I could barely see Mr. Norris. I could also
see that everything in the shop was in its place. The shop was as clean as a pin,
but it didn't have any color at all. His back was to me. He wore coveralls and
had what looked like a nylon stocking over his head.

"Howard, how are you?" he said. I said I was fine. He said, "I don't look
very good, but I just have to live with that." He turned around, and I was
shocked to see that Mr. Norris had no face. I tried very hard not to seem taken
aback. He told me he had been burned severely during World War II in the
South Pacific. The reason he was unable to paint the bike frames was because
he was blind. He could true wheels because his sense of feel was so acute.

I never did get used to seeing him. The old lady was his mother, and she
took great care of him. She couldn't take him anywhere because he looked so
frightening. His hands were burned. He wore long sleeves and coveralls.

The tower behind his house was for a shortwave radio. He was a ham
radio operator. One night when I visited him we talked to a man in New
Zealand. I knew where that was, and I couldn't imagine talking to someone
from that far away. He talked to another man in England, and I was amazed
because it was like he was downtown on a street corner. This was Mr. Norris'
social life. Through him I really learned a lot. He was a wonderful person.
He just had no social life at all except through that radio because of the way
he looked.

In addition to my bicycle business, I started working on other men's race
cars. As bad as I wanted to drive, I never could get my micro-midget to run
right. When I was fifteen I began going to North Belmont to work on a '37
Ford coupe owned by a racer whose name I no longer remember. Back then
I knew everyone in town who had a race car. Some of the people working in
the mills even had race cars because cars were cheap. You bought everything
from the junkyards.

I started going to the races with the man who owned the '37 Ford coupe.
We would go to the Kings Mountain Speedway, a track about twenty-five
miles from Belmont. He was the car owner, not the driver. One Sunday
afternoon we arrived about eleven thirty. You couldn't crank up the cars until
noon because of the Blue Laws. The track would have made a great movie set.
On the other side of the flag stand was a judge's stand that had three old men

in coveralls playing mountain music. They had a banjo, fiddle, and guitar. It was a real hot day, and half the drivers didn't even have shirts on. When his driver didn't show up, I told him I wanted to drive. I had told him I had raced. I didn't tell him it was only once, in a micro-midget. He let me sit in the driver's seat, and I went out and made a few laps, and I did okay.

The track promoter was a man named Frosty Spearman. We drew for positions out of a hat. I drew 1/1. First heat, pole position. Frosty came over to me and said, "Who are you?"

"My name is Howard Wheeler."

"You ever race before?" I had come too far. I wasn't about to get out of that car. I looked him straight in the eye and said, "You never heard of Howard Wheeler?" He shook his head and walked away. If I had said anything else, he would have jerked me out of the car.

The flag dropped. It was an old dirt track that ran a quarter mile. There were sixteen cars in the first heat. Before I got around to finishing the first lap, every car in the race had passed me. I was really last, but I ended up finishing twelfth because four cars wrecked.

The feature came up, and thirty cars started. The flag dropped, and I stayed out of trouble and finished eleventh. I drove for him a little longer, but it was my senior year in high school, and I had to stop racing to concentrate on playing football. My father had finally let me leave the Abbey school and go to Charlotte Catholic where they had a football team. I kept racing until I was twenty-one, but by then my interests lay elsewhere. I had begun to write, and I did PR for some of the local tracks. This was back in the days when promoters didn't know anything about PR. I could see that anything I did was better than what they did.

CHAPTER 2

The Scotch-Irish and the Segregated South

M Y HOMETOWN OF BELMONT wasn't terribly different from a lot of towns in the foothills of the North Carolina mountains. It's red-clay country. It's where the Scotch-Irish tumbled out of the mountains when the Industrial Revolution came along, and after the New England textile owners went to cheap labor in the South. They began to build mills in the Carolinas, and towns formed around the mills as people came out of the mountains and took jobs.

These were primarily Scotch-Irish people, meaning they had been Scots who went to Northern Ireland, only to find things were just as bad. After living several generations there, they either went to Australia or America. Most of them landed in Philadelphia and didn't like it because it was a big city and the culture was ethnic. These people had never before been around an ethnic mix of people. They were Nordic in nature and not used to the French, Italians, Germans, and Poles, and they began to plod westward in what became the Scotch-Irish migration trail, which roughly follows the Shenandoah Valley down through Virginia. A few were mesmerized by the Virginia Allegheny Mountains because it looked like home. But it was North Carolina, East Tennessee, and the mountains of South Carolina and Georgia that really attracted them, especially the North Carolina mountains. And so they settled there.

The Scotch-Irish people adored misery and reveled in it. They farmed the bottomlands of the rugged Appalachian Mountains, raising mostly corn, cabbage, and some livestock. They lived in hills and the hollows, which made living very, very tough. And because they grew corn, they brought their whiskey-making skills with them. It was another way to make a living off the land, even back in Revolutionary times. The Scotch-Irish raised livestock, and though they didn't want to get involved at the start of the Revolutionary War, toward the end of the war they got mad at the British and came out of the mountains, and the British found out just how tough Americans could be. They could shoot and they could hide.

Flash forward to the Industrial Revolution. Before then, these people had nowhere to go. But when they heard about the mills, they began to flock to these little towns, of which Belmont was quite typical.

A cotton mill town wasn't terribly different from a steel mill town or a coal mining town. Its economic center was the mill, a few of which were run by Jewish people who had migrated from Eastern Europe. The English owned most of the others. The two groups traded among each other, but socially they did not mix. Both groups hired from the same labor pool, and when the laborers needed a place to live, the mill owners were forced to build houses.

You can go to Lowell or Haverhill, Massachusetts, or to Scotland or Australia, and you can find the same kind of mill housing. They were all wood. They used heart pine as the subflooring and mostly New England hard maple for the final floor.

The mills themselves were either high- or low-ceilinged. Low-ceiling mills were cheap, and they are almost all gone now because they could not be converted into warehouses, condos, and lofts. The high-ceilinged mills were cleaner, had more air movement, and didn't cause as many health problems.

Those who worked in the mills suffered from white lung, which they got through the constant inhaling of fiber.

That and the fact that just about everyone smoked. These were poor people, and they would get a tin of tobacco and a pack of cigarette papers to roll their own. Those who didn't smoke chewed, and the women dipped snuff called Sweet Peach. Some of it was made in Connecticut and shipped down to the poor folk. Also their diets were very poor, very high in carbohydrates. They didn't eat a lot of protein. They ate grits, grits, and more grits, and beans, and some ham, which was the principal meat because there weren't a lot of beef cattle around. They had dairy cows but few heads of beef cattle, and they had a lot of hogs.

Carolinians used a lot of Karo syrup—corn syrup—and molasses, which is syrup made of cane sugar. And we used a lot of refined white flour to make biscuits and corn meal to make corn bread.

If you worked the first shift in the mill, a typical breakfast was no breakfast. The shifts ran six o'clock in the morning to two o'clock, two o'clock to ten o'clock, and ten o'clock to six o'clock in the morning. The women usually worked the first shift so they could be home when the kids came home from school. The men worked either the second shift or the godforsaken third shift at night. No one liked working it, but some had no choice.

The mill workers lived in shotgun houses, called that because if you open the front door, you can see all the way down to the back door. Off the hall were two bedrooms, a living room, and a kitchen that also served as a dining area. Again, these houses were built by the mill. Some of them didn't even have running water.

A small mill village typically had two stores: a general store that sold everything but groceries and the grocery store across the street. The mills either owned the stores or rented the buildings to the store owners. Most of them were cashless stores. You could use cash, but a mill worker would usually put it on his bill, and it would be deducted from his payroll.

When a person started working in the cotton mill, he usually started off as a sweeper. A tremendous amount of lint would fall on the floor, and it was important to keep the floors clean so as not to foul up the machines and the manufacturing process. As a result you just swept those maple floors all day long.

Some employees worked in the card room. They didn't play cards in there. They prepared the cotton. Then there was the spinning room where workers spun cotton into thread. At some mills all they did was make thread.

They also had what they called finishing mills, which made products like socks, T-shirts, underpants, and blue jeans. Another group of mills—called knitting mills—made hosiery, socks, sheets, and pillowcases. Having worked in both, I can tell you that knitting mills were a better place to work. They just seemed a notch above.

The minimum wage at the time was seventy-five cents an hour, which is what most entry-level jobs paid. Most of the mill workers earned between a dollar and a dollar and a half an hour.

Nobody ate breakfast at home. They'd eat it at the mill from the dope wagon. A guy came around with a cart full of sugary snacks and carbonated beverages. The dope wagon had the worst possible food you could possibly eat. It had honey buns, moon pies, and Lance peanut butter crackers, and that's what the workers ate for breakfast. Any kind of carbonated beverage we called "dope." Early on, Coca-Cola was reputed to have had traces of opiates in it, so we called sodas "dopes." We'd say, "I'm going to get a dope."

Those on the first shift started work at six in the morning, and the dope wagon would come around at eight, and they'd get their caffeine hit from RC Cola or something called Double Cola. This was when soft drinks had cane sugar in them. Today they have corn syrup. That's why they tasted so good back then. You can still get cola with cane syrup in Mexico. Today they bootleg it into the states from Mexico.

With the cola, they'd eat a honey bun, which was pure sugar, and then finish off with a Moon pie, which was pure sugar. Filled up with caffeine and sugar, the worker's blood sugar would go sky-high, and about two hours later it would start to plummet. He'd get a headache, and that's when the Goody's powder—ground-up aspirin laced with caffeine—would come out. Essentially, they were mainlining aspirin.

Working in the mills, I learned how to make a straw out of the Goody's package, line up the powder, put it on my tongue, inhale it, and swallow it. If you know how to do it, you can take one dry.

So the mill workers lived on this up-and-down diet of caffeine and sugar. Dr. Pepper had a famous advertising slogan back in those days that went "Ten, two, and four." You drank one at ten o'clock, and then at two o'clock, and then at four o'clock. And you were supposed to stay healthy doing that. You didn't get a headache because your blood sugar would go back up.

On top of that, these mill workers smoked incessantly. They smoked either unfiltered Camels or unfiltered Luckys. Many learned to smoke while they were in the armed forces where aggressive cigarette companies worked hard to hook the soldiers. They furnished the troops with cigarettes, though some of them still rolled their own.

There was also a lot of romance and intrigue in the mills that would sometimes turn violent because some guy would start messing with another guy's woman. This was especially true in the hosiery mills where the loopers sat and looped the nylon thread and began the process of sock-making or finish work. The loopers were women who sat at these little sewing machines all day. Most of them had bad eyes and wore thick glasses. The men would come wandering over and start trying to flirt with them, and sometimes that would lead to problems.

I got into a brawl one day in the hosiery mill over a looper. Her name was Sally McCorkle, a cute, little blond girl about eighteen. One of the guys who worked in the mill liked to play cop. He had a car that looked like a police cruiser, but he wasn't a cop. He kept teasing and flirting and messing with Sally, and she told me she didn't like it so one day I told him to stop. He told me to go screw myself, and I told him I wasn't going to do that, but that we had to go somewhere and settle this. Everyone knew if you fought inside the mill, you automatically got fired. We decided to go into the box room, which was where they kept all the empty boxes.

We closed the door and went at it. It was a pretty good fight, lasting about five minutes. Everyone knew what was going on. I earned a technical knockout. I came out with a black eye and a couple of abrasions, but I was okay, and the guy didn't mess with Sally anymore. It was typical of what would happen every once in a while around the mill.

Two families in Belmont controlled all the mills, the Linebergers and the Stowes. Mr. Stowe was real nice to me. He knew I was building a street rod and that I coveted the set of U.S. Royal master tires he had taken off his Cadillac. They were as good as new, and he sold them to me cheap—five dollars each—trying to help me out. I put them on my car as soon as I got home. Of course, when he asked me if I would dig a septic tank hole for him, which was like digging a grave but much wider, I couldn't say no. It took me three days to do it. It also made me appreciate the fact that I really needed to get a college education.

When I was growing up, twenty percent of Belmont's population was black, but we rarely saw them. They lived in one section of town and we lived in another. My father worked at Belmont Abbey College, a school attached to a self-sustaining Benedictine monastery that had its own bakery and dairy, and even grew its own grapes for wine. A lot of black people worked at the college performing the more laborious tasks, and a lot of them converted to Catholicism. They went to eight o'clock mass on Sunday, and that's when our family went. At the Cathedral blacks were welcome, and so they had an integrated mass, which was rare in the South.

My father, who came from Rhode Island, was quite liberal, and he made sure he brought us up to see the equality of man. I went to Charlotte Catholic where there was exactly one black kid in our class. His name was Dan Rose. He was a good student and a very quiet person. He was there when I started at the school in 1955. Though it was a totally segregated society, nobody made anything of it.

The high school in Belmont was all white. The black kids went to Reid High School in the black section of town. They played their football games on Thursday nights, and Belmont played theirs on Friday nights. Same locker rooms. Same seats. Two different worlds.

I can remember going to watch Reid play another black school, Shelby, one Thursday. Reid had a great quarterback by the name of Nelson Craig. We went to church with the Craigs. His brother's name was Angelo Bertelli Craig, named after the great Notre Dame quarterback. Angelo wasn't very good, but Nelson was great. He had "star" written all over him. Bobby Bell, who became a great All-Pro in the NFL, was quarterback for Shelby that night. I got to watch two great quarterbacks battle each other.

Shortly after that, tragedy struck when Nelson Craig, who might have been the best athlete ever to come out of Belmont, contracted spinal meningitis and died. My father came home one night and told us about it. Though white people didn't go to black wakes very often, that night we got in the car and went over to the Craig home to pay our respects. We were the only white family. It was very painful for me, because Nelson was my age, and I knew him well. To see someone die that young and so quickly, someone so talented, was a terrible tragedy. It also gave me greater respect for my father.

SOMEONE ONCE SAID that white people in the South like black people, but won't socialize with them. That was true of some of the people I knew. There's a book called *Hitler's Willing Executioners*. A professor who had studied this subject at length said Germans treated the Jewish people in such a dehumanizing way because they thought they were a subspecies. And to a great extent that was the way white people in the South looked at black people. At the same time this was also back in the day when many middle-class whites hired black maids. The mill workers couldn't afford hired help, but the middle-class whites could.

We had a maid. The maid would come in and do all the dirty work—washing, cooking, and cleaning. The crazy thing was a lot of these black women literally raised the children of the whites. They took care of them, nurtured them, babysat them, and fed them. They were about as close to them as you could be. They didn't get paid much, but the families always gave them their secondhand clothes—whatever they couldn't wear or outgrew—and they acted like they appreciated it. Not having much money, they used it, I'm sure.

Most blacks didn't have cars, so they had to utilize public transportation, which in the South consisted mostly of buses. These buses were run for one primary reason: to get black people to the white neighborhoods to work in the white homes and to get them downtown to work in the white businesses.

People talk about how blacks had to ride in the back of the bus. Hell, there weren't any white people on the bus, not in back or in front. Everyone on the bus was black. Except me. I rode the bus many a time. I had to sit up front, whether I wanted to or not.

When I was boxing, I sometimes traveled with a couple of black fighters. At the matches, white guys fought white guys and black guys fought black guys. One time we traveled to Atlanta for a match. We were riding down Highway 29, and this was when there were signs in front of restaurants and motels that said, "No niggers allowed." The signs didn't say, "No blacks," or "No Negroes." They said, "No niggers." It was lunchtime, and the place was packed with white people. We pulled into the place, and one of the black guys went in back to the kitchen where the black people got their food. Everyone in the kitchen was black so we always got fed instantly. They would put the food in a bag, and the black boxers would bring it around to us. It was like having a fast-food place before fast-food places existed. So even though it said, "No niggers" in the front, everyone who was cooking was black. I always thought that was kind of ironic.

When we had to stay somewhere, I would stay at some high-class place like the YMCA, but my black teammates couldn't. They had their own underground housing—either a boarding house or one of the few motels for blacks.

The one really bad thing about these times for blacks was the scarcity of bathrooms. The same was true of drinking fountains. There were many white drinking fountains but usually there wasn't an accompanying black drinking fountain. Blacks had to go around back and get water out of a spigot.

One time late at night our boxing team went to eat at a barbeque place. There were seven white guys and a big black guy—one of our heavyweight boxers. There wasn't anybody else in the place. They said, "We can't feed you.

Not with him. You all can come in, but he can't." We were a pretty rough-looking bunch. We had already fought, so we were all beat-up-looking. Finally, just through intimidation, they let us come in and they fed us.

THE MORE VICIOUS RACISM could be found in some of the more rural areas. I can remember in 1963 I was doing promotion for a racetrack in Augusta, Georgia. It was totally unsuccessful because road racing just couldn't cut it in the South. Fireball Roberts won the race, and Dave McDonald was second.

The owner of the track was Mr. Payton, an asphalt contractor from Greenville, South Carolina. It was November 1963, and five days after the race he and I were driving back from Augusta and we stopped at a filling station in the middle of Georgia somewhere. The guy who pumped gas came out and said to us, "That nigger-loving son of a bitch got shot. I hope he dies."

We didn't know what he was talking about.

"Who got shot?" I asked.

"Kennedy."

"Which Kennedy?"

"The President, asshole," he said.

Well, that got both of us rankled up. I would have figured Mr. Payton to be prejudiced, but it turned out he wasn't. I thought Mr. Payton was going to knock the guy's block off. So, though not all white people were prejudiced, there were a lot of incidents like that.

IN THE SOUTH in those days, you knew black people well, which was more than you could have said for white people in the North. I know when I'd go north in the summertime with my father, who was from Rhode Island, they didn't know any black people. In the South we knew their names. We talked to them, and we liked them. We just wouldn't let them drink out of our fountains or go into our bathrooms. We'd let them cook our food, but we wouldn't let them eat next to us. They could raise our children, but give them an equal opportunity? That wasn't done.

The only black people who had any money were those who could lay brick or concrete, or build a house—craftsmen who were really good and who were paid a fair wage. The rest of them didn't have any money at all and lived from hand to mouth. There wasn't any welfare. One thing you saw often were black men who had been hurt, but who couldn't afford decent medical care and as a result were left crippled.

I remember a black man by the name of Mr. Mercer. He lived in a little bungalow near the Charlotte Motor Speedway—a little house with a little garden—and he had a little tractor. He would sit out in his yard under an oak tree every afternoon, and I used to stop and talk to him. He had been in a bad motorcycle wreck. He was crippled, and he just never had it fixed right because he didn't know how to get it fixed right.

One day I rode past his house and there was a sign, "Funeral today." He had died. Perhaps if he could have had decent medical care, he wouldn't have died. But that was common.

As a boy I used to fix bicycles in my shop for black people. They were all very poor, and during the summer I would go around and collect every junk bicycle I could find, bring them back, sand them down and paint them red, put chrome fenders and new tires and wheels on them, and I'd sell them for $19.95—as opposed to $35.00 for a new bicycle at the BF Goodrich store. My customers would pay me four or five dollars a month until the bike was paid for, and I would deliver it just before Christmas.

Usually I would put the bikes under the houses so the kids couldn't see them. One Christmas when I was sixteen years old, I took a bicycle over to the Imperial Mill Village to a typical house owned by blacks, never painted, roof half fallen in, the screen door bent. This house didn't have the usual three stairs going up. This one had a door that opened on the ground. It was a one-room shack, and the floor was dirt.

I was invited into the house, and I could see a little boy who was about ten. He didn't know I was bringing him the bike. They had a little Christmas tree they had cut down, but they didn't have electricity. They had hurricane lamps. For trimming, they had cut up little pieces of tin cans to look like ornaments. And the man was so happy. He came out to get the bike, and he got his wallet out, and in it was a twenty-dollar bill and nothing else. He was trying hard, but times were tough. It was like that for all the blacks.

I said, "Is that all you've got?"

He said, "I've been saving for this. I've been waiting on this day. I got everything else done. This is the last thing to do before Christmas."

I felt bad for this man, and I just could not take his money.

I said, "Here's the bike." And I started walking away.

"You ain't giving me that bike," he said.

I said, "Yeah, I am." We argued for about three minutes, but he made me take the money. He was wearing old overalls, and as I turned to go, I brushed past him and shoved the twenty back in his pocket, and I left. It was the best Christmas I had in a long time.

TO SUPPLEMENT MY MEAGER INCOME at the bicycle shop, one summer when I was sixteen I went to work for City Supply Company, a construction company. You could get a work permit and a job when you were sixteen. I started off working on a ditch gang along with twelve black men helping to dig a basement underneath a mill. Even the foreman was black.

The foreman was called Shotgun, and some of the other men were called Pick Man, Grunt, Shackle—I presume the guy had been in prison—and Sleepy, who had droopy eyelids. The nicknames like Too Tall, Long Boy, and Runt most often came from physical features. They all wore the same clothing—wide-legged Levi blue jeans, brogans, and white socks. Each wore a T-shirt with a denim shirt over it. Their clothes were well-worn, threadbare at the knees and elbows. While they worked, they would sing or tell jokes sometimes, anything to break up the monotony of this very, very tough existence. In a way it was like working on a chain gang.

These guys I worked with were large. Even the one they called Runt was large, though he wasn't tall. He was big horizontally, really wide. I'd look at those guys and think, *This one is a middle linebacker; that one is a left guard. There's a fullback.* But of course, none of them ever played anything. But they were very strong and had a lot of endurance, and I thought they were really old, though they were probably in their thirties.

This was in 1955, and it must have been the days before backhoes. We had to dig the ditch by hand. The first day I was there Shotgun came up to us and said, "Okay, boys, we're going graveyard deep." I didn't know what that was, though it was common sense: six feet deep. They all knew. They laid out a string and worked in two-man teams. The guy in the front had a pick and the guy in back had a shovel. One picked into that hard red clay, and the other shoveled it out.

They didn't trust me with a pick, so I started off with a shovel. It was all very methodical, in rhythm and unison. From my perspective, they looked like they were working very slowly. Everyone worked at the same pace— except me. I was giving my usual one hundred percent.

Since I was the only white, my nickname was White Boy. Runt, the man behind me, said, "White Boy, you better slow down. You ain't gonna make it through the day if you don't."

When we started at six o'clock in the morning it was cool, but by ten o'clock I found out what Runt was talking about. I had taken my shirt off, and one of the other men said, "Boy, you better put that shirt on." I couldn't figure out why, but it was because I had white skin and was going to get a painful sunburn.

I had boxed and played football so I thought I was in good shape, but I found out that this work was a whole different deal. By about two o'clock I found out what these men were talking about. Because I was about dead. I didn't think I could get out of that ditch. At the end of the day it took every ounce of energy I had to stagger to the truck taking us back to City Supply.

We were sitting in the back of this truck on the floor, and one of them said, "Tomorrow, you're going to learn about pacing yourself." Well, I had already learned. A couple days later I was finally in sync with them. It wasn't that they were lazy or slow. That was the pace they needed to follow to get through the day.

During the next week Shotgun said to me, "White Boy, do you know how to drive?" I said I did. He said, "I want you to drive the truck to City Supply and get a whole truckload of postholes." I was overjoyed. All I could think of was that I was getting out of that damn ditch. Man, anything to get out of that hole!

I jumped out of there, got in the truck, and about halfway to City Supply, I got to thinking about postholes. *Postholes? Postholes?* I pulled up to City Supply, and I said to the man on the dock, "Willy asked for me to get postholes."

He just started laughing, cracking-ribs laughing. *Aw shit*, I thought. *I've been had.* I turned around and went back, and when I returned, the guys were bent over laughing as though that was the funniest thing they had ever seen. I was sixteen years old, and they were men, and they had tricked me. I was enraged and they knew it. To calm me down they said, "We were just teasing you."

"It made me feel stupid," I said.

"You ain't stupid," one said. "You know how to read and write."

It turned out that not one of them knew how to read or write. We went back to work, and after that they were real nice to me. But it was their way of bringing me down a notch without taking the humanity away from me. They were having a little fun, because those guys had *no* fun in their lives. Just living one day to the next was a tough deal for them.

For a while after that they called me Posthole. I didn't mind because I had gotten tired of White Boy.

We would take a break about ten. The guys all had beat-up old metal lunch boxes. They had a thermos, and most of them ate corn bread for their mid-morning snack. For lunch some of them had sandwiches or else canned meats—Spam, potted meat, or Vienna sausages. Usually it was sandwiches because the potted meats were more than they could afford.

If I brought something different, they all wanted to know what it was and asked to taste it. One time I brought pecan pie, and they all wanted a taste. I felt for these guys, and once in a while our cook would make a pie, and I'd bring the whole pie and we'd share it.

During lunch they'd sit around and talk about this guy or that guy in the local black community. I particularly remember Mule Man, who had a wagon pulled by mules. He would go out to the farms and pick up the sharecroppers' produce, and he'd take it to the grocery stores and sell it. He'd then go back to the farms carrying a full load of what everyone knew was corn whiskey, which he got from bartering produce for it. The cops knew what was going on, but they looked the other way, which they did a lot back in those days.

I'd see Mule Man going downtown, but I never knew him. The guys did, though, and they told funny stories about him. They said he would get drunk on Friday, and he'd lose his wagon somewhere. It would always be at someone's house where he'd leave it after delivering his goods, and after he'd start drinking somewhere, the next morning he couldn't find his wagon. That was Mule Man, and the guys would talk about him and laugh and laugh.

They were interesting men. They also talked about their social lives, so they also talked about church. Going to church for black people was different than going to church for white people. They would go at eleven o'clock in the morning on Sunday, and lots of time they didn't leave until after three. They'd eat there, and it was their social gathering place for friends and family. Generally they were very devout. They may have told ribald jokes, but they believed in "Da Lord."

Some of the ditch diggers had been to prison, and they talked about that fact. Evidently being a black man in a southern prison was really horrible, so bad they didn't talk about their experience except to say, "I ain't ever going back to that damn place again."

These men lived this terrible, gruesome life, but they counteracted the gruesomeness with humor, religion, and a self-deprecating manner. They were very humble and deferential around white people. But since I was a kid and we had become friends, when they saw me, it was like I was one of them. They were very interested in what I did, how I lived. They knew where I lived; they just didn't know what was going on behind the front door.

I never invited them over. You just didn't do that. A couple of times I invited them to come see me box, but they wouldn't go.

The job lasted the summer, and the next year I worked inside a hosiery mill. It was a lot better because it was cooler. Air conditioning had just been installed in some of the mills, including mine. I was an oiler, which was a plum job. During my entire shift I would go around and squirt oil in the machines. When I went home, I would be covered in oil. I also learned to do simple mechanical things to keep the machines working. They broke down and needed constant adjustment. I was mechanically inclined, and I liked to work with tools. After a while it was something I could do.

As bad as the racism was, it wasn't nearly as bad in North Carolina as it was in some of the states of the Deep South. It was less harsh in North Carolina and Tennessee than it was in South Carolina, Virginia, and Georgia because North Carolina and Tennessee weren't plantation states. Rather, they were states with small farms and small farms did not need slaves, nor could the farmers afford them. South Carolina, Virginia, and Georgia had vast plantations that required tremendous labor, and therefore slaves, and those plantation owners feared the potential of a slave uprising. As a consequence, they were very hard on the slaves—and just as hard on the blacks after they were freed.

After the Civil War, even though the slaves were given their freedom, most of them didn't go anywhere. Some went north, but generally they stayed in Mississippi, Alabama, and South Carolina, so you ended up with places with huge black populations—particularly in the old South Carolina plantation counties where you might have had a ninety percent black population. That's why there were such onerous laws to keep blacks from voting. Some counties made it impossible for black people to vote because, if they hadn't, the white candidates would have been crushed at the polls.

In North Carolina, we didn't have such a large black population, and as you went up into the mountains, there were very few black people. There was no reason for them to settle in the mountains as there was no work for them to do.

The mill villages generally had a twenty-five percent black population, and they were at the bottom end of the totem pole. The mills hired them to do menial tasks like maintenance and garbage pickup. I never saw a black looper in a hosiery mill. I never saw a black person in the card room of a cotton mill until much later, when white people stopped working there.

WHEN THE BUS BOYCOTT of Birmingham began in 1961, followed by the sit-ins at lunch counters, you read about it in the newspapers, you saw it on TV, and people talked about it, but you didn't see many changes. As the civil rights movement crept along, blacks gained certain freedoms. Eventually they were able to ride anywhere on the bus they wanted, but in fact, they tended to stay in the back of the bus anyway. They continued to stay in their own neighborhoods. It was a very, very gradual process, even though I know to the rest of the country it looked like the civil rights movement had moved into the South and things were really starting to change. The truth of the matter was, in its early stages, the civil rights movement was mostly symbolic.

When I went to work for Firestone after college, I went to a significant number of NASCAR races. One of the drivers I got to know well was Wendell Scott, the only black on the circuit. I used to provide him with free tires. Wendell had started racing at Bowman-Gray Stadium in Winston-Salem. Alvin Hawkins was the promoter. One thing that the white South was never unabashed about: selling tickets to black people as long as they sat separately. In the movie theaters white people sat in the lower balcony, blacks in the upper balcony. At Bowman-Gray, Alvin took a section of the grandstand and assigned it to black race fans. In order to draw those black fans, Alvin needed a black driver, and that's when Wendell emerged. It wasn't long before he began racing the entire circuit all through the South.

His race car operation was typical of a black body shop in a small town, a black barbershop, or any black small business. There was very little money, so the enterprise was tattered and torn and barely making it. Everything was used. When I began to work with Wendell, he had hand-me-down stuff from parts supplier Holman and Moody—cars, engines, rear ends, and pretty much everything else. It was the worst equipment. He bought a lot of equipment from junkyards—not that other people didn't do that—but he could just about barely make it from one race to the next. The other problem Wendell had was that he never had enough guys working for him. It was a tough, tough existence, and he was always pretty dirty and greasy because he had to work on his car himself. By that time a lot of drivers didn't have to do that.

As a result he couldn't compete. He just tried to stay in there and be around at the finish to make a little money, and then he'd move on to the next place. He had to conserve the car, because he couldn't afford to fix it. One time on a pit stop he was so short-handed that he got out of the car and helped with the tire changing—which would put him another two laps down.

I can remember being at the Spartanburg Fairgrounds—a half-mile dirt track—a place that could not have been more segregated. It was all white people, and mostly from the lowest of economic circumstances. Wendell was driving one of those beat-up cars from Holman and Moody. He was in the race because not that many cars entered, so everyone who signed up automatically was accepted. Wendell went down in the first turn and flipped, and tore his car up pretty good. Before the race resumed, several drivers went up into the grandstand with their helmets to try to raise some money for him. It was quite a gesture, but it didn't produce much money. Last year his wife told me exactly what it was: $300. He was able to get back in the race because he had an uncanny ability to fix things and make the most of what he had.

Wendell was an extraordinary person to be able to put up with all he did. The other racers didn't pay much attention to him one way or another. Some of them would give him their hand-me-downs—like you gave maids your used clothes—and think they were doing him a big favor.

Richard Howard, the promoter who preceded me at Charlotte Motor Speedway, actually put a deal together once for Wendell where he was supposed to get a well-prepared car from Holman and Moody. In practice he did fairly well. There was no doubt in anyone's mind about his ability to drive a race car. Even when he was driving junk, he was competing at Daytona, Atlanta, Charlotte, and Rockingham. He had to have skill just to get around those tracks. I don't doubt he could have been a fine race driver had he come along at a different time.

The race he won at Jacksonville is still talked about today. Wendell won, but Jacksonville had the culture of South Georgia, and they would not declare him the winner because they didn't want him kissing Miss Something-or-Other in the winner's circle. They said Buck Baker won it, and Buck got to kiss Miss Something-or-Other. The next day they declared that Wendell had won the race.

His not being declared the winner in the first place was pretty fishy. In those days, NASCAR scoring was pretty meticulous, and it was pretty difficult not to figure out who won the race. It was two hundred laps and only twenty cars. How do you miss something like that? I never learned the whole story, but it was not a pretty chapter in the history of NASCAR.

I never asked Wendell about it, and he never talked about it.

The interesting thing about Wendell Scott was that he was able to live in a totally white male world that mostly looked down on black people, and he was able to swallow real hard and ignore such things as not ever being invited to race at Darlington Raceway by Bob Colvin.

I remember an incident after Bob's death. Diane Sawyer was coming to Darlington to do a piece on Richard Petty for *60 Minutes*. It was during the week before the Southern 500, and Darlington was always a redneck carnival. One of the attractions was called Dunk Leroy. A black man, Leroy was his name, sat in a chair, and for a dollar you were handed three balls to hit a target. If you hit it, Leroy would drop into a tank of water. As soon as I saw Dunk Leroy, I went over to Scrunt Shipman and Red Tyler, two men on the Darlington board who worked the garage and infield for the track, and I warned them that they better get rid of Dunk Leroy before Diane Sawyer and her camera crew arrived. I could see CBS jumping all over that and accusing NASCAR and the track of being racist as a result.

I said, "Good God, they will rip us apart." This was at a time when we were trying to do what we could to upgrade our image, which wasn't very good at best. It was bad enough with the Confederate flags flying every-where. And when they told Leroy he had to leave, he got mad as a hornet. Leroy didn't want to give up his livelihood. He was not happy, and I don't think he ever came back. So some things work the other way. We denied the man a bountiful weekend.

Had Wendell Scott won races, he would have been like Jackie Robinson. The fact he didn't win allowed white people to feel comfortable. "Well, don't worry about this nigger. He ain't gonna win any races. Let him be."

The great tragedy of Wendell Scott was that Talladega did him in. He was in a terrible, terrible, multi-car wreck there, and suffered terrible, terrible injuries. He almost died, and he never raced again. In the early days of Talladega, a lot of bad things happened, and he was one of the victims. The extent of his injuries wasn't disclosed after the race, but that wasn't racism. That was the policy of the tracks—injuries were bad PR. He was taken to the hospital, and after he got there, they found out he had a fractured skull.

So Wendell certainly paved the way to an extent, but what did he pave the way for? Nothing of consequence has happened since. I often wondered, *Did Wendell die in vain*? I will never know his feelings unless his wife talks about it, and she and their daughter have remained tight-lipped about all that.

CHAPTER 3

Learning the Ropes

A S A YOUNGSTER I FANCIED MYSELF an entrepreneur. In addition to my bicycle business, I also liked to buy and sell cars. In the spring of 1956, I found a '39 Cadillac LaSalle coupe in a car lot. It was a really nice car, but cheap because the owner said there was something wrong with the clutch and you couldn't shift it. He said he thought something really bad was wrong with it, but I knew it was just a throw-out bearing, so I bought the car for twenty dollars. I got the car home, and it took me two days to take apart and put back together again. It cost me nine dollars to fix.

Again, this was back in the days when I didn't have any money except the little money I earned at the bike shop and whatever odd jobs I could do. I had the LaSalle parked in downtown Gastonia, and the owner of the local radio station saw it and said he had to have it. So, when he offered me $700, which was a lot of money in those days, I took it.

So I was well-heeled by the time I began college at the University of South Carolina. I arrived at Columbia, the state capital, and the move to the big city opened up my life. I had come from a small-town environment, and it was just wonderful getting away from that.

We started spring football practice. The guys were so much bigger and faster than in high school, and everybody hit like a Mack truck. Even though I knew I was a marginal player, I enjoyed playing and managed to stagger through my first semester. The coach, whose name was Warren

Giese, called me into his office and said, "I understand you race stock cars." I told him I did. He said, "I don't want you doing it." So for a time I stopped.

The summer went by, and I started the second semester of my freshman year. Practice started again, and I was enjoying it, except that Columbia is probably the hottest place in the world to play football. It's in the hill section of South Carolina where the heat is just brutal. Getting through it was tough because the coaching staff wouldn't give you any water. All they would do was let you suck on a lemon. Some days we were out in a hundred-degree heat facing full contact.

By fall I had run through my LaSalle windfall. The school gave the players on the football team fifteen dollars a month for what they called laundry money. I had bought a '53 Hudson Hornet, which was the scourge of NASCAR. My dorm was about three-quarters of a mile from the football field and it was all downhill, so I would get five guys—the heaviest I could find—and we'd pile into that car, and we'd coast down to the practice field to save money on gas. Most days we made it without cranking the motor, though sometimes we wouldn't quite get there, and we'd have to start it.

There was a gas station across the street from the practice field. We didn't need much gas to get back to the dorm. The gas was full-service, and there were times when I would run out of money, and I'd say to the attendant, "I don't want to dry up your tanks, so I need a quarter's worth of gas." That used to really tick him off.

The gas station also sold beer, which we were absolutely prohibited from drinking—a prohibition which absolutely no one paid any attention to. You could buy beer at eighteen.

I enjoyed living in Columbia. I didn't get home very often, even though it was only a hundred miles away. You had to drive the back roads. There were no interstates in those days.

I began to accumulate some interesting friends, mostly football players. A lot of guys had been in the service in Korea and had played service football, so they were quite a bit older. Some of them were twenty-five or twenty-six. One guy, Corky Gaines, had been on the all-Marine team in Honolulu. He looked like the Neanderthal man. He was 5 feet 11 inches tall, weighed about 245 pounds, and had a huge jaw and a real huge head. He taught me a lot and helped me a lot.

I was a guard. Back then you played both ways, and I was marginal. He gave me tips that made me better. He didn't know how to drive, so anywhere I went, he went with me.

There was another player by the name of Tom Perry, a tackle who everyone called Mot, which was Tom spelled backward. He was 6 feet 3 inches tall, weighed 270 pounds, and had a huge stomach and an insatiable appetite. He knew the short-order cooks in the college mess hall, and when we got our laundry checks, Mot and I would go up to the counter and say, "Fill her up," and they knew Mot wanted chocolate pie. He'd think nothing of eating twelve pieces, and then we would somehow make it back to the dorm room.

Another student by the name of Booty discovered that at exactly five minutes before eleven the second shift would leave the school cafeteria kitchen. For five minutes no one was there to guard the place because the workers on the first shift wouldn't get there before eleven. Booty figured he had four minutes to get to work, and as soon as the second-shift workers left, he and a friend would rush into the cafeteria's freezer, steal as many pies as they could, and carry them back to the dorm where he'd sell them at a deep discount. Booty's record was twelve. Of course, Mot Perry's room was the first one they went to, because Mot would buy three or four of them for a quarter each.

The campus police began to investigate, and one night Booty went for the record and stole fourteen. The cops caught him and his friend on the way out, but not without a chase. Booty tripped, and his friend ran into him, and the pies went everywhere. From that point on to this day, the University of South Carolina has never left its kitchen unguarded.

We got our books free as part of our scholarship, but one of my teammates sold his books just as soon as he got them because he had no intention of ever reading them. To my knowledge he never opened a book. He managed to make it through two years of eligibility before he finally flunked out. He took some exciting courses like Physical Education I, Physical Education II, and First Aid. We sure did have a lot of characters there.

There were no black football players at the University of South Carolina even though a consensus All-American winner in the fifties was J. C. Caroline, who came from Columbia and whose father worked at our stadium. J. C. had to go all the way to the University of Illinois to play football. If he had played at the University of South Carolina, we might have won the national championship. But in those days of segregation it was impossible.

I went to a black barber, and as soon as I walked into his shop, he would start joshing me, saying, "Do you know who's the best football player in the state of South Carolina?" I had to go through this every time I went for a haircut. On the wall was a great big picture of J. C. Caroline.

One weekend, when South Carolina had a bye week, our line coach wanted a group of us to see South Carolina State, a black school, play because he wanted us to watch this lineman who was 6 feet 6 inches and 260 pounds, and who could move faster than any back on our team. His name was Deacon Jones. Before the game, I said to one of their players, "This Jones. I understand he's quite a lineman." He looked at me and said, "He is the line." And that day Deacon was unbelievable.

We were down on the field after the game, and their guys were glad to see us. They knew who we were. I said to our coach, "We ought to take him back to Columbia."

"I wish we could," he said.

MY COLLEGE EDUCATION was interrupted my junior year when I got hurt real bad scrimmaging during football practice. We were getting ready to play Army, and I was one of the players mimicking the Army team. This was when All-American Pete Dawkins was playing for Army, which featured Bill Carpenter, the Lonesome End, and a no-huddle offense, which no one had ever seen before. South Carolina was the first team to see it.

I was on defense, getting ready to make a tackle, and as soon as I made the hit, my teammate from behind drove his helmet into my back. I was in so much pain I couldn't move. I injured two vertebrae, and that ended my playing career. I tried to come back, but I was in too much pain to play.

After my spinal injury kept me from returning to the team in the spring, I entered one more boxing match. I went down to Kingstree, South Carolina, and I fought a heavyweight from Yonkers, New York. He wasn't very good, and I barely beat him, and right then I resigned myself that very night to switch from a physical career to a mental one.

For me to keep my scholarship even though I was hurt, I had to work. Like most of the football players, my assignment was to work in the laundry room washing jocks and T-shirts. I didn't mind doing that, but I had a better idea. I saw there was an opening in the sports information department, so I went to Coach Giese and asked him if I could work there instead. Coach Giese talked to the head of the department, and I got the assignment.

That's when my life changed dramatically. My job was to promote the football players as well as the basketball and baseball players. I learned a lot about promotion, and I began to develop a serious interest in journalism. I also had a burning interest in stock car racing.

Russ Catlin was the PR director at Darlington Raceway then. He had been brought in from Indianapolis to put Darlington on the map. This was 1958, when it was the only paved superspeedway in the United States besides Indianapolis. Daytona was still running on the beach.

Russ had been editor of *Speed Age Magazine*, which was the only racing magazine back then. He'd also worked in the PR department at Indianapolis. He was from Pennsylvania. He really knew racing, and he was a superb publicist. I don't think there was ever a better one than him.

When school ended, I decided I wanted to work for Russ during the summer. After I wrote him a pretty persuasive letter, I wondered if I would ever hear back. About a week later he wrote back, asking me to come down and see him.

I hopped in my '55 Chevy and went down to Darlington to see him. He lived right by the track off the first turn in a place he called The Copperhead Manse. Russ would sit on the front porch at night, and we'd talk about all the things he'd done, and he'd talk to me about what I was doing. He offered me a job for the summer, and I gladly took it.

I learned a tremendous amount working for him. Back then, the big Darlington race was always on Labor Day, so I was able to work right through it.

Getting that job allowed me to meet the drivers of the day. Fireball Roberts was one of the first to greet me. Fireball was the type of person to reach his hand out to people. Tim Flock was another very friendly person who always had time for the fans. Junior Johnson didn't talk much in those days, but he was pretty friendly. And then there was Tiny Lund, a big bear of a man who always had time for you. Tiny loved to fish and so did I. Everybody liked Tiny because of his happy bearishness.

Tiny won the 1963 Daytona 500 when he replaced Marvin Panch, whom he had rescued from a burning Maserati during practice at the speedway. For most of his career, Tiny drove with a chronic bad back after a terrible accident at a track in West Memphis, Arkansas. It was the largest dirt track in the country—a mile and a half—and he was going into a corner in a '57 Chevy when something broke in the front end and the car began flipping violently. Some say it flipped fifteen times. Tiny was thrown out of the car onto the track and was run over by another car. He broke his back and other bones. Had it been anyone else, he would have been killed. Being Tiny, he miraculously made it through.

Sadly, Tiny died in August 1975 in a crash on the eighth lap at a race at Talladega. His car came to a stop in the backstretch, and another car smashed into his driver's side door. He was killed instantly.

I'll tell you who else I met, and they weren't old enough to race yet: Cale Yarborough and Richard Petty. Cale, who was sixteen, was always around Darlington, and Richard, who was fifteen, came to the races with his father, Lee. And I also got to know a teenage Bobby Allison who had come up from Miami to sweep floors for car owner Carl Kiekhaefer. I have known these guys literally my whole life.

Carl Kiekhaefer was one of the most unusual people we have ever had in racing. He owned the Mercury Outboard Engine company, based in Wisconsin, and when he came into NASCAR in 1955 he about revolutionized the sport. Unlike most car owners, who counted their pennies and scrimped and used parts over and over, Kiekhaefer spent whatever it took to win. For him, money was no object. He was Rick Hendrick before Rick Hendrick was even born.

Kiekhaefer's cars were immaculate, and so were the white uniforms his drivers wore. He was the first owner who had what I call a West Coast shop on the East Coast. It was an eat-off-the-floor shop with everything in its place. His cars were brought to the track in expensive, brightly painted carriers.

He hooked up with Chrysler, and his cars were beasts to say the least. These were the famed Chrysler 300Bs, which had the powerful hemi engines in them. They were big cars that looked like tanks. Kiekhaefer painted them cream white, and when you saw one of them, you thought to yourself, *This might do okay on the big tracks, but it hardly fits on a track as small as Bowman-Gray Stadium in Winston-Salem or a half-mile dirt track.* But it not only fit, it was formidable. Tim Flock won the racing championship in 1955 in Carl Kiekhaefer's Chrysler 300B.

Carl Kiekhaefer did more to change the MO of racing operations than anybody who preceded him. He changed the way owners and crew chiefs related to their drivers. He demanded his drivers win, win, win, or else. He set the stage for the factory wars that followed from 1964 to 1970 when Ford and Chrysler went at it.

§

BILL FRANCE, THE MAN WHO invented late-model stock car racing, was always coming up with newfangled ideas, and one of them was a sports car circuit that ran on oval tracks. He ran a race at Raleigh, a one-mile asphalt track that wasn't open long but made its mark. It was a dangerous track, and during the first race two Modified drivers were killed. Kiekhaefer entered Tim Flock in a 1955 Mercedes Gull Wing, and he won the race overwhelmingly. It was a very expensive car, but it didn't make any difference to Kiekhaefer. It was the only time a Mercedes ever ran in a NASCAR race.

Kiekhaefer, who was very dogmatic, very Prussian in his attitude, almost caused Tim to suffer a nervous breakdown. His demanding nature did not sit well in the South. He was resented for it. He demanded his drivers not sleep with their wives the night before the race and ordered them to be in bed at a certain time. Since he paid more money than anyone else, the drivers did as they were told.

Though Tim Flock was the driving champion in '55, Kiekhaefer wasn't satisfied with winning only eighteen of thirty-eight races. He wanted to win them all, so he hired six of the very best to drive his cars, including Herb Thomas, Speedy Thompson, and Buck Baker. That year Kiekhaefer cars won twenty-one of the first twenty-five Grand National races. From March through May, he won sixteen consecutive events. But then the other car owners began to complain, and the fans got bored and started booing his cars, and Bill France began to panic.

Buck Baker won the championship driving for Kiekhaefer in 1956. When they made him, the mold was thrown far, far away. Buck was a feisty, hard-drinking, temper-tantrum-throwing guy who gave no quarter to anybody. I knew him well enough never to turn my back on him. He was capable of anything. He was the kind of guy who acted like he would slap the crap out of you anytime.

He and his wife, Margaret, who was a big woman, would get into fights. She wouldn't take any sass from him, and they fought just about anywhere they wanted to. Buck's anger was more than on the surface. He wore it on both sleeves.

He was born down near Florence, South Carolina. He had wavy, dark black hair. I suppose you could call him handsome. He was a great Modified driver who had an unbelievable mean streak. It showed up in the race car and out of the race car; it just showed up whenever it wanted to show up.

If you ever bumped him, you were going to get spun out or smashed or pushed into the wall. I can remember him hitting guys, flipping them, and creating havoc—often. I particularly remember when he drove stock cars that they called "jalopies," '29 and '30 Model A Fords. They didn't have fenders on them and didn't have a top. They were never allowed to run in NASCAR. They were nasty little race cars that you could really get hurt in, and I can remember seeing Buck drive one of those. Most drivers didn't like them because they were so dangerous, but Buck wasn't bothered at all. As he sat in that car, I thought, *The devil himself is behind the wheel.*

Buck drove a city bus for a living. He worked for the Charlotte Transit Authority, and he finally quit when he won enough races. He raced from 1949 all the way until 1976, winning 46 Grand National races and 44 poles.

I can remember him finishing fourth in the standings in 1953 even though he was driving a '53 Chevy, a terrible race car. It had a vacuum-shift and a six-cylinder inline engine. I could not imagine why he was driving that car. But he ended up driving some pretty good cars, including winning fourteen races and the championship in Carl Kiekhaefer's '56 Chrysler 300B.

You might wonder how the combination of Buck's temper and Kiekhaefer's Prussian demeanor won a championship. What Buck did was swallow hard time and again. The one thing that always improved his mood was winning. He also saw that Kiekhaefer had genius. People will put up with a lot to be part of that.

In 1956, the booing got to Kiekhaefer, and his entry into NASCAR didn't do much for his Mercury Outboard Engine business because most fans thought he was advertising Mercury cars. Carl Kiekhaefer's cars won thirty races out of fifty-six in 1956, and then at the end of the season—satisfied there were no more worlds to conquer after winning two championships and tired of fighting with Bill France Sr.—Kiekhaefer left Grand National Racing, never to be heard from again.

THOUGH RUSS CATLIN WAS publicist for the Darlington Raceway from 1953 through 1969, he never saw one lap of competition on the racetrack. He would sit down in a little bunker underneath the press box in the first turn, and he would listen to the announcer with his earphones on and figure out what was going on in the race. He had a Teletype, and he would type up the results and run them up to the press box.

This was back in the days when the sports pages in the South were totally stick and ball sports—football, baseball, basketball, and golf. To get publicity for racing, you had to be really clever, and Russ was clever.

He would organize trips to Norfolk, Spartanburg, and other places, and he would bring together what media there was, and he would always bring along a couple of drivers. His favorite was Joe Weatherly, and if he couldn't get Joe, he'd get Curtis Turner. He would introduce the driver, but he'd see that the driver didn't have to make a speech. I learned that trick from him. He would get up and say, "This is one of the greatest drivers ever to hold a steering wheel. He risks life and limb." Russ was like a carnival barker. He'd build the guy up like he was immortal, and then he'd say, "Ask this fantastic athlete anything you'd like," and that made the driver comfortable because all he had to do was answer questions, something he could handle.

Many a night I would sit on his back porch as Russ imparted his great wisdom. One time he said, "I want you to learn some things at that university you're going to. I want you to learn meteorology, because a racetrack doesn't have a roof over its head and you're going to need to know about the weather, and I want you to learn about television. Right now everything in the media is newspaper driven, but it won't be long before it's all television driven." This was back in 1958 when big urban markets might have three stations. Back then a station would do news, weather, and sports in fifteen minutes. But Russ kept impressing on me the need to gain experience with television.

Russ was also a great storyteller. He had written more about the days of the board tracks than any man alive. Those old board tracks were the precursor to the superspeedways of today. Had they been made of concrete instead of wood, racing would be completely different today. He knew every one of the Indy drivers, and he would tell tales about them—how Ted Horn got killed—and how when they investigated, they discovered he had knocked down thirteen posts.

He always had a story; many were laced with superstition. Peanut shells or something green in the car was always the reason a driver was killed.

One night I was with him on his porch along with Bob Talbert, a brilliant columnist with the *Columbia State* who later went to the *Detroit Free Press*, and Joe Whitlock, another fine reporter. It was dark by the track, and Russ, in all seriousness, said, "Where there's been a violent death on the racetrack, there is always an aura at night. If you go to that spot, you can feel it."

We were sitting there with our eyes bulging because a year or two before Billy Myers had been killed in the third turn at Darlington, so obviously the three of us had to get up and walk over there to see if Russ was right. I will say we had a few beers, although Russ drank nothing but bourbon, as was the custom in South Carolina.

We walked over to the third turn. It was pitch black. No one was in the place. We got to the spot where we thought the accident had happened. Bob, Joe, and I were like three ten-year-olds. One of us said, "I feel it. I feel it. It's here. There's a life force here." And we were scared to death that Billy Myers or his spirit would come out of the asphalt.

That week was race week at Darlington. Junior Johnson had just come out of prison, convicted of a moonshine offense. Junior was racing for Ray Fox in a Dodge, which everyone called The Goat back then. In those days Junior was heavyset, brooding, and taciturn, with black hair and thick eyebrows.

I was over in the pits gathering information for Russ Catlin while the race teams were practicing. I'd call him on the phone and tell him what was going on. If there was an accident, he insisted I measure the skid marks so he could write, "Fireball Roberts this afternoon lost control in the second turn and skidded 611 feet and slammed into the wall with the right front fender, totally destroying his car." Russ always said that wrecks, if they were spectacular enough, got more publicity than who won the race.

All of a sudden the yellow flag comes out, and there's a big commotion. Junior's car had broken a right rear axle going down the back straightaway. The car dug into the racetrack, went way up in the air, and left the track. I hauled my butt down to the third turn and ran to where his car landed in a ditch beside the county road.

There was no telling how many times Junior had flipped the car, but when I got there he was still in it. The car was a wreck, and Junior didn't know where he was. The rescue team got him out of the car and took him to the hospital. The next day he came to the track, and he was black and blue. He had bruises everywhere, but he didn't break any bones. Both of his eyes were black. He looked like a raccoon.

Russ made a big deal of it in the papers. I remember what I had told him, and his description sounded a whole lot different—and better—than what I had said. He wrote, "Coming out of the second turn, the rear axle broke violently, sending the car into a terrible spiral, flipping it high in the air. Some estimated as high as thirty feet. It sailed completely out of the track, landed on its top, began a series of violent flips, and landed in a ditch beside County Highway 210. The driver was unconscious at the scene when the attendants got there."

Now that's promotion at its finest, I thought, as he described this spectacular wreck that he had never seen. He had put just the right twist on it. When you think back, in those days there was little TV, few reporters at the track, and the photographers only had 4x5 Speed Graphic cameras, not the fastest camera in the world, so you had to capture the moment in words. And Russ was a master at it. From him I learned that to get tremendous attention you had to take the ordinary and make it extraordinary.

Fireball Roberts absolutely dominated at Darlington in 1963 in the Southern 500. It was the worst race I had ever seen. It ran 500 miles without a caution flag. I thought, *Oh my God, what can Russ say about this? This race was terrible. No one will ever come back to this place again.*

His opening paragraph: "Fireball Roberts, the master of asphalt, ran the most perfect race ever run in the history of NASCAR." He put the "perfect race" spin on it, and I was so impressed. For me, learning under Russ was like a young artist back in the day learning to paint with colors under Raphael. Long after I left him and came to work for the Charlotte Motor Speedway, Russ would write me long letters on that old rag paper with his old manual typewriter. The *J* was always up in the air because it was stuck. I remember in one letter he wrote, "Always go where the money is. Never go where there's no money." And every time I followed his advice, things worked out, and every time I didn't, things didn't. He also kept pressing me about learning TV.

I went back to college for my senior year, but I continued to work for him. I would go down for the spring race and work that week, and I'd work summers and race week. By my senior year I had decided to major in political science because I was thinking of going to law school. South Carolina had a three-and-three program where you could get out in six years. But the more I looked at law books, the more boring I thought law would be, and I cannot stand boring. I decided to change my major to journalism, but that meant taking eighteen hours of journalism in two semesters.

In addition to my part-time job with Russ, I also had two other jobs. I did sports information at the university, keeping my scholarship, and I also had gotten a job with the *Columbia Record* as a sportswriter. Ron Winzel was the sports editor, and I was his only employee.

The good thing was that most of my journalism professors worked at the *Record*. I took a class in makeup, and the guy who taught the class said to me, "Look, you're making up the paper every morning, so I'm going to grade you on how you do that." He said it was going to be much tougher than if I was in his class. The feature writing professor told me the same thing, so I didn't have to go to that class. He'd just grade me. And those two guys would just rip me apart for what I was doing to their newspaper. This was back in the days when there was no playing around. The editors told it like it was. They'd say, "You screwed up. You're using too many adjectives. You're writing too long," and they'd cut your copy in half. And God forsake you if you misspelled a word.

I screwed up so often, I decided to invent a fall guy by the name of Michael Dillon. I even gave him a byline. If someone would call in and say, "You didn't put my son's name in the paper even though he hit two home runs for the Battery Park Little League team yesterday" or if a complaint came in saying, "You misspelled my daughter's name in the softball agate," I would always place the blame on Michael Dillon.

One day there was a softball tournament that I didn't feel like covering, so I had a stringer cover it and I put Michael Dillon's byline on it. Michael screwed up a couple of facts, and the managing editor came in and said to me, "Who the hell is Michael Dillon?" I fudged a little. I said, "He works part-time for us."

The editor said, "He does? He isn't on the payroll."

"I pay him out of my own pocket," I said.

"What does he look like?"

"I don't know. He calls the stories in."

"What's his address?" Now he had me. Of course, he knew full well there wasn't any Michael Dillon. He was just busting my balls. He finally said, "I want you to make him dead without having to write an obit. As far as I am concerned, Michael Dillon is dead." And so I didn't use Michael Dillon anymore.

ONE OF THE MOST memorable stories that I wrote was about Hank Aaron, who was with the Milwaukee Braves. Milwaukee was playing an exhibition game against the Columbia Reds. After the game I went up to him and said, "Mr. Aaron, I would love to interview you." He was very friendly, but reserved. I was persistent. I was not going to leave without interviewing him, and he could sense that. I said, "I want to interview you about what it's like to be a black player in the South today." That got his attention. This was 1960. He said, "Okay, but you don't need this right now, do you?"

I said, "No, but I need it today." He gave me an address where I could meet him in two hours. I knew from the address it was a residence in the black neighborhood. I couldn't figure out why he wanted me to meet him there.

I arrived there two hours later. Turns out it was a boarding house. I figured out that this was where the black players stayed. I was incredulous. I thought, *This is one of the greatest baseball players in the world, and he has to stay in a boarding house in Columbia.* Aaron wasn't allowed to stay in the hotel downtown because of segregation.

We sat and talked on the front porch of the boarding house. He was very guarded in what he said, because he didn't want to come straight out and say his life was filled with prejudice, but you could tell it was there. We talked for about three hours, and I wrote the story. The next morning I brought it to the paper and shoved it into the first edition, which had a very limited circulation. The first edition was a trial run, and if the editors didn't like a story, they pulled it before it was given prominent play. I knew the Aaron story was going to hit a nerve, and I couldn't help wonder whether the editors would kill it before it made the second edition.

The managing editor came storming over to me, fire in his eyes. I thought, *Oh shit, it's hit the fan. He's going to lay me low, and he's going to pull the story.* Because of the racial aspect. He looked at me as though he was going to rip me apart. What he said was, "Your damn paragraphs are too long."

I almost dropped out of the seat. And every time I read *USA Today*, I think that the ghost of this man must be doing the editing because when you worked for him, you did not write long paragraphs.

CHAPTER 4

Moonshine and Racing

I DON'T THINK WE CAN ever measure fully the contributions bootlegging made to racing, not only technically, but in the drivers it provided. Wilkes County was the center of the moonshine trade in North Carolina, and the early 1950s was the peak of the moonshine business. The greatest moonshine bust in federal history occurred in 1935 when the feds raided Junior Johnson's father's house. Junior himself was arrested at his Dad's still in 1956. He served almost a year in Chillicothe, Ohio, a federal prison.

It was a two-story farmhouse up there in Wilkes County, and somebody tipped off the feds that he had a huge stash. The feds raided the place, and they seized 17,000 gallons, a record. Junior must have been sleeping on top of the stuff. For a long time he wouldn't talk about his moonshining activities. It was a federal felony offense. He couldn't vote, couldn't do a number of things, so he wasn't real happy talking about it. Even after Tom Wolfe wrote about him, calling him the Last American Hero, we would sit around many a night during a tire test with nothing to do, and Junior just would not talk about it. Only lately has he opened up about it.

His biggest problem, he told me, was buying sugar, which was an integral part of the moonshine manufacturing process. The Internal Revenuers began to concentrate on looking for buyers of larger quantities of sugar. They figured whoever was buying the sugar was making the moonshine. Today it's become part of his life story. He's even proud of it. As much as we glamorize it, it was a bunch of guys working real hard at night being as elusive as possible.

To reach the stills, you had to go way back into the hills. The routes to the stills weren't paved, and in most cases there was no road at all, just a trail. You had to walk the supplies up there and build the still after you got there. There was a tremendous amount of hard labor involved. It was a very rough life, one Junior said he was glad to get out of. And it was racing that got him out of it.

He's very proud that he never got caught in a bootleg car. He made a lot of runs, and there were a lot of chases, but nobody ever caught him.

There were a few other legendary bootleg figures. There was one bootlegger called the Gray Ghost. No one knew who he was. The legend is that the feds finally trapped him in a roadblock on a bridge, and he jumped out of the car into the river, and no one ever found hide nor hair of him. Nobody on the mountain thinks he drowned, and nobody will even confess to knowing him. I don't know if Junior will admit it even happened.

I was curious as to which car the bootleggers favored most, so a few years ago Junior set it up for me to go up to Wilkes County and talk to a group of old bootleggers. Turns out most of them favored the '39 Ford over the '40 Ford because it was a hundred pounds lighter and it had a painted, rather than a chrome, grill. NASCAR Modified racers also loved that '39 Ford. In the early days of racing, the bootleggers and the racers used similar engines—the old flathead Mercury. Then came the overhead valve engine in the Olds Rocket 88 and then the Cadillac, and as soon as they hit the junkyards, the bootleggers pulled out their flatheads. What finally put the Fords out of the bootlegging business was the Dodge hemi engine, which had so much brute horsepower.

Back in the 1940s and 1950s there was very little traffic on the roads, so another reason the bootleggers liked the '39 Ford was that it was a plain-Jane-looking car. They did not want to take anything showy on the roads. And a truck surely would have tipped off the revenue guys big time.

There was talk that the bootleggers put tanks in their cars to hold the moonshine, and that did happen, but most of the time they simply filled the big mason jars and stuffed them in the trunk, the back seat, and the passenger seat, because the customers mostly were the shotgun houses in the mill villages. Each shotgun house would buy four or five jars. His customers weren't buying fifty gallons. So basically they were making a milk run. They did all of this at night, driving from customer to customer.

When I talked to the old bootleggers, they made it clear that the King of the Mountain was Junior Johnson. All were his friends, and they all looked up to him. One time I invited eight of them to the Charlotte Motor Speedway for an exhibit. I put up a real still. We had bootleg cars. I promised each of them a steak dinner.

We were sitting around the Speedway Club, and the subject of prison came up. They all had been there at least once. One guy said, "I didn't mind getting caught north of Charlotte. I didn't like getting caught south of Charlotte." I asked him why. He said, "When you got caught south of Charlotte, you had to go to Atlanta. When you got caught north, you went to Chillicothe." I asked him why he would want to go to Ohio in the cold weather. "Because there was always somebody from Wilkes County there," he said.

Under federal guidelines, the first time you got caught they gave you a suspended sentence. It was usually three to five years, and they'd suspend it. They seized the car, kept it, and used it to chase your buddies or they sold it at auction. Once when I was in high school I bought one of them, a '40 Ford with a Rocket 88 engine in it. The car had never been washed. That's the way they liked them.

The second time you got caught, the suspended sentence was activated, and you went to prison, usually for a year if you were on your best behavior. That's why so many of the drivers were teenagers; they had no record. And that's why so many of them quit after the first time they were caught.

Your chances of getting caught at the still were slim. I knew Stanley Noel who for years was an internal revenue agent. Hollywood always made a big deal of the supposed camaraderie between the agents and the bootleggers. Stanley said that was BS. He said he and another agent were going through the woods one day looking for a still, and the next thing he knew he woke up in the hospital in Winston-Salem. Somebody came from behind a tree and hit him right in the temple with the flat edge of a shovel. However, most ATF agents said the bootleggers in the Carolina mountains were gentlemen compared to the crooks they encountered in Philadelphia, New York, and Cleveland.

Hollywood also loves to play up the chases, but the bootleggers would do anything to avoid them. If a bootlegger found himself being chased, the first thing he would do was to get off the main roads, which were paved, and head for the country roads, which were dirt or gravel and kicked up a lot of dust. If they could stir up enough dust, that's all they needed to do to get away. And don't forget, radio communication wasn't very good in those days.

Junior said he was always into stealth. Most of his runs were out of Wilkes County, down the mountain into the Piedmont and on into the dry counties, particularly the textile mill villages where you couldn't legally buy booze. The only way the poor guy in the mill village got any relief was to go to a shotgun house and pay fifty cents for a drink. The bartender would fill up a glass with white whiskey, and then he'd chase it down with something— everything from lemon-lime soda to Kool-Aid. The stuff would hit your throat, and it would light a fire so bad, you had to chase it down with something.

One time I attended the retirement party for a North Carolina state trooper by the name of Clyde Shook. The usual assortment of troopers was there. When there's a retirement party, you can drive 200 miles an hour down the interstate anywhere within 60 miles of the place, and no one will stop you because all the troopers are at the party. Some of my bootleg buddies who I had gotten to know were also there. All in attendance were older red-faced Scotch-Irish guys who knew Clyde.

The troopers' job was different from the internal revenue agents, who were there to stop them from selling alcohol without the tax. The troopers' job was to enforce the speeding laws. They weren't as involved with the boot-leggers, but sometimes they cooperated with the feds in trying to catch them.

Part of the tradition of the retirement party is to bring a gift. I brought Clyde a Speedway jacket. After me came an old bootlegger carrying what we call in the South a poke, an old paper bag that has been around forever and is crinkled in a way that no one in Hollywood could make crinkled. It's been used over and over because these people in the mountains save everything. They were into recycling before they knew what the word meant. So this bootlegger comes up to the podium with his poke, and he says, "Clyde, do you remember that roadblock you set up in 1951? It was up on 421 coming out of Boone. And that car done run that roadblock on you, and you got mad and you threw a flashlight at it, and it went into the car." And then he reached into the old bag and pulled out the old flashlight. "Well, I want to give it back to you!" And when he did that, the place went wild. It had been Clyde's flashlight. The bootlegger had run past him, Clyde had thrown it at him, and it had landed in his car. And here he was returning it all these years later.

§

FOR MOST OF THE PEOPLE who lived in Wilkes County, there wasn't any work to be had. None. And you couldn't think of a place that was more difficult to farm. Those mountains of North Carolina were tough because the only places that were flat were the valleys, and they were prone to flooding. You could grow crops, but chances were you would get flooded out. It was not an easy life.

What brought economic change to Wilkes County was Holly Farms, which set up a vast network of independent chicken raisers. The farmer would go to where his pasture once was and put up big, long chicken houses. He'd raised chickens, and Holly Farms bought them and processed them, and that enabled the farmer to use the land in a very productive way. And it gave people a living.

If you asked someone in Wilkes County what he did for a living and he said, "I have a public job," that didn't mean he worked for the post office. It meant he got a steady paycheck every week as opposed to piecework where he'd be paid in cash. For some reason the people from Wilkes County were so damned independent they didn't like coming down from the mountains and going down to the mill villages. They maintained a ferocious independence that still exists today.

Several things put the bootleggers out of business. Law enforcement began to have better communication, and it was getting harder and harder to outrun the lightning speed of a radio. Also the roads were getting paved. But the other thing that really ended the era was that in the late 1960s counties began to vote in whiskey. Today I don't even know if there's a dry county anymore in the state. So there was no real need for moonshine, though there has been a resurgence way back in the mountains. College kids have started drinking it because it's so cheap.

Here's a good ending for the bootleg story: A guy I knew who was once brand manager for Winston cigarettes was on the Internet a few years ago, and he noticed that a federal liquor license for the manufacture of distilled spirits was available in the state of North Carolina. And he bought it. He paid $500 for it. The first call he made was to Junior Johnson. So he and Junior went into business and today they are making legal corn whiskey. They have two brands, one called Cat Daddy, which the college kids love, and the other one is called Junior Johnson's Midnight Moon. You can go to any North Carolina ABC liquor store and buy it. You can also buy it in Virginia, Tennessee, South Carolina, and parts of Georgia.

Moonshine had become legal!

Junior is doing well fifty years after he was jailed for making the same whiskey.

BILL FRANCE WOULD NEVER talk about the impact moonshining had on stock car racing, and Bill France Jr., his son, went to his grave refusing to talk about it. The Frances didn't want to admit that moonshining had anything to do with NASCAR, and that's the biggest bunch of hogwash that ever was.

There were actually two bootlegging centers, Wilkes County, North Carolina, and Dahlonega Georgia, near Atlanta. Because of the moonshiners, Charlotte and Atlanta had the greatest concentration of driving talent in the United States outside of Indianapolis and Southern California. We're talking right after World War II when bootleggers in both areas made oval, red-clay dirt tracks to race on to see who had the fastest cars. That natural red clay was as much a factor in the proliferation of stock car racing as the moonshiners. There was this great vein of red clay from down in Alabama all the way up through Atlanta, Georgia; Greenville, South Carolina; Spartanburg, South Carolina; Charlotte, North Carolina; and on up into Virginia and the foothills of Appalachia.

The further east you went from Atlanta and Charlotte, the more you began to run into loamy, sandy clay, which was not as good as the red clay. Nobody had any money back in those days, so if you found a good area of red clay, it was easy to carve out a track. It was also great as a base for road-building material, and it helped the Piedmont areas of Georgia, North Carolina, South Carolina, and Virginia develop and grow.

Atlanta had a mile track, the Lakewood Speedway, and a number of short, red-clay dirt tracks in the area. The Atlanta area is where the Flock brothers, Ed Samples, Red Vogt, and a driver by the name of Jack Smith came from. And Raymond Parks, who was one of early successful car owners. He's still alive. He's in his nineties. Parks is an interesting character, because he was the link between the two bootlegging centers. He was a man who didn't go to college, so he wasn't a college football fan. He liked cars and racing, and it was a good outlet for him. He liked to be the boss.

Most important, Parks had a lot of money. He bankrolled bootleggers, and he was also big in the vending machine business. Vending was big, whether it was pennies, nickels, or dimes for cigarettes, soft drinks, or bubble gum. Raymond Parks was the King of the Vending Machines in Atlanta, just as Lee Smith was King of the Vending Machines in Charlotte. And both were involved in stock car racing.

Vending machines provided Raymond Parks with a lot of cash, and the bootleg business was a cash business. I had heard he was also involved in numbers, which proliferated in urban areas.

Parks was always immaculately dressed, always in a coat, tie, and hat, and I don't care if it was 20 degrees or 110. He didn't drink, didn't smoke, and if he had vices, I don't know about them. He was quiet and reserved. If you met him, you'd have thought he was a banker or the local Ford dealer—certainly someone of means—by the way he carried himself. What I remember most about Raymond Parks' cars was that they were always really neat and clean, well-painted, and looked first-class. This was back in the days when this was the exception.

His chief mechanic, Red Vogt, was a stockily built, muscular guy who always had a crewcut. He was a very, very hard-working guy, with mechanical talent right up there with Smokey Yunick, Banjo Matthews, the Wood brothers, and Bud Moore as far as knowing what he was doing. Red was one of the most successful Modified mechanics in the history of the sport. That was his real forte. I don't know that he ever really loved Late Model racing, because you couldn't change those cars as much.

Raymond Parks and Red Vogt were very successful. They were particularly good at Lakewood, one of the nastiest racetracks we had—nasty because it was a mile, very fast, and dirt. But Parks not only won races with Red Vogt in Atlanta, he ventured out. Those cars came up to Charlotte and raced. They went over to Daytona and raced. They were successful wherever they went. In 1949 their driver, Red Byron, won the driving championship the first year of NASCAR.

Raymond did not stay in racing long. He got out, and I don't know why. But it was Raymond Parks who was the first successful car owner. He also helped France Sr. financially.

It's INTERESTING. Even though, as the years went by, Atlanta surpassed Charlotte as a cultural center, it did not surpass it as a racing center. The pivotal reason was that the Ford Motor Company located its racing headquarters in Charlotte in the early 1950s, and they installed Pete DePaolo, a former Indy 500 winner, to run its racing program. That program eventually became racing powerhouse Holman and Moody, and it wasn't long before a lot of the race teams had set up shop in Charlotte.

CHAPTER 5

The Robinwood Speedway

I TOOK RUSS CATLIN'S ADVICE and went to work in TV at the CBS affiliate, WBTV, in Charlotte. I got bored real quick, because there were no sounds of engines over there. By then TV had been around for fifteen years, and it had gotten dull and boring, so I needed something else to do. I always liked to have two jobs.

In April 1961 I ran into stock car racer Marvin Panch, who was running the Robinwood Speedway in Gastonia. I had moved back to Belmont, and Gastonia wasn't far away. Marvin told me he wasn't doing very well financially.

I had always loved that track because it was an anomaly, a hippodrome track, more like a big bicycle velodrome than the typical flat quarter-mile track. It was a beautiful red-clay dirt track with corners banked at twenty-four degrees. The straightaways were at about ten degrees, and it was real fast.

Robinwood had been built after the war as a midget track. This was the short period when there was a war between the midget and Sprint cars and the bigger stock cars. The midgets did well in the Northeast, the Northwest, the Midwest, and the far west, where there was money. Where there wasn't money, as in the Carolinas, people couldn't afford to race them.

"I'm finished," said Marvin. "I'm not going to run it anymore. If you want it, you can have it." He was leasing the track from a lady named Mrs. Quinn, who had an adjoining farm. I went over and talked to her. I had no money at all, but I gave her twenty dollars and rented it for a weekend.

I knew that making a success of the track would take a lot of work. I had done some work on the side for a drag racing promoter and car dealer by the name of Bob Osiecki. He later owned the first car to break 180 miles an hour at Daytona, a winged car that Curtis Turner drove first, and then Art Malone drove it to break the record. I went to see Bob, and he agreed to be my partner. I sold a race car I owned and all the parts for $3,000. Now I had to figure out how to put on an event that would make me some money.

I thought, *What I need to do is race cheap race cars.* I started something called the Junior Grand National, because Bill France and NASCAR were running the Grand National circuit. I decided that drivers could enter 1949 to 1953 model cars because they'd be cheap to buy, and I encouraged everyone to paint them like the cars of yesterday. Some did. Some didn't. And they had to use a straight inline six-cylinder engine, a plain old engine you could find in most trucks. It had a lot of torque, which meant you could pass easily. You could buy one in any junkyard for $150.

By race week I had spent my $3,000, and I kept waiting for Bob to put his money in, but he never did. The week of the race he told me he couldn't do it, so there I was by myself. I got out my pick and shovel, and there I was back to digging ditches again. It was the day of the Indianapolis 500 in 1961, and I was listening on the radio, and I was digging a ditch down in the infield to lay some wires as Jim Rathmann won the race.

I promoted my race like it was the last race I would ever run, which come to think of it, it might well have been. I was thinking, *If it rains, I'm up the creek.* I wrote stories for the *Gastonia Gazette* and the *Charlotte Observer* every day, and also for the WBTV news because I was still working at the station. I also dropped flyers from an old Piper Cub. We flew over the mill villages in Belmont and Gastonia. The flyers said: BIG RACE SATURDAY NIGHT $1.50.

I was determined not to have dust on the track the day of the race. I had an old truck with a 1,500-gallon water tank on it, and Friday night me and this big, old African-American guy named Clarence worked all night long putting water down because that's what you have to do. Clarence lived up the road, and one day he came by looking for something to do, and I gave him something. We pumped water out of the creek by the track. I got a Ford tractor, and I used it to till the soil and pack it down. I had seen this done so many times I felt like I knew enough about it not to have any dust.

It was a Saturday in early June, and it didn't rain. Twenty-three cars showed up, which was thirteen more than Marvin was getting. And a pretty good crowd showed up. Almost everyone in the grandstands was a mill worker. Nineteen hundred people paid $1.50, and I paid a purse of $300, which was huge.

We dropped the flag. The track was dust-free. It was one of those nights when everything went right, except halfway through the race—a forty-lap feature—a driver lost it coming off the second turn. He never lifted the throttle, went straight into the infield, hit a dirt bank, vaulted over it, and as he became airborne, I said to myself, *He's headed for the main transformer!*

He knocked the pole down and knocked out most of the lights. There was still some light left from lights in the third turn from another transformer. Fortunately, I had hired an electrician, a pole climber—all electricians were pole climbers—on standby. I figured everything could go out but not the power. He was able to set up a new pole real fast. He got the wires up, finishing the job in about thirty minutes. A racer by the name of Bill Monteith from Clover, South Carolina, won the race in a '53 Ford. It was over by eleven o'clock, and everybody had a great time so I held another one the next week and the next and the next.

We ran four straight races without any rain, and the field began to build. All of a sudden, racers were becoming interested in entering my races because their costs were low. The six-cylinder engine was beginning to make a lot of sense because one could run just about all season.

By the fourth race I had forty cars entered. The entry fee was five dollars. I started anyone who showed up.

A LOT OF TRACKS were sanctioned by NASCAR. I decided to invent my own sanctioning body, which I called the Carolina Racing Association. I had licenses printed up that looked better than NASCAR's.

I was beginning to take a bite out of attendance at the Hickory Speedway, a NASCAR track right up the road run by a man by the name of Grafton Burgess, an old bootlegger. I knew him from when I worked at Darlington. I assume it was Grafton who complained to Pat Purcell—an ex circus promoter, whom Bill France had hired to run NASCAR—because all of a sudden I got a letter from Purcell ordering me to cease and desist in the use of the phrase "Junior Grand National racing." It was addressed to the operator of the Robinwood Speedway. Purcell didn't know I was running the track.

I decided to call him.

"What are you doing running that damn track?" he said.

"Trying to make a living," I said.

"You can't use that name," he said.

"Yes, I can," I said. "You all borrowed it from England from the Grand National Steeplechase."

I never heard another word from Purcell. That was the first obstacle. The second, and tougher, one was that the roads leading to my track needed improvement badly, and the problem got worse as the races became more popular—teaching me that success can bite you in the butt as surely as failure.

THE ROBINWOOD SPEEDWAY was a really fast racetrack, one with two grooves where cars could pass, and the racing was phenomenal. Drivers would really get going down the backstretch, and they'd come out of the fourth turn and slam into the wall and cartwheel down the front straightaway, flipping end over end and sideways. Every night we had four or five flips.

The fans absolutely loved it. After two months, if you weren't there by seven o'clock, you didn't get a seat. But because we were so successful we were congesting the roads, which made it very hard to get to the orthopedic hospital where kids went if they contracted polio. I remember passing by there and seeing the kids on the porch in their iron lungs. It was still a very active hospital, and they didn't like the noise. These are the problems you get when you start to become successful promoting stock car races.

Another problem I had was a demand by a majority of the drivers for a bigger part of the gate. They saw all those people in the grandstands, and they came to me as a group. I argued that I had lowered the cost of racing, that they were having fun and making money, and let's leave it at that. I was investing a lot of time and money, and I thought what I was getting was fair and what they were getting was fair.

There were some troublemakers. There always are. The following Saturday night eight of them conspired against me. This was back in the days when the drivers brought their cars over on low-boys, and they blocked the main entrance, the traffic piled up, and no one could get in.

I had anticipated that something like that might happen, so I had readied four wreckers—two at the entrance—just in case. It was only a two-lane road, and their primary job was to move any car that might have broken down on its way in or out.

We told the troublemakers that if they didn't move their cars, we would tow them, and in typical Scotch-Irish tradition, they said, "You ain't towin' nothin'." They tried to intimidate the wreckers, but I sent out a bunch of beefy guys to make sure they got moved, and they did, but it really screwed us up that night.

The next week we had another incident. The two race leaders, Bob Cooper and Jim Dimeo, had an accident, and they spun out, and we put them in the rear of the field. Angry and feeling I was being unfair, they decided to take it upon themselves to block the track, so they parked their cars side by side at the start/finish line. They sat in the cars, and said they weren't going to move them until we put them back in the front where they had been.

Four or five times they were ordered to move. I really lost my temper. I went down personally and I told them if they didn't move, I would take the water truck and run it right over them. I got in the water truck—it had 1,500 gallons of water in it and weighed about 10,000 pounds. I took off and went by them twice like a stunt driver does before he makes his jump, playing it up, but I was determined to ram them. I had my seat belt on, and there was a gap between them of about six feet. The truck wasn't much narrower. I don't know how I made it. As I drove between them, I shook my fists at them. They knew the next time around I was going to hit them. As I was coming back around, they cranked up, backed down, and got out of the way. I have always wondered what I would have done if they had stayed there. Actually, I know exactly what I would have done because in those days I had quite a temper. But until this evening I had no idea how badly things could get out of hand.

I had another incident. Preston Humphreys came from Forest City, about forty miles away, and he was a heck of a racer. After he won three straight features, the local boys got together and decided they were going to take him out. Preston was leading the race, and as he was lapping this one guy who was chosen to hit him and knock him out of the race, Preston anticipated what he was going to do, and the guy went out of control in the third turn and cartwheeled out of the racetrack going down a thirty-foot bank.

We had to stop the race. The cars stopped out front, and five guys from different race teams came out of the pits and started beating the crap out of Preston with their fists while he sat in his race car. I had hired a policeman, and I was yelling at him to break it up, but he didn't move. So, I jumped off the flag stand, and I went down there, and I broke it up myself. I laid one of them out, and I grabbed another one, and I was about to pop him when I heard this crunch behind me. A guy was getting ready to hit me with a Stilson wrench when my brother, David, who once played guard on the University of North Carolina football team and weighed 240 pounds, cold-cocked him with a forearm. That stopped everything. They had to take him to the hospital along with the driver who had crashed trying to take Preston out of the race.

Preston won the race, and we got through the night. It was one thirty in the morning and my brother and I were counting the money in this little pine shack by the track when we saw headlights coming down the road. We were apprehensive because of the money sitting there. We had a shotgun, but as soon as the lights got closer, I could see it was a police car driven by the cop who wouldn't stop the fight. He was back on duty.

"I have a warrant here for assault and battery," he said.

"You do?" I said. "Who is the warrant for?"

"A guy named Daniel Wheeler. Do you know where he is?"

I said, "Yes, that damned cousin of mine, he's probably in Georgia by now."

The cop said, "I thought so."

What happened was when the guy with the wrench—who my brother, David, hit—got out of the hospital, he went to the police. He thought my brother's name was Daniel, and that's what they put on the warrant. Of course, the cop knew this. He said, "Where do you think Daniel is?"

"Somewhere around Atlanta." I said. How were they going to find anyone, much less a nonexistent person, in Atlanta? They weren't going to look anyway. The cop left, and as far as I know, that warrant is still outstanding.

THE TENSION AT THE ROBINWOOD SPEEDWAY was high, and one night a driver even shot at me with a .38.

I don't even remember what it was over, but he had been drinking, as was the case in too many occasions among drivers and spectators. He had said something to me, and I ordered him to leave the track. He said, "Make me." He was just a little guy, and I grabbed him, and he didn't like that, so I dragged him over to where his truck was. His car wasn't hitched up yet.

"I can't find my keys," he said.

"Then I'll bust in the windows," I said, because I wanted to get rid of him. We had a race to run, and I didn't want to fool around with him anymore. I was looking around for my brother or for the deputy I had hired, and I couldn't find anyone.

"You find your keys and get the hell out of here," I said. "When I come back, I don't want to see you're still here." I should have stayed there with him or gotten someone to make sure he went out, but as is the case with short tracks everywhere, I was trying to run a race and I didn't have much follow through on a lot of things.

I went back upstairs to get the race going, and I forgot about him.

Looking back, the guy obviously had his car keys because he got into his car where he drank more booze. Next thing I knew, somebody was shouting, "There's a man with a gun."

That's when I became concerned because the unwritten rule in the South back then was that you used your fists. You never used a gun, a knife, or a blackjack. And frankly there were a lot of guns around speedways, and still are, but most of the time people don't use them.

I figured it must be the driver I ordered out of the track. And then I saw him. He was screaming and hollering at me. I told him, "I know you have a gun. I don't want you touching that gun. I'm watching your hands." I had several people around me, and I'm looking around trying to find the deputy. This was before the days of radio. There was no instant communication.

Someone said something to the guy, and he pulled his gun and fired two shots. One of the shots came awfully close to me. Thank heaven, no one was hit. Then a couple guys grabbed him and detained him and the deputy sheriff finally showed up and handcuffed him and took him in.

THERE WAS SO MUCH TENSION at the track during this time I started to think that if things kept going like this someone was really going to get hurt. I had created too much drama—the place was too full of tension—but the irony was that was why so many spectators were coming. But I felt like I was standing on the edge of a cliff. How many people had the balls to ever stand there? Not many. I was proud to be standing so close to that edge, but at the same time I was scared to think what might happen if I fell off. I feared someone—maybe me—could get hurt or killed. I could sense I needed to tone it down and back off, and that's what I did.

I did it several ways. I could afford it, so I did pay more money without admitting defeat. I backed off from having to get so involved personally by hiring a few extra security guards who knew what they were doing. Then at the drivers' meeting I was less outspoken. I let them know I was in control, but I wasn't so dogmatic about it because again, with Scotch-Irish people, you have to be careful. They wanted me in control, but they didn't want me shoving it down their throats.

Gradually, over a period of time, things began to get better. There was still high tension because of the way the track was built and the large number of cars we had, and because of the type of drivers we had and the kind of spectators—and the amount of alcohol consumed.

AT THE PEAK, I was getting sixty cars in the field and Robinwood was becoming the most successful track in the greater Charlotte area. Everyone wanted to be there for the racing. My philosophy was to try to do something different every week. Before this one show I learned there were three of Smokey Yunick's Hudson Hornets in a junkyard called Ball Creek Salvage, and I went up there and paid about $1,000 for them. I brought them down to a friend who owned a service station, and I had them painted up. I let Jim Duncan, another friend of mine with whom I played football, drive one of them.

We picked numbers out of a hat, and Duncan picked number 1, the pole position. That was a big mistake on my part because everybody thought it was a put-up job since I owned the race car. As a result the other drivers decided to take him out on the first lap. He was going down the backstretch, and they tagged him going into the third turn, and the car went into the air and flew out of the racetrack. I jumped out of the judge's stand and ran to where the car was. I was mad as a hornet, no pun intended, and when I saw that the car still ran, I decided to drive it myself. Another mistake. I got in, cranked it up, got Jim's helmet, and headed back out onto the racetrack. I shouldn't have done that.

I had to start in the rear of the field. And it was fun because my Hornet had a lot of torque and could fly. I passed about half the cars before someone hit me and knocked me up into the wall, and that was it for the car. I had had enough for the evening, so we parked it. But I kept running those cars, and it added a lot of flair, because no one else was running those Hornets, and that put some pizzazz into it.

One week I decided to run the Chinese Upset Race, a race that had never been run before. I sent out a letter explaining exactly how it worked. The winner's purse would go to the *second-place* car. The first-place car got zero.

I had been sitting around thinking about what would happen if I did that. This was another of my bright ideas that was a mistake. It was a hundred-lap race, and I hired the best scorer I could find, Lee Smith, who scored all the big-time NASCAR races. Lee was an absolute fanatic for detail. He always knew who was in the top ten, and he never had to write anything down. He was almost a savant.

I went to the driver's meeting, and repeated the rules over and over. I held up two fingers. And I looked at the dumbest driver there, and I asked him, "Do you know what I said?" He said, "Yeah, whoever wins the race finishes second." I said, "That's right." I said to him, "What does it mean if you finish first?" He said, "It means you lost the race." I said, "Good." I figured if he could understand it, everyone else could too. I repeated it about four more times for good measure.

We dropped the flag. It was a heck of a race with crashes and flips and excitement. The usual drivers were up front. Ervin Carpenter was in the lead, and Bryant Wallace was second, and in the race was Jim Dimeo, the only Italian in Gaston County. Everyone else was full Scotch-Irish. The only diversity was black. Since nobody could pronounce anything outside of English words, everyone called him Jim Domino. Or Jim Die-mo. I asked him, "Why don't you just change your name to Domino?" Well, that was an affront. He wouldn't do that, but I was able to get a sign painter to paint dominoes on the top of his car. Which satisfied me. Jim was running third, and Harold Dunaway—whose father, Glenn, won the first Grand National race Bill France ever ran but was disqualified for having the wrong springs on the car—was fourth.

We came down to the ninety-ninth lap, the one I was waiting for. Carpenter was in the lead, and as they came around for the checkered flag, everyone put on their brakes as Bryant Wallace pushed Jim Dimeo down the straightaway over the finish line. Meanwhile, Bob Cooper came flying around the track—obviously he didn't get the message—and he thought he won the race, which would have made Jim Dimeo—the second-place finisher—the winner. Bryant Wallace also was sure he had finished second and was the winner.

I ran over to the ticket office because we had a packed house. My mother was guarding the gate receipts, and I wanted to check if she was okay and the money was okay. As I was rushing over there, the announcer, John Moose—a Modified driver and the first man with a master's degree ever to race in NASCAR—intoned over the loudspeaker, "Ladies and gentlemen. We've had a mistake here tonight. We've run an extra lap." In which case Jim Dimeo was in second place and he was the winner.

I thought to myself, *This can't be happening. Why did I leave the judge's stand?* Because I never would have let John make that announcement if I had been there with him.

I charged back over there, and by then the pits were in an uproar. All three teams thought they had won the race and wanted the winner's money. I was sure there was going to be a riot. They were threatening to beat everyone they could see working for the track if they didn't get paid.

As I stood on the judge's stand, they were all screaming and hollering at me, and I'm thinking, *Let's be cool. Why the heck don't you just pay all three of them the three hundred bucks? And have a run-off by just the three of them the next week. You'll fill the house. And everybody will be happy.*

And I did that, but they were still ticked off because there wasn't one winner. I said, "There can't be. We messed up. It's our fault. We're paying you 3 guys $300 each. Next week we're going to have a rematch and the winner'll get another $300." Oh boy, they liked that.

I had learned that you needed to show some force to these people, and so I did. I had a long-nosed .38 with a big, long barrel. I had had it nickel-plated, and it was shiny. I kept it polished. My brother and I drove my '55 Chevy into the pits to pay everyone off. I laid that .38 on the dashboard and made sure the light reflected off of it, and I rolled down the window and paid. If someone came up who we didn't particularly like, I'd roll the window up halfway. They'd see that gun, and that kept them pretty well contained.

Everyone went home happy, and the next week the place was absolutely packed. Everything would have gone great except that the day before the race my workman, Clarence, went over the guardrail with the water truck, and it turned upside down. He was knocked cold, and he was bleeding. He had a concussion, but after I got him to the hospital he was okay. Even though he was black, they administered to him because I wasn't going to let anything happen to him.

I needed a tanker truck desperately to water the track, and none were available, so I hired a septic tank truck owned by a man who was a race fan. It was the day of the race, and I told him, "Make sure you clean it out good first." I made the mistake of going home and leaving him for about three hours. When I came back, the track was coated with the worst smell I ever smelled in my life. It was a stench. I wished for rain, but there wasn't a cloud in the sky. I said to the guy, "Can't you smell that?" But he had been around foul odors so much he didn't smell the difference. I didn't know what to do. The smell would not leave the track.

People were starting to come in. The officials showed up. The ambulance drove up. Everybody was saying, "Where does that smell come from?" I didn't know what to do or say. "I don't know," I said. I couldn't say a sewer line broke because there was no sewer out there. Everyone started coming in, sniffing, smelling the odor. Oh, man, it was bad. I thought, *Maybe the wind will start blowing.* But there was a dead calm.

The drivers came in, and they wanted to know, "What did you do?" I didn't know what to say though the word was getting out that I had used water from a septic tank. The drivers came over and said, "We're not driving on a track covered with septic." I said, "Well, you can go home if you want to." That shut them up. Meanwhile, the people kept streaming in, and I was hoping once they started drinking the corn liquor they brought in their paper sacks and poured into the Dixie cups they bought at the track, the smell would go away.

The announcer, John Moose, came on and said, "I want to apologize for the smell here tonight. Seems like the paper plant is acting up again." I thought, *Who told him to say that? Where did that come from?* But then again, I also thought it was pretty ingenious and that I'd keep the guy around for a while. There was a notorious paper plant about twenty miles away, and every once in a while when the wind was blowing wrong, the smell would get up into Gastonia.

It turned out to be the most uneventful night the Robinwood Speedway ever had. Nobody raced anybody. It was like they were all on valium. We didn't even have an incident. There wasn't one fight in the grandstand. I don't even remember a car turning over. And around eight thirty that night, who walked into the pits but Clarence, all bandaged up.

"Your doctor told you not to leave the house for a week," I said.

He said, "I wasn't going to stay at home."

I told my brother, "This is one night I'll never forget."

ABOUT TWO WEEKS LATER I decided the track should undergo its first modernization. In the early 1960s someone once asked me, "What is the definition of a superspeedway?" The real answer is a track a mile or more that's banked. But my answer was, "It's a track with flush toilets." Because there were very few dirt tracks with flush toilets.

I decided to build Robinwood a ladies' room. I went to the sawmill, got the lumber, and I went to City Supply where I used to work and got shingles, and we built this real nice ladies' restroom. I put four flush commodes in it. I was really proud of that restroom.

That night my announcer was sick, so I had to do the announcing. One of the drivers was named Jungle Boy Lane. He was from Belmont. I knew him as a kid, and the way he got his name. We used to go to the movies on Saturday afternoons, and usually we saw Gene Autry, Roy Rogers, and Hopalong Cassidy, but the best was Tarzan, starring Johnny Weissmuller. After the movie was over, we'd go home and play whatever we saw, whether it was cowboys and Indians or Tarzan. Lane loved Tarzan, and he'd put on what looked like a loincloth with no shirt. He was real skinny, didn't look at all like Johnny Weissmuller, and we started calling him Jungle Boy. The name stuck, and he became a wild race driver. He made his living as a mechanic. Still does today.

I was on the PA system. I said, "Bryant Wallace is in the lead, Jim Dimeo second. Coming up in the second turn, they are coming down the back-stretch, and Jungle Boy Lane is trying to pass on the outside. He's losing it folks, oh shit . . ." I threw the mike down because Jungle Boy was exiting the track. He hit the wall in the third turn, went airborne, and was headed straight toward you know what—my brand-new, state-of-the-art women's restroom. And he hit it square on. Oh, my God. He just absolutely flattened it out.

And someone was in it. A twenty-seven-year-old woman got out of the rubble on her hands and knees. Through some miracle she didn't get seriously hurt. She had bruises, which were fixed up in the ambulance. She wouldn't even leave the track. She wanted to watch the rest of the races. And for some reason, she never did sue us. Which was incredible. But the whole restroom was lost, and I was so mad at Jungle Boy, but then I started thinking, *Why should I me mad at him? I put the thing in the wrong place.*

§

NOT LONG AFTERWARD I held a race card noteworthy for two events. My wife-to-be attended for the first time, and a little boy was killed in the stands. It was the beginning of the end of my stewardship of the Robinwood Speedway.

My wife-to-be's name was Pat Dell Williams, and even though she was dating a friend of mine, I thought she was fantastic. He was at law school, and I badgered her into going out with me to the mountains, and at the end of that first date I asked her to marry me. When she said no, I asked her out for the next night. She did agree to that.

We went out six straight nights, and then I asked her to go to the races with me at the Robinwood. She had never been to a race. An axle broke on one of the Hudsons, and a wheel somehow went over the top of the wheel fence, and it hit a six-year-old boy and killed him. I just felt terrible.

Insurance provided for $10,000 in the case of a death at the track, and I settled with the boy's family the next week. The boy's father had absolutely no money, so he took it and said, "Maybe I can do something for the rest of my kids now."

But that soured me on the place real bad. And then Pat, torn between two lovers, told me she was going to leave Charlotte and go to New York to work for Chase Manhattan Bank, leaving both her boyfriend and me on the curb. That was her way of solving the problem.

I went down to St. Peter's Church. I was really depressed. I made a promise to the Good Lord that I would do something every day if He would only keep her in Charlotte. I got back to my office an hour and a half later, and I had a message to call her. She said, "I have thought about this, and I have decided not to go to New York, and I will marry you." I had promised to do something every day, and for 47 years I have done it. It's been a wonderful marriage that began with tragedy.

MY RUN AT THE ROBINWOOD SPEEDWAY didn't last much longer. I had been lucky the parents of the dead boy didn't sue, and not long afterward another wheel went into the grandstand, hit a spectator, and broke his arm. He sued, and we wound up in Superior Court where he won a judgment of $150,000. I had $100,000 worth of insurance, and I had a judgment against me for the difference. We appealed to the North Carolina Supreme Court. Right before I took a job working in Ohio, we settled for a total of $70,000. But I was still stuck with the anguish of having that judgment against me. I also had other rather significant bills against me, and I was forced to close down.

I was twenty-four years old. I thought I knew a lot about business, but it turned out I didn't. I had lost a lot of money because of suits. I had few accounting skills. I had my famous system of drawers. I put the money in the top drawer and the bills in the second drawer, and if I had more money in the top drawer than the second I figured I was making money. I ended up owing a significant amount, but before I left Charlotte I went to my creditors and I promised to pay them off.

I owed the most money to a guy by the name of Bob Hilker. He owned a chain of radio stations on which I advertised a lot. I owed him thousands of dollars. After I got to Akron I was paying everyone off, and eventually I paid off everybody but him because I owed him so much.

One Christmas he called me and he said, "I have a surprise for you. I appreciate very much your paying down your debt. A lot of people wouldn't have done that. And as a Christmas gift, I'm writing off the rest of it."

Years later I repaid the favor. I made a deal for Turner Broadcasting to televise the World 600, and it was supposed to be blacked out within a hundred miles of the speedway. Well, a small cable company that serviced Lake Norman goofed up and ran the race. I was going to sue until I found out that the cable station was owned by Bob Hilker. We made a deal: if he put on the weather channel, I'd drop the whole thing. He did, and I did. That wouldn't have happened in New York City.

AFTER I CLOSED THE ROBINWOOD SPEEDWAY, I started promoting a track in Monroe, North Carolina, called the Starlite Speedway. It didn't last long, and there was little that was memorable about it except that the farmer who had built the track put up an irrigation system around the outside so he wouldn't have to use a water truck, and on the very first night of racing a driver went through the wall and knocked down his irrigation system.

I also took a job at the bankrupt Charlotte Motor Speedway. Curtis Turner and Bruton Smith had been ousted, and the track was in trusteeship. The track was technically owned by the Honorable Judge Red Robinson. I got a call from Earl Kelly, who was doing publicity for the track, and he asked if I'd be interested in handling the advertising.

The Charlotte Motor Speedway had maybe five employees. It had no money, and it was barely able to put on a race. There was constant upheaval among the stockholders, and while I was there Richard Howard, who eventually took it over, began buying up the stock at twenty-five cents a share.

The track's decisions were being made by Duke Ellington, not to be confused with the jazz great. Duke was an attorney from Washington, D.C., who had been appointed general manager of the Speedway. He got caught up in the southern art of being a promoter, and he decided that what the Speedway needed more than anything else was a cheetah, the world's fastest animal. Duke bought a full-sized, supposedly tame cheetah. I can tell you firsthand there is no such thing. One of my jobs was taking care of the cheetah.

Duke used to let him run wild inside the Speedway after it was all locked up. Some nights he would take the cheetah home with him. He kept telling me how tame this cheetah was.

Most of the time the cheetah was housed in a place called the Nature Museum in Charlotte. During the day people could see it, and in the evenings, I would go and get it and take it to various and sundry places in the hopes of gaining attention for the Speedway and selling a few tickets. When you ran a speedway in those days, there were two things you always carried with you—brochures, which you would hand out to anyone who could walk and see, and tickets.

One night in late November I had to bring the cheetah to Shoney's drive-in restaurant in Charlotte. It was getting dark. I walked maybe twenty-five yards down a little gravel path to the cheetah's den at the nature center. I had been around the cat long enough to sense he was feeling moody that night. I attached his chain to his collar, and we started walking back up the path to his trailer.

This night the cheetah wasn't acting like himself. He was agitated, snarling. I didn't like his whole attitude. I had to half drag him up the hill, and a couple times he growled. Finally I got him into the trailer for the ride to Shoney's.

We were met at Shoney's by Miss Charlotte Motor Speedway. We were showing off her and the cheetah. When I went to bring the cheetah out of the cage, he began yanking on the chain and trying to get away. We weren't but a quarter mile from downtown Charlotte. I was risking life and limb if that cheetah got loose.

The cheetah lurched at one of the customers. Afraid the cheetah was going to bite him, I grabbed it by the neck and held on as best I could. I weighed about 175 pounds, and it was everything I could do to keep him from escaping.

The madder I got, the madder he got. He was growling, and I had a feeling he was going to bite me. And then from out of the kitchen this black gentleman, who had more common sense than anyone I ever met, brought out a raw steak and threw it into the cheetah's cage. When the cat saw the steak, he stopped caring about our war of wills. I let him go, and he vaulted right into the cage.

My night wasn't done. I had to get him back to the nature center. I had to let him out of the cage and lead him down the hill. I couldn't just leave him in the trailer, because the cage was too small. I held the cheetah by his chain and as I started down the hill, I slipped on wet leaves, fell down, and watched the cat run off into the bush.

It was about ten o'clock at night. We were in a hoity-toity section of Charlotte. A cheetah was running around in the wild, roaming through the tall grass out of my sight. I knew I had to call the cops, but what would they do to him when they caught him?

I remembered the steak. I knew where they kept the raw meat in the center, but all the doors were locked. At that point I didn't care. I saw a shovel, and I used it to bust out a window. I ran inside as the alarm started going off, grabbed a couple pieces of meat from the food locker, came back outside, put the raw meat in his habitat, and waited.

Fifteen minutes later, here he came. He loped into his habitat to grab the meat, and I locked the cage door behind him. I wanted to kill that cat, and if I had had a gun, I would have shot him right between the eyes. Around the same time the police arrived. I told them what happened, and they had a good laugh. I turned off the alarm and left.

I suggested to Mr. Ellington really strongly that he get rid of that cat. He chose not to listen to me, and a few months later the cheetah bit a kid at the North Wilkesboro Speedway. Only then did he donate the cheetah to a zoo.

The only other memorable event that occurred while I was working at the Charlotte Motor Speedway was a wreck that Fireball Roberts had on October 15, 1961, during the National 400. Fireball was driving for Smokey Yunick in his black and gold Pontiac. It was a typical Smokey car, too strong for the tires. Fireball was leading a third of the way through the race when he crashed into the fourth turn and ended up sideways and perpendicular to the oncoming cars. A driver by the name of Bill Morgan came off the fourth turn, never lifted, and drove right into the passenger door of the car. He literally pushed the passenger door into the driver's seat. From the grandstand no one who looked at Fireball's car could have imagined he could have survived. Smokey came running across the grass to the car before the safety crew got there. Fireball was shaken but unhurt, and when he climbed out of the car, the people began cheering like crazy. From the stands arose a tremendous ovation.

Smokey did a very unusual thing with the car. He took it to a scrap yard in Charlotte and had it baled into a square. He then took it back to his garage and kept it there as a souvenir. As far as I know, it's still there.

THOSE WERE MY MOST MEMORABLE experiences during my first stint at the Speedway.

I ended up getting fired. They wouldn't tell me why. I didn't even know who fired me. A couple years later I applied for jobs working for Ford and Firestone. Ken Gregory, who worked for Ford, said to me, "You ought to clear up something at the Speedway. They said you stole a movie projector."

I was mystified. No one had told me that. I was in the habit of taking 16-millimeter movie projectors to the Rotary Clubs to show films of the races because they weren't on TV. I had always returned them. But apparently one went missing, and I got the blame. Later on someone who worked at the Speedway found it in his closet. Since it wasn't widely known, I didn't say another word to anyone. I just forgot about it. That's the way it is sometimes in the South.

CHAPTER 6

Slick

THERE WASN'T A LOT a smart boy from the country could do if he didn't
go to college. Most country boys graduated high school because in those
small, country towns they made damn sure everybody went through and
graduated. Had he gone on to Harvard, he would have ended up running a
bank somewhere. But because he didn't, he would end up in the mills or he
might try dirt farming, as my mother called it, though you couldn't make
much money doing that.

He might have opened a grocery store —this was the era before the big
franchises like McDonalds and Burger King. Franchises eventually would
be what would pull the South into the middle and upper-middle class. In
the post–World War II South, franchises were the bulwark of the economy.
But before that began to occur in the 1960s, the only franchises were Ford
or Chevy dealers, which were given to college guys who finished Chapel Hill
or the University of South Carolina. The guy with the high school diploma
could open a used car lot.

Richard Howard, who owned the Charlotte Motor Speedway after Bruton
Smith and Curtis Turner went bust, was a smart guy without a college degree.
He opened a country furniture store out in Denver, North Carolina. Richard
was smart as a whip, and he made a lot of money selling furniture to people
in Charlotte even though he was forty miles away, because everyone knew
you could go up there and buy furniture, and he'd deliver it the next day. Or

if you wanted a refrigerator, he'd sell it to you for cost-plus, whatever it took, and he'd deliver it the next day and set it up in your house. And if it broke, he'd fix it. Richard Howard would go well beyond the call of duty.

There were other entrepreneurs who we called "slick." That was a country guy who didn't have an education but who could outtalk everybody. You didn't want to be called "slick." It had a connotation that you weren't as honest as you should have been. If you were honest, they'd say, "That boy is smart." Slick meant smart too, but it went beyond that. And it was the slick boys who inevitably showed up to run racetracks because they were slick enough to go to the farmer with thirty acres of flat pasture with nice red clay in it and lease it, and they were slick enough to get grading equipment, and they would give the grader part of the deal. They were slick enough to buy the lumber to build fences and put up a grandstand and guardrails, and slick enough to rent a wrecker and get a rescue squad to come out and "help" them. This guy had no money whatsoever, but before you knew it, he got all these other people to pitch in, and he had a racetrack. Or he went to a state fairgrounds that was making money one week a year with a fair, and it had a quarter-mile pony track or a half-mile pacer track, and he talked them into leasing it to run stock car races.

The bootlegger usually wasn't the best guy in the world. He had cash that never saw the shadow of the inside of the bank, so some of it went into the underground economy of the South—bootlegging—and he would cash-roll the bootleggers. The bootlegger needed the money because he might have had his still blown up or his cars seized. He himself was never arrested, but he was always in need of cash, so he went to these people and borrowed money from them, or the bootlegger might invest in his enterprises. And inevitably some of these men showed up at the tracks.

To say they were rough was an understatement. And these were the promoters I was competing with. These guys were rough as the dickens. Sometimes the roughness went beyond the call of duty to the point of violence, of outright fraud, outright theft, all the things you're not supposed to do. It seemed that the early days of stock car racing really proliferated with this kind of people. There were some good people, but there were an awful lot who you would not turn your back on. Again, they were smart people without education. And if you opened up a track, inevitably one of these guys was going to open up a track down the road, compete against you, and try to take your drivers.

One of the most brutal battles took place in Charlotte when Bill France and Bruton Smith were operating against each other. I can remember Bruton had a Modified race at the Concord Speedway, north of Charlotte, on the same day France had one at the Charlotte Speedway, south of Charlotte. Highway 29 is the main road from the north, where a lot of the drivers came down from. Bill France had advertised that certain top drivers were going to be at his race, and Bruton would call them on the phone, offer them money, or stop them on the road, and try to convince them to run in his race. Whatever it took to get them, he would do it. There was nothing Bruton wouldn't have done, and Bill France was the same way.

This tough dealing happened every time I tried to run a racetrack, and sometimes it would get downright nasty. There was a promoter from Charlotte by the name of Buddy Davenport. Buddy, a great concessionaire as well as a promoter, would run a race just to make money off the concessions. But being a promoter was always very difficult, in large part because two rainouts could take you from swimming in cash to flat broke in a short period of time.

BUDDY DAVENPORT HAD LEASED the Gastonia Fairgrounds, a fairly nice place. The track, a flat quarter mile, wasn't worth a damn but the facilities were nice with good lights and a good grandstand. They even had stage lighting, which allowed the promoter to highlight certain places on the track. And it had a beautiful infield, half of it a lake and the other half green grass. The cars pitted on the outside. It was a very pleasant setting.

Buddy had leased the place from Jack Partlow, the owner of the fairgrounds. Jack himself was a real character. He weighed about 350 pounds, and he was an electrical genius as well as being a good promoter. But Buddy was really losing money, and when he was unable to pay Jack the money he owed him on the lease, Jack busted the lease and threw him out.

Jack called me up and asked me if I wanted to take over the track. He told me he had voided the lease. I was looking for the next mother lode, and I was thinking the Gastonia Fairgrounds just might be it. So I told Jack, "Yes, I'll take it over."

I was twenty-four years old. I decided to go for it wide open. I didn't have much money, but at the time demolition derbies had begun to filter down into the South, and they were beginning to draw some people. Larry Mendelsohn had started holding them at the Islip Speedway out on Long

Island in New York, and he had been very successful with them. I studied how he did it, and I decided I would have a one-hundred-car demolition derby, the largest one in history.

I announced I would pay the huge sum of $1,000 to the winner. That was a big deal, because you could buy a car to enter in the race for fifty bucks.

I was inspired. I advertised the race with ten-second ads on TV. I rented a crane, and I bought the body of a '58 Chevy and painted it red, and from a distance it looked brand new. I had it pulled a hundred feet in the air, and then the crane let go, and it crashed to the ground on top of three old junk cars that were filled with water barrels. There was a huge explosion, Boom! And then the announcement: "Gastonia Fairgrounds, two dollars. Kids under twelve free." And that was the commercial, which I ran over and over, and the people watching TV loved it.

To get a hundred cars in the race, I made a deal with Joe Williams, who had a big junkyard in Charlotte. The deal was I would give him forty dollars a car for fifty cars, and at the end of the day I would sell the crashed cars back to him for twenty bucks. I called every race driver I knew and put them in the cars. I was figuring that there would be fifty other drivers who would show up in their own cars.

This was a gamble. I had spent everything I had and borrowed even more. I was absolutely broke.

The race was on Sunday. On Friday afternoon at four thirty the sheriff showed up at the track with an injunction taken out by Buddy Davenport saying I was barred from running the race on Sunday because he had a valid lease, which was bullshit. This was all a con deal, and everyone knew it, but there didn't seem to be much I could do about it except make a deal with Buddy if I wanted to run the race.

I had called Jack Partlow, and he had said to me, "No way, shape, or form does he have a legal leg to stand on. I voided his lease."

The problem was that we couldn't adjudicate whether or not he had a legal lease until Monday, and the race was on Sunday.

I called my lawyer, Basil Whitener, and by the time I got down to his office it was five o'clock. How was I going to find a judge? I couldn't. Besides, the judge we wanted to find was up in the mountains fishing.

Buddy Davenport's lawyer was a man by the name of Grady Stott. When we called his office, he was very available, and so was Buddy. How convenient. We had a meeting, and Mr. Stott said, "I'm sorry you can't have this race." Then he paused. "But there may be a way to have this event anyway." I knew then that the other shoe was about to drop.

Stott made a proposal to me. Buddy would get fifty percent of the gate. I thought to myself, *This is as bad as if he was holding a gun to my head.*

I asked if I could confer with counsel. I had a plan, and I asked him if he thought we could do it legally. He said he saw no legal reason why we couldn't.

"But you better be ready," he said, "because this isn't going to be fun."

"I'll be ready," I said.

I went back in and told Buddy I would agree to his fifty percent. But he would get paid after expenses, and I told him my expenses had been $20,000, and that included rental of the fairgrounds, the cost of the cars, and the advertising. Buddy demanded that Joe Williams pay him the twenty dollars a car for the fifty cars. He would get one hundred percent of that money as part of the negotiations. I agreed, but I stipulated the money we would split would be money taken in at the front gate. Buddy agreed to that. Why not? It was the only gate in the whole place because a fairground only needed one gate, which then took customers to the midway, and then you bought a ticket going into the grandstand.

The next day was Saturday, and that day I made a deal with the man who owned the land adjacent to the backstretch of the fairgrounds. It was a small area, but I needed it in order to build a second gate on the back side—which my 240-pound brother ran.

Sunday arrived, and when Buddy Davenport tried to get into the track, we barred him and his henchmen. He started screaming. I told him, "There is nothing in this agreement that says you can come in." And there wasn't. His lawyer showed up and jumped up and down like a shortstop. But he couldn't do anything about it either.

Meanwhile, a huge crowd was flocking in, and the good old local police began directing a considerable amount of the traffic to the back side of the track, where people were buying tickets through the back gate. It took Buddy a little while to figure out what I was doing, and when he finally noticed, he started going crazy. Again I pulled out our agreement. I said to him, "It only says we split the money coming in the front gate. It doesn't say I can't have a back gate or that we split total revenue."

Davenport was fuming. In the meantime the cars showed up. One hundred and three drivers entered. The weather was beautiful, and the place was totally packed. Buddy was beside himself.

My announcer was John Moose. I was over in the ticket office when a driver, who was one of Davenport's goons, ran up to John in the judge's stand and pistol-whipped him. This was Mr. Davenport's way of getting me back. The sheriff hauled him off to the local jail, and the ambulance hauled John off to the hospital.

I sent my brother and a couple of my USC linemen over to the judge's stand to make sure this didn't happen again, and I put another announcer over there. I went over to Mr. Davenport and warned him and his two goons that we were watching him, and that if anything else happened, he was going to get the hell beat out of him. I wanted to make sure he got the message.

Through the whole race he fumed about that back gate, but he wasn't prepared for the rest of the story. The race was completed, and everyone had a wonderful time. It was the cultural event of the season for Gastonia County. Eighty cars were completely torn up. In the end one car was left, and he was the winner.

Now it was time to settle up. After the race was over I finally let Davenport into the track so he could go to the ticket office. We found out we took in $20,000 at the front gate. And we subtracted the $20,000 of my expenses as was provided in our contract.

Finally Davenport said, "I want my damn cars."

"You've got them," I said.

"Well, where are they?" he wanted to know.

"They're in the lake." While we were settling up, I had Joe Williams' wreckers dump every one of those cars into the deep end of the lake in the infield. The deep end was forty feet.

He went ape shit. He couldn't believe they were actually in the lake. I'm sure he was wanting to kill me, but he would have had to tangle with me, my brother, and my linemen friends. He ran to look for the cars. Those brought in privately were still out there, but none of Joe Williams' cars.

Joe said to Davenport, "I will dredge them out of the lake for twenty dollars a car." Of course, that would have been zero money for Buddy, who left with no purse money and no car money. None. Zero. And we left with about $20,000 from the back gate, enough to pay our bills and get ourselves established. And later that day I drained the lake and pulled the cars out. So we did okay, and Mr. Davenport didn't. He should have known not to mess with the Belmont Boys. And I never heard from him again.

§

AFTER THAT I STUPIDLY DECIDED to start driving again. I don't know why sometimes I do the things I do. A track operator should never race at his own track. Nor should any relative connected to him. It just does not work out.

I resurrected one of the Hudson Hornets I owned. I went out on the track and got around pretty darn good. Everybody was giving me bad looks, and I was very careful about drawing for positions. I drew number three, but I put that in the pocket and then I pulled a higher number. I was in third place most of the race, and I was determined to win it. I can't remember the name of the guy who was in the second, probably for a good reason.

I knew the only way I could get around him was to bump him. He went a little bit high, got in the cushion, and as I went into the corner I hit him, his car flipped six or seven times, and it was nasty. I came back around, and the red flag was out, and that's bad. They were cutting him out of the car, and it made me feel just awful. I knew he was hurt. In fact he broke his arm and a couple of ribs. At that point I decided never to race at Gastonia again. I told myself I would never race anywhere again. I really felt bad.

After racing that night, I was determined to make Gastonia safer. During that race I recalled thinking, *Gee whiz, if somebody goes off the backstretch, there's only a teeny weeny rail fence between them and oblivion.* Just outside the track was a stand of trees and a drop off, and the car would go into those trees about halfway up.

I decided to put a chainlink fence up all the way down the backstretch. It looked so good and shiny, and I was so proud, because those were the days when nothing around a racetrack looked pretty or shiny.

During the first lap of the first heat, a driver came off the corner, leapt over the pitiful little guardrail, and started into that chain link fence. He began flipping, and as he did, the car was wrapped all around it by the chainlink fence. I was thinking, *If the car catches on fire, he'll never get out.* Fortunately, there was no fire, but the only way they were able to get the driver out of his car was with chain cutters. Believe me, he'd have been better off going into the trees.

AFTER THAT I HAD THREE RAINOUTS. I was at the low end of my career. Making things more financially difficult, my former partner at the Robinwood Speedway, R. P. Harrison Jr.—a dairy farmer who everyone called Junior—built a new track called the Carolina Speedway about eight miles away. He ran Saturday nights, and I ran Friday nights, but Gaston

County isn't very big, and neither of us was making any money. It was 1963 and times were tough.

I decided to roll the dice, gamble it all, and hold a big race. Most of my events were forty-lappers, and so I held a one-hundred-lap race I called the Piedmont 100. I really promoted the heck out of it, spending a bunch of advertising money. I threw leaflets out of airplanes and ran half-page ads in newspapers and ran ads on TV. I was trying to make a mountain out of a molehill, and I could feel I was succeeding.

This was around the time John Kennedy launched the Bay of Pigs invasion. There I was, broke, spending other people's money. The week before my race I got a call from my wife, Pat. The draft board wanted me to report for induction. I was ordered to report to the Charlotte Armory in two days for a physical and I should prepare to leave for Fort Jackson immediately afterward.

This was a complete surprise. After I was hurt so badly playing football at the University of South Carolina, I could no longer participate in ROTC. This was back in the days when you knew you were going into the service, and I had wanted to go in as an officer in the air force, not a private in the army. My spinal injury made that impossible.

The physical was two days before my big race. Here I was, broke, with a wife and a five-month-old child at home, and I'd been drafted.

I packed my clothes and arranged with my brother, David, and a friend to run the speedway while I was at Fort Jackson. I and a hundred other guys went over to the Charlotte Armory, destined to go someplace no one wanted to go.

I went to take the physical. I was still having a lot of problems with my back. The doctor said, "You seem to have stiffness in the lower part of your back." I told him about the injury. He examined me a bit more and said, "I don't think we'll be taking you today." He didn't say anything else. The recruiter who had my papers ordered me to go home.

Friday night was one of those days you dream of when you're a promoter, particularly after you've been rained out three times. And after you've been sent home by the army. It was perfect, beautiful. All the advertising worked, and the people started streaming in. It was astonishing to see people piling into the place. I was smacking my hands together thinking, *I've made it through this week.* The huge crowd allowed me to pay off some of my debt.

§

THE NEXT NIGHT Junior had an event at his track, and he didn't do very well because I had taken away all the money. It was time for us to have a meeting, and we agreed that Gaston County wasn't big enough for two tracks, so we decided to join forces at his track.

We ran a few races together, didn't make any money, and at this point I was still broke. I decided it was time to get out of the short track business.

I was married, and I had a child, and I was at the end of my rope financially. Richard Howard, who was running the Charlotte Motor Speedway then, called and said, "Hey, a guy in Augusta, Georgia, needs your help bad. I told him he needs to hire you for at least six weeks." His name was Harold Payton, a contractor from Greenville, South Carolina. This was the same man I would be traveling with when Kennedy was killed.

He had built a track in Augusta called the Augusta International Raceway. It was a great big old road course. In late November he was running a 500-mile NASCAR race. No one had ever made any money on road racing in the South.

When I called him, he said, "I really need your help. Richard said you know how to promote. I'm not selling any tickets. Come on down." I made a deal with him on the phone. He'd get me a place to stay with my family. I loaded up Pat and my daughter, Patti, and we headed to Augusta. I borrowed a car from a Ford dealer and drove to the Howard Johnson where the manager had a trailer in the back of the motel that he would rent to me.

This was the low spot of my life. We moved into the trailer, and the third night we were there a rat bit my daughter's hand when she was in the crib and I had to take her to the hospital. Pat was beside herself that we had been reduced to these circumstances. But I stayed the course, and she stayed with me.

When I got to the track, as soon as I saw it, I thought, *What in the world has this man gotten into?* It was built on a terrible piece of land. The front straightaway was up a hill. You had to go downhill through a swampy area on the backstretch. I had never seen anything like it, and it had gotten very little publicity. I thought how hard it would be to get a crowd to come to the race. We had a test, and Fireball Roberts and Joe Weatherly came down for it. Weatherly was racing for Bud Moore in a Pontiac. He drove off the course into the swamp, not a very bad wreck, but when I went down there, I saw an alligator, not a very big one, but it was all I needed.

I wrote a press release that said, "Joe Weatherly crashed today, went into a swamp, and narrowly missed an alligator." The media picked it up, and before they got done, you'd have thought the alligator had attacked him. One writer nicknamed that section of the track Alligator Alley, and it stuck. It got us a tremendous amount of publicity, and at least got people curious about the event.

We had the race and a decent crowd showed up, considering it was a road course race held in November. Fireball won it, and Dave McDonald, who was killed at Indianapolis the following May, was second. We sold around 12,000 tickets, which wasn't bad, but it wasn't enough to keep the place going. So after that race, the first and only race at that track, in December 1963, I found myself fighting to keep my head above water.

CHAPTER 7

Witness to Disaster

C HUCK BARNES, THE PR MANAGER for the Firestone racing division, was a friend of mine. One day he called and said, "I'm going into the agency business. I'm going to represent Parnelli Jones, A. J. Foyt, and Rodger Ward." Three Indy 500 winners during a time when the Indianapolis 500 was *the* event—Indy racing was so far ahead of stock car racing it wasn't even funny. He wanted to know if I'd be interested in coming up and talking to Firestone about replacing him. Firestone was involved in all kinds of racing and had been in racing longer than any other sponsor. They were on the cutting edge, the forerunner of today's sports marketing. Every June, their ads had all the Indy 500 winners. That was their big deal.

At the same time, I had a job offer from the Ford Motor Company to work in their racing division. The Firestone job seemed more promising, and so we moved to Akron, Ohio, in January 1964. Pat had never lived outside of Charlotte. We rolled into Akron on January 5, and it was snowing sideways. We pulled over to a Gulf station on Main Street with the wind blowing off Lake Erie. It was a full-service station, and a guy came out with coveralls on, and the tips of his grayish beard were frozen with ice. Pat looked at him, and she looked at me like, "Where have you taken me?"

Three days after we moved into an apartment, I took off for sunny Riverside, California, for the first race of the NASCAR season. I had never been to California. I got out to the Riverside track and was met by two men I knew, Les Richter, the promoter, and his assistant, Roy Hord, who had played football with Richter for the Los Angeles Rams. Roy was from Charlotte and had played at Duke and was an All-American. I was the only Southerner there to speak of as far as anybody who could write. No writer had come out of Carolina. I wasn't too sure what I was doing there myself. I was working for Firestone, but I had been an employee for less than five days.

After surviving my first trip driving on the San Bernardino Freeway, I arrived at the Riverside track, and upon my arrival I was taken for a run around the circuitous road course by Tiny Lund. The track blended into the scenery, but as I rode, there were two things I didn't like about it. One was the esses going uphill, and the other was a long backstretch that went downhill and ended with a wall of boilerplate. Rather than building a concrete wall, the track owner—to save money—bought some boilerplate from a ship and laid it up against the dirt embankment. It was most unyielding when someone hit it, and I watched uneasily as the cars slid all over the track during practice. This was the only road race of the season, and the first race on the NASCAR schedule, so a lot of the drivers made the long drive across the country because they felt they needed to be there.

One of the fastest cars in the race was owned by Bud Moore and driven by Joe Weatherly. Bud, who was a big man, had a tenacity about him. If someone had said to me, "Call Central Casting and get me a Scottish guy who was at the right hand of the King of Scotland in the Battle of Glen Morgan," they would have sent Bud, and he would have showed up with a blade about seven feet long. He had fought on the beaches during D-Day and had won a Silver Star for bravery. Over the years I often tried to talk to him about it, but he never would discuss it.

Bud had a tremendous ability to transfer his talents from oval racing to road racing, one of the few old-time crew chiefs who had that ability. His cars would dominate a road race. I can remember one year when Parnelli Jones drove for him, and no one could catch him.

That week Joe Weatherly was his usual jovial, clown prince self. Joe, whom I had known since I was a teenager, was a guy who enjoyed life. He never said so, but my feeling was that he didn't particularly like road racing.

In 1962 I went down to Daytona with Max Muhleman, who was a reporter for the *Charlotte News*. Max was a good friend of Fireball Roberts and Paul Sawyer, who was running the Richmond Fairgrounds. I hit it off with Max pretty good, and he and Joe were dear friends. Max and I went out with Joe a couple of times. Joe was reverently called the Clown Prince of Racing because he was so funny. He had a real red face, with a terrible scar down the right side of his cheek from a motorcycle accident. He looked like Barry Fitzgerald, the little Irish guy in the movie *The Quiet Man*. He had a twinkle in his eye and he was always up to something. He loved to party and have a good time. He and Curtis Turner were inseparable, and they were great racing against each other.

Joe called everybody Pops. That way he didn't have to remember anybody's name. If you saw him, you were Pops. He was just a very funny man. And he was a very good race driver. He won the Grand National racing championship in 1963 in Bud Moore's car. He was the last guy in the world you'd think would get killed in a road race. But Riverside proved to be a deadly place for a number of people.

Early in the race Weatherly crashed on the driver's side into the boilerplate wall. Ordinarily with an accident my job would have been to find out if it had been caused by the Firestone tires, but since Bud Moore's car used Goodyears, for me the question was moot.

When something bad happens on the track, you know it because no one will talk about it. Then the whispers start. If there's a fatality, someone will say, "He bought the farm." There was no NASCAR television contract back then, and little discussion of the crash on the radio. The race was halted, and Joe was air-lifted to a nearby hospital.

He had been riding uphill through the esses when his car hit. The two toughest places on the racetrack for impact were in the sixth and ninth turns, and both were on the driver's side. Joe crashed on the sixth turn. The left side of his car was bashed flat. Joe lost it, the car hit the wall, and he paid the ultimate price.

Anyone who knew Joe knew he didn't like to wear a shoulder harness. He wore just a seat belt, and on impact he flew out of the car head first. There was no window netting at the time to keep him inside the car, and when his head hit the wall, he was killed instantly.

Bob Russo was the PR guy at the track, one of the really good ones. He had worked with Russ Catlin at Indianapolis and Darlington. Bob grabbed me and said, "You have to help us. All these southern papers need copy on this tragedy." I wrote the story of Joe Weatherly's death, and twenty papers picked it up. I had known Joe well, and it was the first of a series of tragedies

I would have to endure. Joe's death began a terribly bloody period, one of the bloodiest in the history of auto racing.

I could tell that Bud Moore was very shaken by Joe's death. He didn't show a lot of emotion, but again, that's the Scotch-Irish thing. Car owners and crew chiefs tend to blame themselves when a driver is killed.

But mainly, he and Weatherly were friends.

WEATHERLY'S DEATH TOOK ME ABACK, but I kept moving on. I got back to Akron, and right around the corner was the Daytona 500. In those days I spent a month at Daytona. First came practice, which started early. Then there was a twenty-four-hour race—a meaningful event in those days—a face-off between the Ferraris and Porsches, and Carol Shelby showed up with his Cobras. I rented a condo down there for the month, and that proved to be an interesting race, because Goodyear jumped into the picture. They had been in stock car racing since 1957, but not very successfully.

This was the beginning of the great Factory Wars that spread through stock car and Indy car racing. It was Firestone versus Goodyear and Ford versus Chrysler in stock car racing. Speeds picked up, and there was some tire trouble. That was my first encounter with tire trouble and how sensitive the tire companies were to this. Blown tires were very, very bad for business.

While working for Firestone I was traveling 250 days a year. I went to perhaps 40 races. Early on I attended NASCAR, Indy, and road racing. The job gave me the chance to see all of the drivers up close.

One of the most talented and most interesting was Curtis Turner. Curtis only knew how to drive one way—all out, hell-bent for leather. If he had had the temperament to try to save the car and finish more races, who knows how many races he could have won? But that wasn't his way. More often than not his engine would blow. But if the car would hold together, he would win.

Curtis was also a driver who didn't mind moving you out of the way if he had to. I can recall a race at the Lakewood Speedway in Atlanta. Toward the end, Curtis tore up Tiny Lund's car, as he liked to do, and he probably didn't even know it was Tiny he was doing it to. After the race Tiny grabbed him around the neck and dragged him to the lake in the infield. Curtis didn't like water, and Tiny knew it. He kept dunking Curtis' head in the water, telling him he was going to drown him if Curtis didn't buy him a new car. Of course, Turner said he would. Curtis would agree to anything. If Tiny had said, "I want the Chrysler Building," Curtis would have agreed, "Okay, you got it."

Curtis never could fight. He avoided fights. But he could talk his way out of anything. You'd be mad as hell at him, and then he would talk you out of it, and you would end up thinking it was your fault.

Someone once said to me, "Curtis never made any money in the racing business; he made all of his money in the timber business." But I don't know if the man made any money at all. I know he always had money in his pocket, but outside of his pocket I don't know if he ever had any at all. Oh, God, was he a character.

He was so funny, so loose. Curtis didn't worry about anything. He was like a great big Labrador retriever. Dogs don't think about anything except what's going on in the present moment, and that was Curtis. Whatever was going on at that moment, whether it was CC and ginger ale or whatever other wonderful thing was happening. Whatever was going to happen later that night, that was another thing. Whatever bad thing happened yesterday, that was gone, and he didn't worry about it. It was the CC and ginger ale right there that was important. He was just hilarious.

I'll never forget one race at the Columbia Speedway. I was working for Firestone. I told Junior Johnson and everyone else that they could only run certain compound tires. Since we were giving the tires away, we had a perfect right to do that. And Junior, who was brilliant, was his own tire engineer. I went over to where the cars were sitting, and I noticed that Junior's car didn't have the correct tires. Junior's brother, Fred, was in charge, and I told Fred he couldn't do that, and he started giving me a bunch of lip. Fred was a little guy. Words were exchanged, and he wasn't going to get the best of me. The next thing I knew, Fred pulled a knife.

I said, "Do something with it, Fred, or put it away."

Well, nothing happened. Meanwhile, Curtis was driving for Junior. This was right after Junior had retired as a driver. Curtis hadn't arrived at the track, and the race was about to start. Junior was known to get back in the race car, though getting through the window for Junior wasn't as easy as it had once been. But Curtis was late, late, late, and finally he showed up. He was wearing his brown pinstriped suit, his cordovan wingtipped Oxford shoes, and his brown silk socks with garters. Under his jacket was a button-down white shirt with a banker's tie.

Curtis, who was trying to look like the vice president of the North Carolina National Bank, arrived with a shit-eating grin on his face. He didn't have time to change into anything. He took off his coat. He didn't take off his brown pinstriped suit, didn't take off his cordovan wingtipped Oxford shoes, and didn't take off his brown silk socks with garters. He got in the race car, went out to qualify, and broke the track record. It was the only time in history a track record was broken in a tailor-made suit.

He came back and changed into his driver's uniform. Junior acted like it was something that was supposed to happen. Everyone around Curtis knew him, so it wasn't a big thing. But Curtis was liable to do anything at any time. I was surprised he didn't land his plane on the backstretch.

I was with Curtis another time at Darlington. This was in 1965, four years after he had been banned from NASCAR for life and allowed to return by Lord High Bill France. Darlington was the toughest track we ran, and Bob Colvin, Darlington's owner, decided to bring back Red Vogt to serve as Curtis' crew chief. Red had been very successful working for Raymond Parks in the early 1950s. This was fifteen years later, and Red was long in the tooth. They were running Firestone tires, and while Curtis was running, the car was flying but it was all over the track. Curtis came in, and after I tested the tires, I said, "Curtis, we took the tire temperatures, and they are awful." The right front came in at 300 degrees. Curtis said, "The car is pushing a little. It's going to be okay." Curtis had no clue what was going on underneath him, and he couldn't have cared less.

I looked at the tires, and I noticed that Red had put the tires on backwards, which is just like putting your left sneaker on your right foot and your right sneaker on your left foot. When I pointed that out to Red Vogt, he was a little embarrassed. I never saw him at the track running a race car again. But Curtis didn't care. I said, "Curtis, you have your tires on backwards." He looked at me and he said, "Yeah, well it's okay. I'm running pretty good." I couldn't believe it. If it had been Freddie Lorenzen, he'd have jumped out of the car and would have been dancing on his left ear, foaming at the mouth. With Curtis, if there had been a bottle of CC around, he'd have said, "Open it up, Pops, and let's have one."

The funny thing was that after they put the tires on the right way, Curtis didn't run a bit better. He was just unbelievable.

Curtis was known for his parties. I don't remember them being anything special, though I probably left too damn early. His parties involved drinking, smoking, loud music, and trying to have a conversation with Joe Weatherly who talked in his guttural Tidewater accent. You needed an interpreter if you wanted to understand it. Curtis would stand around with that shit-eating grin on his face holding court, talking about this and that, mostly about the money he didn't make.

It reminded me a little bit of a heavyweight champion's party. There was the champ, Curtis Turner, and his sparring partner, Joe Weatherly. He has all these hangers-on, and the trainer isn't there because he doesn't want to have anything to do with him, and the guy is just having a good time, smoking cigars and passing out ten-dollar bills.

The Pit Poopsies were always in attendance at his parties. They were the reason women were barred from the pits until recently. It was because the wives of the drivers, the real women of NASCAR, didn't want them there. The Pit Poopsies would assemble at the pit gate where they couldn't even think about getting in, but they could stand there front and center and show their stuff.

Sometimes they would get in fights with each other, real cat fights. I can remember thinking if this one gal could throw just one left jab, she could conquer everybody, but they were always throwing roundhouses, and usually a shoe was involved. I still don't know why women hit each other with shoes.

But these gals would show up at the parties. Today it's different. Most of the drivers are married. If they aren't they have the South Carolina Miss Universe on their arm—all blonde hair, high heel shoes no matter what form of dress, looking serious, and walking very close to the driver.

In 1964, Richard Petty began to show some potential as a superspeedway winner for the first time. There was a lot of speculation whether he could win at Daytona. He had only won at the short track races. A few years earlier his dad, Lee, had been terribly injured at Daytona, which led to his retirement.

Daytona was an interesting place. At first no one could understand why Bill France would build a banked track two-and-a-half miles long. But all you had to do was understand Bill France, who wanted his track to be faster than Indianapolis, which was a flat track. He had tried to run Indy cars at Daytona with tragic results, and so he confined his racing to stock cars. The competitors knew very little about running superspeedways. Darlington had been around since 1950, but it was a weird track, and you could hardly count it as a superspeedway. When Charlotte and Atlanta opened in 1960, it was just those four.

A lot of bizarre things happened on those tracks, particularly Daytona, because they were the only tracks where the drivers didn't lift. That was alien to any driver, and it was the biggest hurdle they had to overcome. That and drafting, which produced blistering tires. The Firestones weren't blistering, but the Goodyears were.

The 1964 Daytona 500 race started, and Richard Petty shone. This was the first year of the big hemi engines. It was Ford versus Chrysler, and Richard's Chrysler was brutally powered. At the 200-mile mark you could tell he was going to be the car to beat—until his Goodyear tires began to blister. I had known Richard for a long time, and it became my goal to get him to switch from Goodyear to Firestone during the race.

This was back when you could talk to a driver when he came into the pits. When he started blistering tires, I started talking to his brother, Maurice, and to Dale Inman, his crew chief. I said, "You need to change your tires." I worked on them hard but I never could convince them to do it. Richard ended up winning the race anyway, and it was the start of his majestic career. He left no doubt that he could win on a superspeedway.

AFTER DAYTONA IN FEBRUARY 1964, I moved over to the Indy circuit. I had a tremendous interest in it because as a boy if you were playing with a model race car, chances are it was an old front-engine roadster, not a stock car. As a boy I had read about the Indy 500 so often and listened to it on the radio that I knew its history, knew the names of most of the winning drivers, and when I got up to Indianapolis, I was enthralled.

I brought my wife and daughter and moved into the Holiday Inn across the street from the Speedway for six weeks. Practice started on May 1, and they ran seven days a week all the way to race day on Memorial Day weekend. You never got a day off.

Two things blew my mind. One, each car had its own enclosed stall in Gasoline Alley. Since you couldn't watch them work on the cars, I couldn't help wondering how anyone kept the mechanics from cheating. The NASCAR cars were worked on in the open. The other thing that blew my mind was that there was no rule book as far as what car and engine they could run. Some teams even entered rear-engine cars. I wondered, *Don't they care about the safety of the drivers?* Here were crude-looking race cars, the engines in the back, the driver laying out, his feet closest to the front, and on each side of his body were gas tanks. The only thing between the driver and the fuel was a thin piece of aluminum, and the only thing between the car and the wall was a piece of fiberglass.

Colin Chapman brought in a Formula 1 car modified for Indy racing. Jimmy Clark was the driver. It was a repositioned Formula 1 car with a Ford engine in the rear, and I was amazed that Chapman was allowed to do that.

Qualifying came a week before the race. It was Sunday, and qualifying continued while back home in Charlotte there was the running of the World 600. Smokey Yunick—with whom I became very close, one of my best friends in racing—had brought a car to Indianapolis.

Smokey was an integral part of the early days of racing. He was one of the first people I knew who made a living doing it full time. And he was the only person involved in NASCAR who was also successful in Indy racing. NASCAR and Indy are two entirely different mechanical species. That Smokey could do both to me was incredible. And also that he could do it with virtually no sponsorship.

I can remember sitting at the Auto Racing Hall of Fame dinner in Detroit last summer where they were honoring Paul Goldsmith, who drove Smokey's 1958 car in the Indy 500. The car's only sponsor was the City of Daytona. I was thinking, *How could he have done that?*

Smokey didn't give a damn about anything or what anybody thought. He was as free a spirit as existed in the world. He had a fierce independence, coming from flying bombers in World War II. He was Polish and hard-headed, and he absolutely hated Bill France. For a long time he would not attend a NASCAR race. In 1977 I called him. I said, "Smokey, come up to Charlotte. I want you to come and see the place, see what we're doing, and I'll take care of everything."

He finally agreed, and once he came, he began to come around. But you still never saw him at Daytona or any of the France tracks. After our company bought Atlanta, he would go there too.

I can remember sitting in the control tower of the speedway during the Coca-Cola 600. We had a TV set on the floor, and while the race was going on Smokey would be sitting on the floor watching the Indy 500. He'd say to me, "Foyt just hit the wall." Smokey was so into it.

He was always doing something oddball. In 1964 at Indy, Smokey put Bobby Johns in his car as the driver. It was the last day of qualifying, and Smokey was trying to get into the field with this oddball car of his. He was real proud of the car. Everyone was talking about it because it was so weird-looking. It was equipped with a sidecar, but Bobby lost it going into the first turn and crashed. Smokey was devastated.

Shortly thereafter I got a frantic call from the Firestone garage. It was Max Muhleman who was working for Ford. Max called to tell me that Fireball Roberts had been in a terrible accident at Charlotte on the seventh lap of the Coca-Cola 600 and he didn't think he was going to live. Fireball had been terribly burned. He had driven for Smokey for so many years, and they were both from Daytona and extremely close. As the 1964 season rolled around, Smokey was trying to get Fireball to retire. Fireball had only a few more races to run before he hung it up when he crashed and burned. It was my task to go up to Smokey's garage and tell him about Fireball.

When I got up there, all the guys in the garage who worked for Smokey were outside, and they said, "You don't want to go in there." This was because of his wrecked Indy car. I said, "I have to go in there."

They said, "You don't want to go in there." Smokey could get pretty cranky.

I went in the door, and I thought, *Oh boy, this is going to be a terrible day.*

I said, "Smokey, I have something to tell you. You have to listen to me."

He said, "What?"

I said, "Fireball has been in a terrible accident at Charlotte. I don't think he's going to live." Well, that was like I had sent a spear right through his heart. He said, "You have to be kidding." I said, "No." I told him everything I knew, and I said, "I'll tell you if I hear anything, but it doesn't look good at all." I turned around and walked out.

This was late May, and Fireball lived until July, then he died. This hit me so hard.

Meanwhile back over at the Holiday Inn in Indianapolis where most of the drivers were staying, my neighbors in the next room were Eddie Sachs and his wife, Nancy.

Eddie was originally from Greensboro, North Carolina, so we became good friends. We'd see each other every day at the track and then at the Holiday Inn. We were together a whole month. But going into the race I could sense a fear at Indianapolis in the drivers that I hadn't seen before. The Indy drivers were different from the NASCAR drivers. If you look back at the history of Indy, you see that an awful lot of Indy drivers were killed or seriously injured. As a result, they had a cockiness that was different from anything I had been around.

My mission on race day was to get as much publicity for Firestone as I could. That meant making sure all the drivers wore Firestone uniforms and Firestone caps, and had tires with the Firestone name. I also had to get releases from all the drivers for the ads. I didn't know whether that was going to be hard or not, but I found out that you can get a driver to sign anything right before a race. He would have signed his last will and testament to you personally if you had walked up to him and handed him the paper to sign. They were all scared to death, or they had so much adrenaline going they just did what you asked them to do.

The pre-race ceremony for me was quite an event. They had the Golden Girls from Purdue, and the crowd sang "Back Home in Indiana," and there were marching bands. That was right down my alley. At the same time I could feel the fear and worry that was in the air, particularly from the veteran drivers like Rodger Ward and Parnelli Jones, who didn't like those rear-engine race cars.

I was in the pits when the flag dropped and the race started. Dave McDonald started passing cars in the backstretch. Dave was driving Mickey Thompson's car. In the *Indianapolis Morning Star* that morning, there was a double-truck ad that showed Mickey's cars. The ad said, "They will be riding with 110 gallons of Marathon gasoline."

Dave went into the third turn, got through, and I looked up in the fourth turn—because at Indy you're waiting for the cars to come out of the fourth turn—and all of a sudden there was this enormous napalm blast that went off. Dave McDonald lost it in the fourth turn, slipped down on the inside of the track, hit the wall on the inside, vaulted across the racetrack, and was T-boned by another car, causing every bit of those 110 gallons of gasoline to explode. After the huge explosion, cars were flying through the air. What no one could see was who was in the car that had T-boned Dave.

They red-flagged the race. All the cars were stopped on the third turn. Everyone was parked, including Johnny Rutherford.

I went up to the fourth turn. Indianapolis had a seasoned safety crew. Joe Quinn was the safety director. He had his yellow-shirted security team surround one car in a circle so no one could see it. He didn't want photographers shooting any pictures of the car.

When I got up there, Joe said to me, "We don't know whose car this is." I said, "Let me look at it." I went through the cordon of safety guys and looked at the car—it was completely charred and so was the driver. But Eddie Sachs had the only rear-engined car in the field that had a finned oil cooler on the left-hand side of the car, and I recognized it immediately. I knew that horribly charred body was Eddie's. I told that to Joe. It just stunned me.

Johnny Rutherford was riding right behind Eddie Sachs when it happened, and Johnny told me he saw Dave come across the track, and he was looking at Eddie. The next thing he knew, he was flying over both of them in the air.

"I don't know how I got through it," Johnny said.

We didn't know that Dave McDonald had been taken to the hospital. He died too. Johnny Rutherford's car wouldn't restart and they had to take it back to the garage. When Johnny got back to Gasoline Alley, his crew chief started looking at his car. Johnny still wasn't sure who he had flown over, and no one was saying anything. His crew chief looked underneath the car, and he pulled Eddie Sachs' kerchief out from under it. That's how Johnny found out for sure that Eddie Sachs had perished.

I went back to the Firestone tire station on Gasoline Alley. I was irate. All the things I had seen the whole month came back to me in a bad way. I knew this tragedy was inevitable. It wasn't a premonition. The lack of rules and concern was just so apparent.

Raymond Firestone, the chairman of the company, had come over there. He took a tremendous interest in the racing program. He was upset, but he was much calmer than I was. I went ballistic when I saw him. I said, "I cannot believe something like this can happen."

Bill McCrary, the director of racing for Firestone, came over to me and said, "You have to calm down. You have to get through this." I thought to myself, *These guys hadn't seen what I saw.* They, too, had a callousness about Indianapolis. Their attitude was: This is what happens here. It was the attitude that surrounded the whole place. A great bitterness sank into me that I couldn't get over.

The race restarted a couple hours later. It was anticlimactic. No one raced anybody. Everyone went through the motions. The grandstand was numb. The pits were numb. It was a ritualistic "let's get it over with" kind of deal.

A. J. Foyt was in the lead, and I knew my day had not ended because A. J. was on Firestone tires, but he was wearing a Goodyear uniform. A. J. was one tough Texan, and I thought to myself, *This is going to be terrible when we get in the winner's circle because I'm going to have to fight with him* (because A. J. was really anti-Firestone). There had been a big brouhaha the year before over tires, and Foyt had almost single-handedly brought Goodyear into Indy car racing. A. J. just didn't like the way Firestone did things, and you either did things his way or it was the highway. There was no in between.

Foyt won the race. I was in the winner's circle when he drove in there. Bill Neely, the PR guy from Goodyear, was trying to put the Goodyear hat on his head. Finally, after he went through the ritual of drinking the milk, he put the Firestone hat on and they took his picture, but he didn't keep it on very long. That ended my day.

THE AFTERMATH WAS INTERESTING. After the two deaths at Indianapolis, the anti-racing press came out and really stuck it to them big time. And rightfully so. The others were looking for answers. What do we do about these cars? How can we make them survivable? Ideas abounded, such as coating the walls with rubber, which is a little like we have today. But that didn't go anywhere. And after that we had a number of horrific problems. Bobby Marshman, a bright young Indy driver and a good friend of mine, was killed at Phoenix during a Ford test in one of Chapman's Lotus cars. Something happened to the car going into the third turn, and he hit the wall, and the car exploded. He went to Brooke Medical Center in San Antonio with terrible burns, lived terribly for about five days, and died. I went to the funeral, thinking, *This is not going to end until someone comes up with a solution.* Then Jim Hurtubise hit the wall up at Milwaukee, and the car napalmed on him. He suffered terrible, terrible burns, but fortunately didn't die. Through lots of morphine, he told the doctors to fix his hands in a way that he could drive a race car. After that his hands had a permanent wrap-around-the-steering-wheel look to them.

Billy Wade was killed at Daytona while testing. He blew a right front tire, submarined the car, and was killed. All the while Firestone and Goodyear were working to make their tires safer. One of the big problems with the tires was that when you blew one on a superspeedway, the car would go into the wall with the right front, and it was never pretty.

Finally Goodyear came up with the solution of the inner liner, and then an interesting thing happened at Firestone. They had a coated fabrics division in Spartanburg, South Carolina. An engineer had gone back to World War II fighter planes, which had had a problem. Those planes had wing tanks, and the tanks would take bullets, and if the tanks were partially filled with fuel, the fumes would explode and knock the wing off. Firestone came up with a coated rubberized fuel cell that they put the gasoline in, and that kept the oxygen from building up. When a bullet or a piece of shrapnel went through it, there wouldn't be enough oxygen in the bladder to set off an explosion. To a great extent, that solved the problem of enemy fire.

Firestone took that concept and applied it to the fuel tank of a race car. But they needed one more improvement. They needed to add a substance called foam—a sponge-like material in the fuel cell—and once they did that, it about eliminated the fire hazard. The coated-fabric fuel cell was the greatest safety innovation in racing since the seat belt.

But the problem with the Indy cars didn't end with the fuel cell. The problems continued because of the position of the driver. The following year there was a tragic accident involving Bob Hurt, who was movie star handsome. He was coming down the front stretch, and the car got out from under him, and he slid down the front stretch, and hit the wall backwards. A supporting rod for the engine went into his spine and paralyzed him from the neck down. Bob would come to the Daytona 500 every year. He'd come down to the pits in his wheelchair. Most racers once they get in their cars say to themselves, "I'm in the cocoon. I'm not getting out," but one year A. J. Foyt was so moved when he saw Bob that he got out of his car before the race and went over and spoke with him. People have mixed emotions about Foyt, but that was a special moment.

ONE OF THE OTHER INTERESTING THINGS that happened in 1964 was that a smallish guy showed up at Indianapolis. I walked up to him and said hello. He had his foot up on the pit wall, and he said he wanted to be an Indy racer. I introduced myself. He said his name was Mario Andretti. We talked. He had been trying to run a dirt car on the Indy circuit, and he wasn't doing too well at all because he didn't have any money, so I invited him out to Phoenix for a Firestone tire test. It was November 1964. Al Dean was testing in a front-engine roadster. Not everyone had gone to the rear-engine car yet. Don Branson was Al Dean's driver, and Don had run at the Ascot Speedway that weekend in a Sprint car race. This was Monday after Ascot, and we got a phone call that Don wasn't going to be able to make it because he had broken his elbow.

We were sitting there with the race car looking around. Steve Petracek, the Firestone engineer, had taken the call, and he looked at me and said, "What in the world are we going to do?"

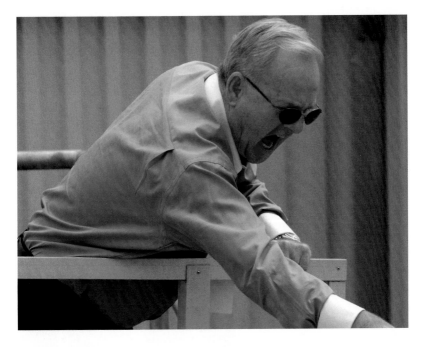

Humpy yelling at NASCAR officials over a call at a three-hundred-mile race in 1999.

Grand Marshal Humpy at the Martinsville 500 with wife Pat in 1984.

With wife Pat after their wedding in Charlotte in 1962.

A very young Humpy learning to enjoy the simple things in life.

Humpy's father, the original Humpy, holding Humpy after his Belmont Abbey football team won the National Junior College Championship in 1938: undefeated, untied, and unscored upon.

Former boxer Humpy, while at Firestone, "spars" with Goodyear's
Chuck Blanchard at Atlanta Motor Speedway in 1968.

Master time trialist Humpy wins a
ten-miler at Speedway in 2000.

Humpy, age two, with friend Buddy Eller on the front porch of a house in Belmont, North Carolina.

Humpy prepares to sign the NASCAR sanction for the Winston All-Star Race in 1989.

Humpy (right) with Elizabeth Taylor and then-Secretary-of-the-Navy John Warner in 1977, prior to the World 600.

Humpy announcing his own race in 1962 at the Robinwood Speedway in Gastonia, North Carolina, which he says was the most exciting track he has ever seen.

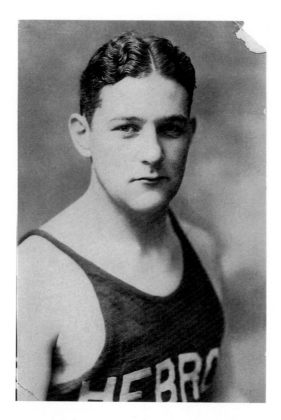

Humpy's father, the original Humpy, was a great
athlete at Hebron Academy in Maine and later played
football on the famous Red Grange, Illinois, team in
the 1920s.

The only driver in the whole place was Mario. He was unproven, untested, and Steve wasn't about to put a greenhorn in the race car to run a test. We called Al Dean and said, "Mario's the only one here, and we need to get this test going. Would you mind putting him in the car?" And Al said, "No, go ahead." Well, Mario got in the car, and ran some practice laps. On the seventh serious lap, he broke the Phoenix qualifying record. And that's how Mario Andretti ended up getting his first Indy ride.

I was at Indy when Mario recorded his first and only victory for Andy Granatelli and handled the postrace press conference.

BY THE MID-1960s Firestone and Goodyear were buying up the Indy racing teams. Remember Firestone's ad where they had a photo of all the Indy winners? Goodyear was the top-selling tire, but we at Firestone always suspected that the reason Goodyear spent so much money trying to put us out of business was to get rid of that ad. The ad ran in May, and that month Firestone would top Goodyear in tire sales. Every other month Goodyear led. That was in the old days when people would change from their winter tires to their summer tires. You're going on vacation with the family, and you want to make sure your summer tires are the best. Even though Goodyear, Goodrich, and Firestone all had tires priced at $29.95, most people picked the Firestones, and everyone figured it was because of that ad. Even if a buyer wasn't a race fan, he'd think, "If Firestones can win the Indy 500, they must make a better tire." Back in those days there were three TV stations and *Time* and *Life* magazines, and for Southerners there was *Grit*, which came out once a week and was bought all over the South.

So during the latter half of the 1960s, Firestone and Goodyear controlled most of the race teams until Firestone finally got tired of the money battle. I was down in Cape Hatteras fishing for redfish on the pier when the constable came out to get me.

"Your boss at Firestone wants to talk to you, Humpy. It's an emergency."

Things were not going well with Firestone because instead of paying the Indy drivers to use its tires, as Goodyear did, it decided to put its millions into the prize money—another points deal. The winner of the Indy championship might win a million dollars of the prize money. But Firestone lost out, because given the choice, the drivers opted for the guaranteed money and chose Goodyear.

"I hate to bother you on your vacation," I was told when I called, "but you better get on up to Akron. I have a board meeting, and it looks like we're going to get out of racing."

I hightailed it to Akron where I got the news. Firestone offered me a job in Washington, D.C., in PR, because Ralph Nader was attacking the tire companies, and we needed lobbying. None of the tire companies had any equity in Washington except to sell tires to the defense department. They didn't have a clue how to operate under governmental regulations.

I went to Washington, D.C., opened an office, and settled into the National Press Building. This was when Washington was in turmoil. The city was very poor, and there were riots.

Usually I drank coffee with my next-door neighbor. He worked for one of the news services, and one morning he was late and never did arrive. Someone had pulled him out of his car, shot him right between the eyes, and took the car, never to be seen again.

I decided at that point I didn't want to bring up my family in Washington, D.C. That's when I quit Firestone, even though I felt I had gotten my master's degree at Firestone. Working there had opened up a whole new world for me.

I returned to Charlotte. I called Gene White, a distributor for Firestone Southeast and a really good friend. I moved my office to Charlotte in a building he owned, and we went into business together. I was glad to be back home in the Carolinas.

CHAPTER 8

When the Rubber
Meets the Road

W HILE I WAS INVOLVED with Indy racing during most of my early
years with Firestone, much of my time in the later years was spent
supplying tires to teams from NASCAR. Among the NASCAR personali-
ties I got to know well were the unlikeliest pair of partners you ever saw,
John Holman and Ralph Moody, the two men who took over the Ford
Motor Company race team from Pete DePaolo. There was a legal reason
why Ford set up Holman and Moody in business. Ford felt that if it dealt
directly with the race teams, the company would be more apt to open
itself to legal liability than if it had somebody from the racing world as a
go-between.

Neither John nor Ralph had any money, and they were an odd couple
if one ever existed. John Holman was a big, beefy-looking guy, an ex–truck
driver from California. He had a big jaw, a crewcut, and a big neck. Ralph
Moody was a proper New Englander, skinny and serious. He had started
out as a midget driver in places like Seekonk and the Old Norwood Arena
in New England, and had came South to race. He became quite successful at
it. Ralph pulled off one of the greatest stunts in racing history during one of
the old Daytona Beach races. He was racing down the backstretch, flipped,
landed on his wheels, and kept going. Amazing!

He and John Holman got together to run the Ford racing operation, and from that moment on I don't know if they ever got along. But aside from that, they were absolutely made for each other. John was the office guy, the front man, and Ralph was the mechanical wizard. Between them they were exactly what Ford needed at the time. John could be as tough as Dick Butkus, but he could also be as much a diplomat as anyone in Washington. I really liked John. Ralph was very good with race drivers. He knew how to get them going and keep them moving.

I can remember one time while I was working for Firestone I went to see Holman. Firestone was very chintzy with their company cars. I was driving a '65 Ford, a straight drive inline six-cylinder engine with no air conditioning. While I drove John to lunch, he said to me, "Where did you get this piece of shit?"

I said, "It's just what Firestone does."

He said, "Let me have this car for a while." Meanwhile, he loaned me a Ford Cortina for about a week.

He called me one day and told me to come over. "I got your car fixed up," he said. I went over there. He had put in a 428 engine with air conditioning—which the auditors from Firestone never saw because they would have had a heart attack.

Another time I was over at Holman and Moody trying to get John to modernize. I told him that what Holman and Moody needed was a catalog. He thought about it and agreed. "You're right," he said, and he asked me to produce it for him.

I finished his catalog, and he liked it, and I said, "That's going to be $1,500, John." I knew I was never going to get paid because he was the barter king of the world.

He said, "Look, Humpy, I got something here you'll probably want." I knew what was coming. We went out back, and up on pallets were five GT-40 race cars that had been run at Le Mans.

He said, "You can have one of those."

I said, "But John, they don't have motors in them."

He said, "Well, someday they will be worth something. Matter of fact, I'll let you have the one Dick Hutcherson finished third in." But I needed the $1,500 more than I needed a junked race car.

He said, "I'll show you something else." He pointed to a Boston Whaler fishing boat, which was in good shape, so I took the boat. If I had taken the

GT-40, today it would be worth a couple million dollars. I kept the boat for four years, and then I sold it for $1,500.

The first prolific driver to star for Holman and Moody was Freddie Lorenzen. He was from Elmhurst, Illinois, and he looked like Robert Redford. He had been quite successful in United States Auto Club (USAC) stock cars, and he came down South. He was cocky, brash, good-looking, and unmarried. He really brought a new level to racing because he wasn't your redneck southern race driver.

Freddie hadn't run on dirt before, and when he entered Darlington—one of his first races down here—the jury was out on him. We didn't know how fierce a competitor he was. I can remember Freddie went out for practice, and when he came back in, Ralph Moody said to him, "You're not driving the car right." Ralph jumped in the car and took it out for four laps, and he cut a second off Freddie's time. That just infuriated Freddie. He jumped in the car, and he clicked off a couple laps faster than Ralph's. But Ralph had made his point. There were few car owners who could pull a stunt like that. That was Ralph. He still had a few laps left in him.

This was an era before radios—teams just used chalk boards to communicate with drivers—and during that Darlington race Freddie got into it with Curtis Turner, who kept slamming into him. Curtis absolutely would not let Freddie pass. There were only a few laps left, and Freddie went down into the first turn, right in front of the press box, and he parked Curtis, caught him in the left rear quarter panel and spun him out—something a rookie driver didn't do. And Freddie won the race.

Boy, Freddie's stock really went up after that, and he became extremely successful. Freddie retired rather early at age 34. He quit after the 1972 season. This was a time when drivers were getting maimed, busted up, and killed right and left, and it left the ride open for David Pearson to fill.

DAVID WAS ONE OF THOSE SCOTCH-IRISH GUYS who came from mill hill near Spartanburg. He's olive-skinned so he probably has a little bit of Indian or Italian or some other breed of ethnicity you didn't see around the Carolinas very often. David grew up in one of those shotgun houses, and at a very early age discovered he had a way with cars. My earliest recollection is of him driving a '37 Ford slant-back sedan with a flathead engine. This was also the favorite car of Ralph Earnhardt—and it was Ralph who David took on for the title of King of the Hill. Ralph had been unbeatable until David showed up.

David was a strange dude who didn't say much. Over the years he didn't change much, except that he gained a lot of confidence. He didn't aspire to race at Indianapolis like Bobby Allison, Cale Yarborough, and Lee Roy Yarbrough did.

He was a good-looking guy, and girls liked him. He spoke that countrified, mill hill English, and he didn't care how he dressed, and a lot of people tried to change him because they were trying to lift the image of racing. These same people wanted to give Richard Petty diction lessons. They would probably prevail today, but fortunately they didn't back then because David and Richard had an inner confidence and wouldn't change. No one was going to make those two talk or dress a certain way.

David almost never showed a temper, but I can tell you he had one. He and I got into it a number of times. I had made a deal with him to drive Firestone tires, and on several occasions he chose not to, trying to tell me the Goodyears were faster. He and I would get mouthy, and it would get pretty steamy. One time I picked up a wrench and threw it on the ground and told him, "You better be glad that ain't you."

David's car was No. 16, powder blue and white with red trim. It was called Sweet Sixteen, and in 1959 he was an absolute terror in it. He ran Thursday nights at the Columbia Speedway and Saturday nights at Greenville-Pickens.

The field at Columbia was formidable. They raced on Thursday nights, so among the usual crowd of racers were Tiny Lund, Tom Pistone, a guy named Dick Dangerfield—one of the greatest racing names of all-time—and the Preacher Man, Marion Cox, who owned a car usually driven by Lee Roy Yarbrough or Little Bud Moore and, of course, Ralph Earnhardt.

The racing was ferocious because the cars were relatively even, and the track was extremely difficult. It was white clay, and got like frozen concrete, which nobody was used to. After Pearson won fourteen races, a watchful and vigilant NASCAR official by the name of Pete Keller, whose job it was to make things as level as he could, ordered David to tear down his engine. They discovered that not only was it legal, it was way *under-powered*. Usually they bore the engine out to what we called 80-over. David's car was only 60-over. What they discovered was that David Pearson was a fantastic young race car driver who had an uncanny ability to get around a racetrack. It was our first glimpse of him, but certainly not our last.

The next year, 1960, David decided to go Grand National racing. He had no money. He had a "shade-tree operation" if there ever was one. It was called a shade-tree operation because usually the garage was a patch of dirt underneath a shade tree. I remember going down to Atlanta and watching David make stop after stop after stop trying to get his car running right. He finished the race near the bottom. I thought, *He's in the big-time now.*

Every once in a while his car would get running well enough to show a glimpse of the driver he was to become. Like when Ray Fox—one of the better observers of young talent, and a fierce rival of Smokey Yunick's—put David in his car in 1961. Ray had the ability to make gobs of horsepower, and it didn't take the two long to show people what they had because in his second World 600 at Charlotte, David did the incredible and won the race.

He went on after that to earn himself the nickname the Silver Fox. Silver because his hair turned prematurely gray. The fox part was the most interesting aspect of David Pearson's driving. Most of the race you'd forget he was even in it. Then all of a sudden, with thirty laps to go, David would come on, and often he would end up winning.

After he left Ray Fox, he went to drive for Cotton Owens, and he did well with Cotton. But the most extraordinary part of his career was from 1972 to 1978 when he won 43 races and took 50 poles with the Wood brothers.

He was racing against some really great drivers—Richard Petty, Bobby Allison, Buddy Baker, Cale Yarborough, Curtis Turner, and more—and so many times he prevailed during this period, and always at the last minute.

It became a running joke in the pit area when halfway through the race someone would ask, "Where's David?" because he was lurking in the back somewhere.

Now David could get feisty if he wanted to, but that's not the way he chose to race. He recognized in the early days of superspeedway racing that these races were four hours long and not only did your car have to be around at the end to win, but it had to have horsepower, brakes, and tires, and he knew how to preserve them.

But when it came time to put pedal to the metal, David certainly did.

MY FAVORITE PEARSON STORY came after my Firestone days, when I was at the Charlotte Motor Speedway. We used to get huge crowds for qualifying for the World 600. All the construction workers would turn out on a Wednesday afternoon. We got as many as 40,000 fans to come watch.

But then from 1972 through 1978 David Pearson won the pole at the Charlotte Motor Speedway fourteen races in a row, and it got to be a joke.

It was awful. Fewer and fewer fans were coming because the outcome was almost preordained.

I was determined to do something about it. I was all over NASCAR to find out what Pearson was doing to get the pole. I knew the Wood brothers weren't cheaters, but something was going on, and I was determined to get to the bottom of it. I even badgered Glen and Leonard Wood. I asked, "What are you guys doing?" I never could find out. And when I'd come around, David Pearson would look at me and laugh. I finally enlisted the aid of my friend Banjo Matthews, who built the Wood brothers' car.

These were the days when Banjo built most of the cars that ran in the races. It was before the race teams built their own cars. I had done Banjo a lot of favors. He also had a lot of other cars in the field. I was sure Banjo didn't want people to think he was showing favoritism to the Wood brothers.

I badgered poor Banjo to death. For three months it was like a Chinese water torture. He finally agreed to unveil the mystery. The day after Pearson won the pole—again—he called me and said he thought he had figured it out. I can't tell you how anxious I was to hear the answer, because attendance at the Speedway was dropping precariously. Used to be there was a lot of betting on who would win pole, but with David winning every time the odds had to be one to one, and no one was interested in those odds.

"It's the way he's getting into the first turn," Banjo said. "It's the way he's going over the hump."

The first turn at Charlotte had a notorious hump in it. You rode over the hump into the corner. It was also the fastest part of the racetrack. When I heard that, all sorts of flashing lights were going off in my brain. I immediately came up with a concrete answer to solving the riddle: I decided to cut out the hump and re-profile that corner. Which I did that summer of 1975. I hired a guy with a bulldozer, and I went out there with him and made sure it was done right, and I was very proud of myself. I rode my passenger car over the spot many times, and it just felt different. I had a couple other drivers come out and drive over it, and they gave me their opinion of it.

No one knew the real reason I had done it. I did it one hundred percent to try to take away David Pearson's advantage.

I had a new secretary at the time, and she didn't know anyone in racing. It was Wednesday, qualifying day, but I was so busy working on the weekend schedule that I had forgotten all about it. I was oblivious to what was happening on the track that day, when about five thirty in the afternoon my new secretary said to me, "You have a phone call. There's a Mr. Pearson on the phone."

I was thinking it was Harold Pearson from the *Columbia State*. Thinking it was a media person, I took the call. I picked up the phone, and the guy on the other end said, "You picked the wrong place." And he hung up. Of course, it was David.

I thought, *Holy shit*, and I called the media center. "Who the hell got the pole?" I asked. They said, "Who did you think? Pearson."

I said, "You have to be kidding me."

"And not only that, he broke the track record."

I immediately became incensed with Banjo Matthews. I was figuring he had played a huge practical joke on me, though that wasn't in his nature. I finally tracked him down.

"What in the hell is going on?" I said. "You said it was the first turn."

"Humpy," he said, "you know how racing is. It might not have been there."

The next race in October we held a practice, and I was walking toward that first turn, because I wanted to see firsthand how Pearson was going through that corner. He was the only car on the track, and after running a few laps, he slowed and then stopped his car next to where I was standing.

"I want my tow money," he said.

That was an old joke. Back in the days when things weren't quite so fancy, track operators would pay the drivers tow money to help pay for the gas to get to the track. Tow money at the Columbia Speedway had been five dollars.

I got my billfold out, pulled out five bucks, and handed it to David.

"I want you to sign it," David said.

Since then it's become a standing joke. I've probably paid him $1,800 in tow money. Every time I see him, he says, "Give me my tow money."

David wanted me to know not to fool with him and he wanted to let me know I was never going to find out what he was doing. And I never have.

ON THE CHRYSLER END OF THINGS, you had the team of Paul Goldsmith and Ray Nichels, who were Chrysler's official arm, and then you had Petty Engineering, which had its own separate deal. Petty Engineering was owned by Lee Petty, one of the first men able to make a living owning and driving a race car.

Lee could be ferocious. I can remember a race between Lee and Junior Johnson in October at the old Charlotte Fairgrounds. It was a Grand National race, and there was a huge crowd, and the two knocked each other everywhere but upside down. There was so much drama that Bill France Sr. decided to schedule a rematch the next week. There was an open week in the schedule, so he added a race to attract another big crowd. The next week nothing much happened between them. They never got into it, but France Sr. packed the place a second time around. That's the way it was in the old days.

Lee won championships in 1954, 1958, and 1959, running Chryslers, until he was badly hurt at Daytona in 1960. After that he confined himself to playing a lot of golf and turned the primary driving over to Richard, who won seven more driving championships. Richard also ended up winning 200 races, the most in NASCAR history. But Lee was still the patriarch.

Lee was an ornery, feisty guy who gave no quarter to anybody. He was very tightfisted, which was about the only way you could make it in those early days. Despite the onslaught of money from Carl Kiekhaefer and Holman and Moody, Lee Petty remained an independent.

As an example of Lee's independence, I can I remember the time he got mad at the phone company. He went to Fort Bragg, and in an auction he bought a phone system, and he installed it himself and started his own phone company. I was working for Firestone, and I would call up there. I would have to dial zero, and the operator would ask for a four-digit number. I would give it, and she would say, "Oh, you must be calling the Pettys." That was during a time when the telephone operator wasn't from India. When I'd visit Lee, I'd see this girl at the switchboard with a plug she pulled in and out. That was Lee's phone company.

Lee also built the first test track I ever knew about. This was back in the days when drivers would test their cars out on the road—literally. They'd find a back road and go test. But you needed to turn somewhere, and so Lee carved a little dirt track out in the woods behind his house.

Eventually it became one of the world's greatest junkyards. It was filled with cars, wrecked and unwrecked, numbered 43 and 42. If you had those cars today, you'd be worth a lot of money.

When Richard was driving for Lee in 1964, he was earning a salary of $200 a week. That was the year Richard won his first Daytona 500, and going into the race the rap against him was that he couldn't win on a superspeedway. This was only the fourth year of the superspeedway era. Most drivers really didn't know what they were doing. There was drafting, but it was in its embryonic stages. Richard went down to Daytona in a Plymouth, an interesting race car because unlike the '55 Chevy and the '60 Bonneville Pontiacs that Fireball Roberts drove, the engine was off-set just a little bit to the left. That gave the car a little bit of an advantage because it put a little bit more weight on the left side, though no one actually recognized that as an advantage at the time. The car also had that hemi engine with tremendous horsepower. Daytona is where you need horsepower, and Richard won that Daytona 500, dispelling everyone's notion that he couldn't win on the superspeedways.

Richard was also a showman. He learned that from the drivers who came before him—his father, Curtis Turner, Joe Weatherly, and Junior Johnson—who knew how to put on a show and who knew what brought people through the gate. Richard also knew the NASCAR game. He didn't win races by a lot. He didn't tip his hand. He played it close to the vest. Go back to his 200th win, at Daytona in front of President Reagan when he beat Cale Yarborough on the last lap. Everybody said, "My God, Ronald Reagan was there. How could that possibly happen?" Well, it could happen if it was Richard Petty, because he wasn't about to show his hand early. He always waited until the end. A lot of the drivers today don't understand that. And by doing it, he kept the NASCAR officials off his back.

What made Richard Petty so good was that you couldn't intimidate him. He was totally unflappable. I never saw anyone like him. He never got mad at the other drivers. Things could happen to him, and he would maintain his demeanor.

He held his compass and his course, and that enabled him to keep his focus longer and better than most drivers. That ability to focus is what differentiates the great ones from all the others, because for the three or four hours you're behind that wheel, you can't be thinking about anything else. I've seen Richard get out of his race car after someone knocked him into the wall, and he would stand for an interview, and he would act like nothing had happened. Then he would go into his trailer and raise hell.

As time went on he became more flappable, more opinionated, but never in public. And he absolutely set the example for every race driver signing autographs. He had that beautiful calligraphy he learned at Randleman High School, and he would just sign autographs until the last person was standing in line. While he was doing it he would never get upset or cantankerous.

He was also as straight an arrow as ever existed. He was not a womanizer. He didn't drink. He didn't smoke. He was just a small-town boy who made good and set a great example for everybody.

At the end of the 1964 season Lee split the money between him, Richard, and older son Maurice, who served as the team's engine builder. In November 1966 Lee finally stepped away, allowing Maurice and Richard to make the decisions themselves. I know this because I had gone up to Level Cross to make a tire deal with Petty Engineering, and I said, "Where's Lee?" Richard said, "He told us we could make the deal." I was shocked because Lee always had been in total control.

I said, "Okay, I'm going to shut the door, and we're going to make a deal before the day's over, and we're not coming out until we do." We negotiated for six hours, and we finally agreed that Firestone would pay Petty Engineering $50,000 for them to run our tires. It was as much money as we ever paid anyone. But that was the best deal I ever made because in 1967 Richard Petty won twenty-seven races.

People ask me, "How did he win all those races that year?" My pat answer was "the Firestone tires," but in truth one thing the Pettys discovered was left-side weight. Up until that point the left front never did much of anything on a NASCAR race car. But the Pettys and a Chrysler engineer by the name of Larry Rathgab shifted the weight of the engine over to the left side—it was a torsion-bar car—and that gave them an advantage. Couple that with Richard's driving ability and Maurice's talent for finding a lot of horsepower, and they could hardly lose that year. Just how dominant they were became evident at Wilkesboro when Richard fell seven laps behind and then roared back to win the race. Having cousin Dale Inman as the crew chief didn't hurt either.

One of the most unbelievable days I ever had as a track operator occurred in 1984 when Richard won the 500 at Charlotte. I was looking forward with great anticipation to the end of the race, because afterward I was headed to an obscure island off the coast of South Carolina to go fishing with Tom Higgins of the *Charlotte Observer*. I was running the Charlotte Motor Speedway, and the second race, the one in the fall, was always much more difficult to promote. I needed a short break and couldn't wait to leave.

The race ended, and Bill France Jr. called me over to the control tower. He said, "Oh, boy, the inspectors found that Richard's engine is too big." I said, "Oops." Because up to that point Richard had never been involved in the cheating end of it. His reputation was spotless. Bill Jr. said, "Let's you and I tell him."

This was back when you went to Victory Circle first and then went to the press box. The security guards brought Richard over to the control tower where Bill Jr. and I were, and Bill told him about his engine. I could tell by looking at him that he had no idea, and Maurice ended up taking all the blame. Richard had a hard time with that, and it was a huge story.

As soon as I got to my obscure island, the press was waiting. When we got to our final destination—Cape Lookout, which was as isolated as it could be—everyone on the island had heard about Richard's big engine, and they wanted to talk to us about what happened. I was thinking we should have gone to Canada instead. The talk never died down the whole year. It was a big deal.

RICHARD PETTY WON 200 RACES and David Pearson won 105. David retired in 1986. Richard quit after 1992. Richard won seven championships and David three. In the 1960s and 1970s, they were the two top drivers in large part because they both ran all of the races—fifty-something a year—when most drivers refused to do that because the purses were rather small for many of the races held on the shorter tracks. Richard and David would run at tracks like Richmond and Bristol where the quarters were narrow and they had the two best cars, and inevitably they would get into it. You might call it a gentleman's war. It rarely reached the intensity of a rivalry like the one between Darrell Waltrip and Bobby Allison because Richard and David were both pretty level-headed. Yet at the same time it could get ferocious, as it did on that memorable day in 1976 at the Daytona 500.

I was there that day. It was hard to tell who was going to win the race. They battled side by side down the backstretch, so you knew it was going to be close. I frankly didn't think they were going to crash because both were clean drivers and both knew how to get around a racetrack. What I didn't put into the equation was the fierce competitiveness of them both wanting to win at Daytona. Had the race been someplace else, perhaps the end result might not have happened. But at Daytona that day it was quite a slam-bang affair coming off the fourth turn as they raced to the finish line.

One of the cars got into the other one coming off the turn. The way cars drift, it was probably both of them, and once that gets started it usually continues, because if one driver hits another, the other driver usually retaliates. Also the cars have a tendency to bounce back into each other. Particularly if you're on the inside and you hit a guy and you start to lose it, the best thing you can do is lean against him to keep control. And so they hit each other over and over, keeping at it until they finally crashed. Both stopped before the finish line, but Pearson was able to get his car going again, and he won the race.

I was surprised Pearson made it to the line. He had hit the wall, and his car was all bashed in and torn up. After the race Richard appeared to have taken the loss okay, though I'm sure he was upset about it.

Ray Fox called me one day in 1965. David Pearson had left him, and he was looking for a driver, and he asked me what I thought about Buddy Baker, who was Buck Baker's son. Buddy was the most fearless human being I ever knew outside of Bonneville Flats speed record holder Art Arfons. Now I didn't like Buck at the time. I can't say I ever did like him. But I tried hard not to let Buck prejudice me against Buddy, and I told Ray he had talent but "you have to get control of him."

I knew Ray could do that. He was like Smokey, though Ray wouldn't have wanted to hear that because the two were bitter rivals. At the time, Ray was running those Dodges with the hemi engines, and I knew he had to have a driver who would put his foot to the floor, and that was Buddy.

I said, "If you take him on, I will make sure he gets plenty of tire testing." In those days we tested on the big tracks at least twice. We liked to have two drivers, a veteran and a young kid because a tire test was supposed to give the tires maximum abuse, and the veterans were so much smoother you preferred to test the tire with the younger guy. Plus a younger guy hadn't hit the wall that many times, and he was more apt to go all out.

We went down to Daytona, and we started testing, and boy, right off the bat I saw Buddy's fearlessness. These were the days when you could put bigger carburetors on the cars, lower them, mask them off, and do whatever you could do to make them faster. A lot of drivers when they ran at the Daytona for the first time would drive into the pits, get out of their cars, and be ashen. But Buddy relished it. He just wanted to go faster.

Buddy never asked or cared what kind of tires we put on his car. We'd put tires on to make the car push or to make the car loose—all different effects—and Buddy was able to adapt very quickly to any situation, as quickly as anyone I had seen. He would just get in and drive his brains out. If a car had 100 percent in it, he'd get it to 99.9 percent. He must have put in 2,000 laps at Daytona even before he entered his first 500. We tested him at places like

Charlotte, Atlanta, and Darlington—real tough racetracks—and all those laps accelerated his career. He was the best test driver Firestone ever had.

This was a period when there were a lot of drivers' deaths and injuries. In 1969, I brought Don MacTavish, a kid from Massachusetts, down to drive in the Daytona 300 Sportsman race. He was supposed to have come the year before but he didn't feel he was ready, so I brought down Pete Hamilton instead.

I liked to work with young drivers. I was working with Buddy, and Buddy was helping me train Don. I said to Buddy, "Before he takes the green flag we have to tell him not to be overaggressive early in the race." That was the kind of hard-charging driver Don was. When Don was sitting in the car, Buddy and I went over to talk to him. I said, "Keep calm, keep cool. Don't try to win it on the first lap."

Buddy and I went up to the roof to watch the race. On the eighth lap Don lost it coming off turn four, and when you lose a car at a big track like Daytona or Indianapolis, the cardinal rule is to lock the brakes up and go to the inside. You never try to save it and go back outside, which is what Don did, and he hit the opening in the wheel fence and got his car slashed in half. He was sitting there with his body dangling out of the car when another car rammed into him. It was the worst impact ever at Daytona. Don was probably dead even before he got hit.

Buddy and I went down to the wreckage to see what we could do, but Don was lifeless. I was a lot more shook up than Buddy was. We went back to Don's motel room and cleaned it out.

But nothing seemed to faze Buddy, and he was able to keep going.

It was February 1972, and my goal was to get Buddy ready for the World 600 in May. I told him, "Before you start winning races, you gotta get yourself in physical condition. You have to get used to the heat." Buddy had a 1967 Dodge Charger, the same car as his race car, and we would drive around in it for forty minutes at a time, the length of time between pit stops, with the windows up and the heater running full blast while wearing rubber suits. Then we'd stop by a field, put on boxing gloves, and box. One day I got a little carried away, and I really slammed him in the head, and he went berserk. We starting wailing into each other like a scene from *The Quiet Man* with John Wayne. We kept going across a field into the backyard of a woman who called the police. The cops showed up and asked us what the hell we were doing. After we got a drink of water, we started laughing about it. Two weeks later Buddy won the World 600. He repeated the feat again the next year.

Buddy's career came to a premature end after an accident at Charlotte in 1988 at the Coca-Cola 600. Buddy was driving for Hoss Ellington, and halfway through the race in the middle of a multi-car wreck, he tried to knock the first-turn wall down. He was stretched so far in that car that his helmet hit the right side roll bar. He was dazed, and he was taken to the hospital. The doctors checked him out, and everything seemed to be okay. But at Watkins Glen during practice he was going down the long straight-away, and after he came in he told Dr. Jerry Petty, "Jerry, something is wrong. I felt like I was outside the car." He was checked out, and it turned out he had a hematoma. Buddy, who had a deep fear of hospitals, called me.

"I gotta go to the Carolina Medical Center," he said. "I gotta have minor brain surgery." I didn't want to scare him, but I thought to myself, *There ain't no such thing as minor brain surgery*. It saved his life. He ran some after that, but that was pretty much the end of his career.

Buddy won eighteen races, but Buddy was like Curtis Turner. If the races had been 250 miles instead of 500 miles, he probably would have won 50 of them.

CHAPTER 9

Big Bill France

I FIRST GOT TO KNOW BIG BILL FRANCE in 1963 when I was working at the Augusta Speedway. It was a new track, and Mr. France and I talked quite a bit because he wanted to make sure the event wasn't a flop.

Then, after I went to work for Firestone, I got to know him real well. He became a person I could go to for advice, and I went to him quite often. I knew I wanted to be something, and I knew knowing him would help. Every chance I got I went to his office or called him on the phone. I went out of my way to make friends with him, and he was very helpful to me.

He was a big man, about 6 feet 5 inches and 250 pounds. He was an imposing figure, but I never saw him even close to getting into a fight. He was a smooth talker and the first person I ever met who would go out of his way to go see somebody to solve a problem. He was a good pilot, and if there was a problem outside of his home base in Daytona, he would get in his plane and fly to the person he was having a problem with and try to solve it in person. That meant a lot to people.

Bill also didn't duck conflicts. He didn't mind facing someone down. In 1961 Curtis Turner was going to get a lot of money from the teamsters if he could organize the drivers, and Bill France stood up in front of all the drivers and told them that anyone who joined was never again going to race on one of NASCAR's tracks, and all by himself he stopped that union movement cold.

In 1965 Bill Senior got angry when Chrysler pulled out of racing. That really tore him up. He didn't like the tail wagging the dog. And when Ford pulled out the next year, after Chrysler returned, he was just really incensed.

People wonder why Bill was moved to build two huge tracks like Daytona and Talladega. It goes back to a story I heard after Bill had started NASCAR. He went up to Indianapolis to see the race, and allegedly they refused him a credential, and he was thrown out of the place. He never acknowledged that this was the reason he built Daytona to be as long as it is, but what other track was two and a half miles? Indianapolis. Bill made his track faster than Indianapolis by building a high-banked track. Everything he did seemed to point to his wanting to go one-up on Indianapolis. One of the first things he did after Daytona opened was offer $10,000 to anyone who could break 180 miles an hour. Eventually Art Malone won the money in a car owned by Bob Osieki called the Mad Dog, a front-engine IndyCar with a wing on it.

Bill tried to run IndyCars at Daytona, and it was a bloodbath. He even had a midget division. His vision was always to be bigger and better than Indy.

Once Daytona was built, he then was determined to build an even bigger and faster track. He told me that the place where he wanted to build his new track was in the Greenville, South Carolina, area. Greenville was an ideal location, because it was between Charlotte and Atlanta right on highway 85.

But in order to make this happen, Bill first had to change the Blue Laws to allow racing on Sunday in the state of South Carolina. He worked and worked behind the scenes to get that done, but there was too much opposition from the conservative religious interests. And it cost the state of South Carolina a track that would have been the biggest in NASCAR. Because of its location it would have made it the second most important track in America after Indianapolis. Ironically, not too much later they did change the Blue Laws, but by then it was too late.

As a result, Bill started looking around at other places. One day I received a phone call from Fonty Flock, a former racer who was bird-dogging for Bill France. Fonty also worked for Bill at Daytona driving fans around the speedway. Fonty said he had found some land in Alabama.

I said, "Fonty, why the hell would you want to build a racetrack in Alabama?"

He said, "Because I can get the land for almost nothing, and I can get the state to do just about anything we want to do." Bill had worked for the

George Wallace for President Committee in Florida. Wallace and he were close, and Wallace was the governor of Alabama at the time.

Sometime in 1968 Bill asked me to come to Talladega, Alabama, to see the new track he was building. He had put dirt down to form the track, and he was getting ready to pave it. I drove to Talladega, and you have to remember, the atmosphere in racing was terrible then. We had had a number of drivers killed—Joe Weatherly, Fireball Roberts, Don MacTavish, Jimmy Pardue, Billy Wade—and a number of IndyCar drivers as well. It was not a good time for racing. The car companies had been in and out, and there had been a gnashing of teeth over that, so when I arrived at Talladega and saw what Bill was doing, I was just amazed at the gargantuan size of the place—two and a half miles long with this extraordinary banking. I asked him, "Why did you build it so big?" At Daytona we were right on the edge of being able to keep tires on the cars, and this track was going to be even faster.

I was working for Firestone, and I was blunt. I said, "Bill, we are not going to be able to keep tires on the cars here."

"Ah, you guys can figure it out," he said.

I said, "Bill, I am telling you right now, we are not going to figure it out. What's going to happen is the tire companies are going to walk away from this racetrack, and so are the drivers. I'm telling you, these guys don't want to die, and this track is too fast, and we are not going to be able to keep tires on the cars."

He didn't like hearing that. It really pissed him off. And I can understand that, especially coming from a young guy like me. Sure enough, Bill paved the track, and Firestone went down for a tire test, and we could not keep the tread on the tires. The cars were running over 200 miles an hour, and then all of a sudden—bang!—a tire would blow, and the whole tread would unravel from the tire.

I told Bill, "I don't know if man can make a tire to withstand these speeds." As a result, Firestone pulled out, and that really, really got to him, because he was about out of money. Bill never did have much money. Whenever he had any, he spent it. Even though it was a public company, he had his whole net worth tied up at Talladega.

Goodyear hadn't yet run its tire test, but if they pulled out, there would be no race, which would have been an absolute disaster for him. It would have brought him to bankruptcy.

Goodyear ran its test, which was held in absolute secrecy. No one would talk about it. I couldn't learn anything. Of course, with Firestone out, Goodyear decided to provide a tire for the track. I decided that the best thing for me to do was to stay away from Talladega during race week. Because I knew exactly what was going to happen. The drivers ran at top speed, and tire after tire blew. As a result, every factory driver except Bobby Isaac decided it best not to run in the inaugural race at Talladega.

A MAN BY THE NAME of Raymond Pike had called me and asked me to work for him. No one has ever heard the man's name, but he is important in NASCAR history. He started something called the Professional Drivers Association (PDA). His claim to fame was that he had been movie star Esther Williams' manager. A fast-talking New Yorker, he worked for sports announcer Marty Glickman, who worked for a company called Restaurant Associates, which owned Mama Leone's, the 21 Club, and a sports agency. Pike was asked by Marty to come south and become an agent for the race car drivers. Richard Petty became the president of the PDA. All this was brewing as the Talladega Speedway was getting ready to run its first race. All of the drivers except Isaac joined the PDA.

With Richard leading the charge, the drivers announced they were boycotting the race because the conditions were unsafe. Bill France came up to Charlotte and held a meeting with the drivers at a motel on Wilkinson Boulevard. He pretty much laid down the law that a work stoppage like that wasn't going to happen again, or else.

To salvage his race at Talladega, Bill France put Grand American cars in the race—cars with smaller wheel bases that ran slower—resulting in a total mismatch, like boxers and wrestlers entering the same event.

France also announced that if you had a ticket for the Talladega 500, he would give you a companion ticket to the Daytona 500 the next year. It was a mistake because Daytona was France's bread and butter, and giving away free tickets to Daytona would cost him serious money. Daytona was France's whole season, and the poor man had completely run out of money. What saved him was a deal with Union Oil, which bought twenty-five percent of the stock in the International Speedway Corporation. The deal got him through the Talladega 500 and the Daytona 500 the following year.

Bill France made up his mind that he wasn't going to have a walkout by the drivers ever again. To accomplish this, he knew he needed to make sure the drivers ran all the races. Up to that point many of the races were far from Charlotte and paid small purses, and so the most successful drivers like Fireball Roberts concentrated on the superspeedway races that paid a lot, and skipped the others.

What France did was establish a points fund that paid big dollars to the top drivers vying for the racing championship. In 1970 he got R. J. Reynolds to fund it to the tune of millions of dollars. After that, there was never again talk of any pullout.

What sank Raymond Pike and his Professional Drivers Association was the racing economy. With Ford, Chrysler, Firestone, and Goodyear pulling out of racing, no one was making much money. The drivers weren't making much money. And that ended any talk of a drivers' union. At that point Bill France felt he had won a victory as another attempt by the drivers to organize failed. The truth is that had the racing economy been strong in the early 1970s, the PDA would have become established because Raymond Pike was a smart man. But because the economy was bad, Bill France escaped a bullet.

BILL AND HIS WIFE, ANNIE, had a very interesting working relationship. She was always back in the office behind the scenes. He never touched the money. She did. Whether you were at Daytona, or the Charlotte Fairgrounds, or the Raleigh Fairgrounds, you would see her walking around carrying a tin box that held the money. If I needed to cash a check, I'd go see Annie. This was back in the days when, if you were a driver or crew chief and you left town and owed somebody money, the motel or restaurant owner or whoever would call NASCAR, and NASCAR wouldn't let you in the garage until your bill was paid off.

Bill and Annie had a son, Bill Jr., who would later take over for him. Bill did not give Bill Jr. anything. He made Bill Jr. start at the bottom by putting up posters, driving the water truck, or doing whatever else needed to be done. I brought my kids up the same way.

Bruton Smith once decided to build forty condominium units around the first turn at the Charlotte Motor Speedway. I thought he was crazy, and didn't think they would sell.

"Add more seats," I told Bruton.

But Bruton wanted to use the money from the sale of the apartments for capital improvements: paving the track, fixing the drainage system. You might not think you'd make any money by fixing drains, but if fans get stuck in the mud, they won't come back. It's hard to borrow money for capital improvements because they don't bring an obvious monetary return. But Bruton was looking to the future. He realized improvements had to be made.

"I think I'm right, and I want to try it," Bruton replied.

We announced the sale of the units. Four months later, we had sold exactly one—a racing fan from Kansas City who owned a chain of service stations bought one.

We tried selling the condos to race team owners and big companies, even offering a three-year buyback clause. If the purchaser was unhappy, he could get his purchase price back within three years. There were no takers.

We were facing a real disaster. We told each other, "We've always been able to overcome. We need to get creative." I thought to myself, *If they won't write about us, maybe they will laugh at us. Anything.*

I decided to try to get word of the racetrack condos that were for sale on *The Johnny Carson Show* as a joke. You know, have him say there are crazy North Carolinians building condos so they can watch the traffic in front of them running 190 miles an hour. I wrote to one of the show's researchers. We got nowhere.

Then we tried the David Letterman Show. Three weeks later we got a call from a member of his staff. "Is there someone we can call to talk about it?"

We had a guy, Evans Kaiser, who had a great phone voice and he was funny, so David Letterman called Evan Kaiser during the show, and they made a joke about it. You know Letterman. "Are you going to let your kids walk across the street?" He carried on like that.

Well, the next day the bit ended up in the *Charlotte Observer*, and for some strange reason it appeared in the *Wall Street Journal*, and then other newspapers started writing about our crazy idea, and in the next seven months, we sold twenty-eight units.

Around that time Bill France called me and asked if he could come up and see the condos. Bill and Bruton Smith did not get along, but I agreed, and I gave him the grand tour.

Bill France made it very clear he did not approve of the condos. He was very outspoken to me about it. He said, "That's a big, bad mistake. You're giving up valuable real estate to other people that you'll never be able to claim again." And he was absolutely right. Though the condo deal appeared to be successful, there were two drawbacks. One was that Wall Street did not recognize the profits from the real estate because it was a one-time deal.

The second was that you always face trouble from the condo association that represents the owners of the condos. We had to pay a whole bunch of money to get them quieted down.

After that visit, I began to notice a decline with Bill France Sr. It was really sad to see. He was developing Alzheimer's. Sometimes he knew who I was, and sometimes he didn't.

The public didn't know he had it, but everyone in the business knew. We were all greatly troubled by it.

His funeral was well attended. Afterwards we all went back to his office and had a drink. It's exactly what he would have done. Everyone had a good time. I thought it was a good way to pay homage.

Bill's greatest characteristic was his tenacity. He just kept going. He also was a man with tremendous vision, and a third characteristic was that he understood the race fan as well as or better than anyone who has ever been involved in racing.

I remember in 1967 going to Daytona and having lunch with Bill. Afterward we drove by the track, and we saw a race fan in his early twenties walking toward the tunnel. Nothing was going on at the speedway that day, and Fonty Flock wasn't there to give rides around the track. Bill stopped, introduced himself, and asked the fan if he wanted to ride around the track. The fan, who was from Ontario, Canada, had no idea who Bill France was, but he was excited to experience the thrill of Daytona.

Bill took off wide open down the track in his Pontiac. He never lifted, and the guy got a huge kick out of driving 120 miles an hour. I always wondered if the fan ever figured out who had driven him that day.

Bill was that way with fans because he recognized the importance of those people.

He was an extraordinary man, one of the most interesting people in sports of the twentieth century. Before Bill came along, the movers and shakers of racing were wealthy men—Tony Holman at Indianapolis; Carl Fisher who built the Indianapolis Motor Speedway; Eddie Rickenbacker, the president of Eastern airlines; and the other men of wealth who financed racing on the board tracks. Bill France was a man who started off pumping gas in Washington, D.C. Without him, Late Model stock car racing never would have been invented. Stock car racing might have happened without him, but it certainly wouldn't have been the sensation it is today.

CHAPTER 10

Ralph and the Indian

W HEN I WAS A STUDENT at the University of South Carolina, every Thursday night I would go to the Columbia Speedway, a weird half-mile, white-clay track. You weren't supposed to be able to race on white clay, but they did, and because there were no other tracks running on Thursday night, a Who's Who of racers generally showed up there.

Every Thursday night I would be there in the pits, and I got to know the racers. One driver I became friendly with was Ralph Earnhardt, Dale's father, one of the greatest dirt-track drivers who ever lived.

Ralph was one of the first men I knew who made his living racing full-time. For a while Ralph worked in the mills. He couldn't have survived without it. His wife, Martha, told me he came in one day and said, "I want to quit my job, and I want to race full-time." She said, "As long as you don't take food out of my children's mouths." That's all she told him.

He didn't have much money, but his cars were immaculately prepared. I never ever saw him work on his car at the track. He'd pull the car down there, take it off the low-boy trailer, and he'd go racing. Usually he showed up at the track all by himself. He was very quiet, didn't say much. He would sit on the back fender of his car smoking a cigarette.

This was Sportsman racing, and his competitors were outstanding drivers like Little Bud Moore, Tiny Lund, and Tom Pistone. Ralph was a very smart racer, very conservative in his driving, primarily because that was his living and he couldn't afford to always be repairing the car. A typical race was forty laps, and he would sit there back in second place inches away from the leader, putting intense pressure on him. The pressure was particularly great on tracks that were hard to drive, like Columbia. He'd sit in wait until the last two laps, and suddenly the leader would make a mistake because Ralph had been playing with him all night. Ralph would pass and win the race, though usually not by more than a car length. Ralph had learned to play the NASCAR game well, because usually the track officials don't check your car when you only win by a little. It's the guy who runs away with it who usually gets checked.

I got to know Ralph extremely well when I began working for Firestone. I needed someone to test tires on dirt tracks during a race, so I would send Ralph tires. Monday I would call him. I'd say, "Ralph, how did you do at Greenville-Pickens?" Being a man of few words, and fewer adjectives than any person I've ever known, he'd say, "I did pretty well." That meant he won the race.

I'd say, "How did the tires work?"

He'd say, "Don't know if I'd run on them again." That meant they were terrible. If he said, "Might want to send down another set and let me try them again," meant they were kind of good but he wasn't too sure. If they were great, all he'd say was, "I really like those tires."

Ralph just didn't say a whole lot. Back then, drivers would shear axle keys all the time. The axle connects the driveshaft to the wheel and the wheel assembly, and there is a steel shaft that goes into the pinion in the center of the rear end. To keep the axle locked in place, you have to put a little key in it, and the key was a slab of steel about 1/4 inch wide by 1/2 inch high, and it slid into a little slot grooved into the axle. That kept the axle locked in and kept it from spinning. Without the axle key, the axle would spin in place, and the car wouldn't go anywhere. And these things broke all the time, but of all the drivers, Ralph never had that problem.

One time I asked him, "Ralph, you never break axle keys. What's your secret?" He wouldn't tell me until years later, when he was no longer running that rear end, so it didn't make any difference. He said that Bobby Isaac was the only other person to learn his secret. He said Bobby was at his shop one day on a Thursday morning. Ralph meticulously checked his car over and over, and on this day he pulled the axle out and looked at the key, and he saw a hairline crack in it—just a smidgen. Anyone else would have run it, but not Ralph. Ralph looked around for another key, but he didn't have one. He was running late, had to get to Columbia, and like everybody who tinkers, sometimes you have to make something work that's not intended for that use. He saw a Craftsman screwdriver, and he pulled it off the wall, and he said to himself, "This will work." So he cut off the tip and the handle, and it fit right in the slot. After that, he never broke another axle.

Bobby Isaac told me he went down to the Sears store in downtown Charlotte (the only Sears store in Charlotte), and he was trying to buy a certain screwdriver, and the salesman told him he didn't have any left. Bobby couldn't understand that because the store always had them. The salesman told him, "This guy from Kannapolis comes here, and he buys two dozen of them at a time when I get them in, and I don't know anybody who buys so many of the same screwdriver."

"What's the guy's name?" Bobby wanted to know.

The salesman said his name was Ralph, and it was then that Bobby figured it out. That tells you about the ingenuity of the racers back in those days. There were no speed shops. It was all junkyard stuff, and it was known as "getting by."

RALPH, A SCOTCH-IRISH North Carolinian, lived on Coach and Sedan Street in Kannapolis, in an area where the streets were all named after cars or something to do with cars. In the South they named a lot of streets after physical things: Hill Street, Elm Street, Steam Plant Road. Kannapolis was a planned town, as were a lot of mill towns, and by the time they got to Ralph's part of town, they were naming the streets after cars.

Ralph told me one time, "I have a rule. I will never put more than $800 cash into my race car." That meant he bought all the parts, and he did most of the work by himself. Every once in a while Frank Heffner, a guy from Cherryville, would build an engine for him. But otherwise, Ralph, who was a lone wolf, did everything himself. He worked on the race car, made sure everything was right, and he stayed out of trouble. I can't ever remember Ralph Earnhardt having a wreck.

A lot of people said that Ralph didn't like racing on the superspeedways or said he wasn't very good at it, but you have to remember that back in those days it was hard to make any money racing on the superspeedways—and also that it was very dangerous because no one knew what they were doing.

Darlington opened in 1950, Daytona opened in 1959, and Charlotte and Atlanta in 1960. For a long time, they were the only superspeedways, and it was very foreign to everybody. Ralph was not alone in not jumping into superspeedway racing. He was making good cash money on dirt. Why risk it? I have no doubt if he had wanted to race there, he would have done just fine, because he was a top driver.

Ralph would have epic battles on dirt with Little Bud Moore, David Pearson, and Tiny Lund. It was the early '60s, and Little Bud was the first hippie race car driver. Little Bud had long hair when everyone else had crewcuts. Bud had nice teeth, and he had that Geechee Charleston accent, and he could drive the wheels off a race car. I remember one night at Columbia Ralph couldn't just sit back and wait until the finish because Little Bud was passing him, and they kept going back and forth, and that night Bud beat Ralph on the last lap. He beat him coming off the second turn and the second turn at Columbia was a tough place—it wasn't very wide and it had a guard rail on the inside that could get you in trouble and make you wreck—and I thought to myself, *This kid's going to be a racer.*

Lee Roy Yarbrough, who was driving for Marion Cox, was third that night. I asked Ralph, "What do you think about Little Bud?"

He said, "Well, he might make it." That meant he was pretty good.

And I remember another time in May 1959 Ralph and David Pearson were battling in a hundred-lap race. Pearson was driving a '37 Ford sedan called Little Sweet Sixteen. It was light blue with red numbers and a white outline. David was having a prolific year, and he beat Ralph that night. Ralph was at his peak when he did it, and I thought then, *That Pearson is going to make a race driver.*

After the race I ate at a diner on the road between Columbia and Charlotte. Little Bud, Buddy Baker, and I called it "Ralph's Diner." It was the only place open on Highway 21 at night. We'd be going back to Charlotte, and Ralph would either be sitting there eating a hamburger or he had just left.

I would go over to Ralph's house to have dinner, and he would always be back in the garage working on his race car. We'd have what we called a "slick meat" sandwich, like baloney and cheese. He'd be working on the car, and I'd be over talking to him. He'd say, "Let's eat," and Martha would bring us sandwiches or he'd go in and get them. He would work, talk, and eat at the same time, which was not uncommon when you were around racers. They just worked all the time.

There was always somebody wandering into Ralph's garage because Ralph was about the only person in Kannapolis who wasn't on a shift. Everyone else would drop by after or before a shift at the mill, and even though Ralph was a lone wolf and worked on his car by himself, he always had someone around who was willing to help him with the race car. And later on Dale was exactly the same way. He always had buddies who would work for him for nothing, and he'd buy them beer at night.

Watching Ralph and his son Dale interact was interesting. Southern fathers are interesting. Southern fathers don't get philosophical or pontifical. They don't get carried away with a lot of words. It's more: "I'm not going to talk to you much about this. Watch me work on the car and drive it." And every once in a while he'd nudge him.

My father was the same way. He didn't talk a lot either. He had come from Rhode Island, and one day we were up on the roof shingling a house. I put a shingle on wrong, and he said, "You Southerners are all alike—sloppy. If we were caulking a window . . . ." I didn't know why he was talking about windows. We were on the roof. He said, "In the South if you don't caulk a window right, you get cold in the winter. In the north, you die." It was: "Watch me." So I don't remember Ralph ever telling Dale how to do anything, but at the same time, he did.

Ralph was a kind person. He didn't build too many cars for people, but he built one for me, a '37 Ford, flat-back sedan, which was one of his favorite race cars with a flathead engine in it. One of the great regrets of my life is that I sold it to another racer, Little Bud Moore. Little Bud and I were real close, and he loved Ralph and loved old cars. He wanted it, so I sold it.

The tragic thing about Ralph was he dropped dead on the kitchen floor of a heart attack when he was 45. That was back in the days when a lot of men dropped dead. Ralph smoked a lot, but so did a lot of people. I don't remember Ralph ever taking a drink, but he sure smoked those cigarettes. Who knows why he died? They didn't do autopsies back in those days, or at least they didn't do them in the mill villages. It was a shock to everyone. Dale wasn't but 22 when it happened. Ralph must have had some money, but I'm sure he didn't leave a lot.

One of Ralph's best friends was Bobby Isaac, who won the NASCAR racing championship in 1970. Bobby was another one who came up from poverty. He had olive skin and a hawk face. He had the look of an Indian.

He had been brought up by two brothers in a sawmill in Catawba, North Carolina, which is below Hickory.

Bobby was an unusual person, another guy who, like his friend Ralph, didn't say much. I liked Bobby a whole lot. The first big race Bobby won was a Sportsman race. He was driving for Frank Hefner out of Cherryville, the guy who used to build a lot of Ralph's engines.

After a race at the Columbia Speedway, Bobby and Frank stopped off at that diner we called "Ralph's Diner." They sat at a table, and they were given menus, and Bobby didn't know what to order.

Frank said, "I'll have a hot dog." So Bobby ordered a hot dog. The reason Bobby didn't know what to order was that he didn't know how to read. He later learned, but in those days he couldn't.

In 1969 when the drivers went on strike because they felt Talladega was too dangerous to drive, Bobby was the only factory-backed driver to run. I don't care what they called it. It was a strike. Bobby ran in the race, and he did very well. Bill France, who had a great connection with Rolex, gave him a Rolex presidential watch as a gift, rewarding Bobby for his loyalty. On the back it said, "Quitters never win, and winners never quit. Talladega 500. 1969."

Bobby took it home, put it in a drawer, and never wore it.

Bobby retired in 1976 after racing at Talladega. He was going down the backstretch, and he heard a voice telling him to get off the racetrack. He was asked, "Why did you pull off?" Bobby said, "God told me to come in." He got out of the race car, got into his passenger car, and drove all the way back to Catawba. He never ran another Cup race the rest of his life.

AFTER BOBBY RETIRED from Winston Cup racing, he used to visit me at my office at the Charlotte Motor Speedway quite often. We were talking about Rolex watches one time, and I told him how much I wanted one, but I had only been at the speedway a couple of years, and I really didn't have the money to buy one.

A few days later Bobby came in. I was sitting behind my desk, and Bobby said, "I want you to buy my Rolex. I'm getting rid of everything in my house that says Talladega." He felt Talladega had been bad luck for him. He wanted $200 for it. It was worth ten times that.

I said, "Bobby, I can't buy that. Bill France gave you that watch." I knew the whole history of the watch. He said, "No, I want you to buy the watch." I argued with him. "No, I don't want to. It's a trophy." Bobby then walked around the back of the desk, opened the left drawer, dropped the watch in, and left.

About three hours later Tom Pistone called. Tom sold car parts to racers. He said, "I understand you owe Bobby $700."

I was taken by surprise. "I don't owe him . . . ." Then I started putting two and two together. Bobby had bought an engine part from Pistone, and he was thinking he had sold me the watch, and so he had Pistone collect from me.

"All right," I said.

Ten minutes later Pistone was in my office looking for the money. I paid the bill.

I took the watch home and put it away. I wouldn't wear it. Bobby saw that, and he got on me really hard.

"Why aren't you wearing that watch?"

I said, "I don't want to wear it. It's a trophy."

"Nah, you gotta wear it. It don't mean a thing to me." So I started wearing it.

One Saturday at about one thirty in the morning the phone rang. I was asleep. Ned Jarrett who was running the Hickory Speedway then was calling.

"Humpy, I got bad news," he said. "Bobby's dead." Ned said Bobby had been running a 400-lap race, and it was real hot that day. During the race the exhaust manifold came loose in Bobby's car, and Bobby was gassed so badly he had to come out of the car. After Bobby passed out, he couldn't get up, so they took him to the hospital. Ned was a good friend of Bobby's, and he went too. He saw Bobby, who told Ned he was okay, but that he was real thirsty. They gave him a soft drink, which he drank, and then right there he died in front of Ned. They couldn't resuscitate him.

I went to Bobby's home the next morning as early as I could. Bobby had gotten remarried to a beautiful girl named Linda. They lived right next door to his former wife. He built a home next to her so he could be with his daughters.

I went to Linda and tried to console her. I wanted them to do an autopsy, but she didn't want to do it. A lot of people said Bobby had a heart attack, but I'm convinced to this day he died of carbon monoxide poisoning.

I offered to give Linda the watch back.

"No, absolutely not," she said. "He wanted you to have that watch, and I want you to keep it." I still have it, and I wear it all the time.

CHAPTER 11

Bobby Allison

M Y EARLIEST RECOLLECTIONS of Bobby Allison came when I was working for Firestone. In 1966 he came from Alabama to the Carolinas to challenge Richard Petty, Dick Hutcherson, and Freddie Lorenzen—the Ford and Chrysler drivers—in a small Chevelle during a time when Chevrolet wasn't even in racing. For him, a Modified driver, to challenge these guys like that was like Billy the Kid taking on Jesse James with a .32. It was the least formidable-looking race car you could imagine. When you looked at it, your first thought was that it shouldn't even have been there, yet Bobby won two races that year in that car, which he built himself in his garage.

I remember a race at Columbia one night when he gave Curtis Turner fits.

People don't remember Columbia much now because it's been closed for so long. It was difficult. It had a real hard, white-clay track with a terribly tortuous first turn to get into. Bobby didn't win the race, but he was formidable. He really didn't even have a pit crew, only his brother, Eddie, who built the engines with him. I remember looking at Bobby, and thinking, *He's Gregory Peck in* To Kill a Mockingbird.

He and Curtis got into it again at Bowman Gray Stadium, a perfectly flat quarter-mile track that was actually a running track inside the old Wake Forest University football stadium. It is very similar to Soldiers Field in Chicago. Wake played football there until the university moved to another stadium. Now they play high school football there. It's the oldest running track in NASCAR today. It seats 17,000 and has a steel guardrail around it that's been hit five million times. They keep straightening it out.

They used to run Grand National races there, and this night Curtis was in his big Ford. Bobby was in that little, pissy Chevelle, and Curtis just took him out. He quarter-paneled Bobby as Curtis could do so well, and he spun Bobby out.

It didn't take long for everyone to know that Bobby had a temper. Curtis pulled into the pits. All of a sudden you could see a car flying backwards down the track at full speed toward Curtis' car. I didn't think anyone could drive backwards that fast. It was Bobby in his Chevelle, and he just slammed the back of his car into Curtis' grille. I remember everyone scattering real fast. Curtis' car was sure busted up and Bobby's was no better off. Today NASCAR would give you the electric chair or the gas chamber for that, but I don't remember them ever doing anything to Bobby.

Because Bobby and I were both Catholics, we had a mutual interest. There weren't many Catholics in the South back then, certainly not on the racing circuit. When I was at Firestone in the late 1960s, part of our PR campaign was to take drivers to Rotary Club and Elks Club luncheons. We did this to lift up the image of racing.

I remember going out to Rockingham, North Carolina, with Bobby for a meeting of the Rotary Club. I said, "This man works in an office that goes 200 miles an hour and is surrounded by steel tubes." And I introduced him. He got up and answered questions. As was the case in the South back then, particularly in small towns, there were quite a number of pontificating people, men especially. This was back in the days when the Blue Laws existed, and one of the Rotarians got up and asked him, "Do you go to church on Sunday?" He figured that none of the heathens who raced would bother to go to church.

Before Bobby could answer, I popped up, because the question angered me, and I said, "You know, he does go to church every Sunday. So do I. We're both Roman Catholics. That's just something we do."

The guy didn't know quite what to say. He looked at us like we were not quite Christian, because in those days in the South Catholics were very much in the minority.

Once, Father Sebastian, a Benedictine monk from Belmont Abbey College, was over at St. Peter's Church in Charlotte filling in. It was very early mass, about seven in the morning, and he asked if there was anyone in the congregation who could serve mass. Bobby stepped forth and served mass as an altar boy. Father Sebastian didn't know who Bobby was. He told me, "The next day I picked up the *Charlotte Observer,* and on the front page was my altar boy." Bobby had just won the World 600.

Bobby's an interesting guy. As I said he has a temper, and he and I got into a tiff once. Bobby called me and asked for deal money before the Busch race, and I told him that I was stopping that tradition because the Busch race wasn't very profitable, and I couldn't afford to do it anymore. That ticked him off.

He brought his car to the track, drove it to the infield, and parked it right in front of the Media Center with a big "For Sale" sign on it. Then he went into the Media Center and proceeded to tell everybody he was not running in the race and why. When Bobby wants to rub it in, he can really do it.

While he was doing that I had his car towed. When he went outside, his car was gone. I had it put right in the middle of the dump.

I didn't hear anymore about it that day. It was race week, and the next morning I had to make a stop, so I didn't get into my office until nine thirty. There, sitting behind my desk like he was running the Speedway was Bobby, with a big smile on his face, as if to say, "Well, you got me." We sat and talked like nothing had happened. Finally he said, "I did find my car. It wasn't a very good parking place, but now we're even." I couldn't remember why we were even, but we were even.

Bobby was so independent. He drove for a lot of different owners, but he was happiest driving for himself. He always wanted to be the boss, to be in control. I told him once, "If they ever do an autopsy on you, they're going to find your skull is about four inches thick." Bobby always felt he didn't need anyone, that if all else failed, he could go out and do his own thing, which he often did.

Bobby won eighty-five races, third all-time. You have to remember that when he was going strong it was during the awful, bloody period of the mid- to late 1960s. There was a great fear among drivers—who will not admit it even today—particularly when they ran at places like Daytona, Talladega, Charlotte, and Atlanta (real fast places that could hurt you if you didn't know what you were doing or if you ended up in a very unlucky place). I can remember in the years from 1967 to 1970 people in the garage area talking about this driver or that driver being scared, not wanting to mix it up in the draft. For a driver to go through that period mentally was really a tough thing. It was just as bad or worse with the Indy drivers. I once asked Mario Andretti, "How could you go through that?" He said, "Honest to God, there were times I didn't think I would make it." Maybe that's how they handled it. They got in the car and said, "This may or may not be the day."

YOU CAN DRIVE OR YOU CAN QUIT. You can avoid taking too many chances at certain tracks. What made Bobby good was that despite the fear, he was able to drive the wheels off the car. He was particularly good at tire management. He knew how to get the best out of tires, and that's a subject no one talks much about because very few people understand it. But the drivers like Bobby who win a lot of races have the ability to keep their tires under them. Take Martinsville. The standing joke is that whoever has the most brakes at the end of 500 laps at Martinsville is probably going to win the race. A lot of guys use their brakes so much they don't even have brakes at the end. So, that's Martinsville and brakes, but every race is like that with tires. Not Daytona and Talladega so much because the straightaways actually cool the tires, but at tracks like Atlanta—which is fifty percent corner radius—it becomes a series of forty-five-minute races because you have to change tires so often. The goal, and not an easy one, was to go a hundred miles on one set of tires, and Bobby was able to do that. He always seemed to have fairly decent tires at the end of a long run, and this often won him races.

How was he able to do this? Because he had a seat-of-the-pants feel that very few drivers had, and he thought about what he was doing. He thought a lot about tires and their construction. He also was a guy who had come up by his own boot straps on the short tracks, where he had to make the tires last. He didn't have money to buy tires and didn't have anyone to buy them for him.

The other thing that made him particularly good was he had a knack for knowing exactly when to get back on the gas. You hear a lot of talk about a driver going so deep down into a corner you thought he was going to the moon. What you don't hear much about is a driver getting back on the gas after getting off the throttle. Except for Daytona and Talladega, at every track you have to get off the throttle. And knowing precisely when to get back on it is a huge, huge part of winning. It's like someone who plays a very complicated song on a guitar where you have lots of chord changes. Bobby knew when to make those changes, and it was almost musical watching him go through a corner.

And another thing: He didn't roughhouse a car. He was smooth. He was almost Tim Flock smooth. He reminded me of Jeff Gordon or Jimmie Johnson today, like they have the Tim Flock–Bobby Allison gene. Bobby drove so smoothly, particularly toward the end of the race when the adrenalin got going, when guys had to keep from having to pressure the car, which pressured the tires. Because everything you do in a car—getting on and off the throttle, how you exit a corner—affects the tires. And that's what made Bobby extraordinary, plus the fact he could switch into combat mode in a second. He didn't mind mixing it up at all. Had he been a combat pilot, he would not have snuck up from behind. He would have just plowed into the whole squadron. But at the same time he only did it when he had to. His great battles with David Pearson, Richard Petty, and Darrell Waltrip, and to a certain extent Cale Yarborough, came at the precise moment when he needed to wage them.

Sometimes this came at the 200-mile mark, when he did it to show the other driver he was there, and he was going to be there to the end, so don't forget it. And this can be a very important moment, because you can so discourage another driver that mentally he just says to himself, "I can't handle that guy today." No one will admit this, but I know it's true from talking to guys.

So Bobby knew when and how. He knew how to push the buttons. And that's what made him the adversary he was. Guys could get damn mad at him. Other drivers never got mad at Harry Gant, and yet Harry won his share of races. They sure got mad at Bobby. It was his nature. And yet his brother, Donnie, was much more of a fighter than Bobby ever was. Donnie was very combative. But like I said, Bobby knew when to turn it on and off. Donnie didn't have the ability to switch the off button as much as he should have. It's one reason Donnie won ten races and Bobby won eighty-five.

When you look back at it, Bobby raced against the finest talent we ever had, plus he was driving a 4,000-pound race car with huge horsepower, narrow tires, and, for most of the time, no power steering.

AND YET HIS MOST FAMOUS RACE is one he didn't win, the 1979 Daytona 500. At the end of the race, Cale Yarborough and Donnie Allison were fighting for the same space coming down the backstretch. Both of them were total combat pilots who weren't going to give in. When you think about it, it was a race in which whoever was running third—in this case Richard Petty—was going to win the race because of the nature of Cale and Donnie. I wonder if either asked themselves, "I wonder what would have happened if I hadn't been so bull-headed?" Because they were both trying to get to the same spot at the same time in cars that handled pretty well sideways. When they tangled coming off of two, they were sitting so far out on the edge that when the rear end broke loose, there was about a ninety-percent chance they were going to wreck.

Which is precisely what Cale and Donnie did. And then it became a question of two guys with a grudge walking home from school, and they get in a fight, and the big brother is a little distance behind them, and he sees his little brother in a fight. If he has any fighter in him, there's no question what's going to happen. He's going to jump into the fray, and that's exactly what Bobby did.

The Allisons being the clan they are and as tight as they were, there wasn't any question about what Bobby was going to do when he saw Donnie and Cale going at it. He stopped his car, and jumped out into the fight. What made the fight the memorable event it became was that was the day CBS had chosen to televise its very first stock car race live. And there was something else—a snowstorm in the Northeast kept millions of people home, and a lot of them were tuning into the race, and they saw the fight. Up to that point, races were only live if you went to a theater with pay-per-view to see them. Same with the Ali fights. No one got rich off of it, but it was part of the promotion of the race—the live gate as well as seeing it in downtown Cleveland in a theater.

So the race was televised live. I don't know what was on TV that day, but it couldn't have been much, because millions of people who had never watched a race before saw it. In those days, most Americans looked upon racers as less than athletic. They didn't equate them to Mickey Mantle or Johnny Unitas who they saw as real athletes. They said the same thing about golfers because golfers didn't have to run. And the other thing about race car drivers, you can't see them because they're encased in that steel body. This was back before David Hill introduced "facemanship" into sports broadcasts. David is president of Fox Sports, the guy who introduced the electric puck in hockey and started the trend of having close-ups of faces in sports. The quarterback behind the center, or an NFL lineman. All the networks do it today. David Hill started it.

And so after the scalding wreck on the backstretch at Daytona, the three drivers—Cale Yarborough, Donnie Allison, and Bobby Allison—jumped out of their cars and started pummeling each other, and there's nothing Americans like more than to watch a good fight. Had the fight not happened, the race would have caused something of a stir, but nothing like it did. The fight is what made it memorable, not the wreck. It gave the drivers a face, made them seem human, and it showed they were athletes—that they weren't automatons or robots, but people who mashed the gas and turned the wheel. And the fact Bobby and Donnie were brothers gave it even that much more drama. Because people can always identify with their brother getting in a fight and going in to help him out.

You also have to give a lot of credit to Ken Squier, the color announcer on the broadcast. He's never quite been given the credit he deserves. He came along when we needed an anchor in the sport who understood the drama and the color behind it. As soon as it happened, he grasped what was happening and why. He knew the racing people so well. Had it been your ordinary anchor, your ex-NFL lineman, or Howard Cosell, I don't think he would have grasped the entirety of the drama that was unfolding.

By the way, who won the race that day? Once the fight got underway, no one really cared, except the Pettys. America got a taste of what we all thought was rather extraordinary, just as those of us did who had seen Bobby Allison drive backwards and hit Curtis Turner in the grille, or those who had watched one driver go after another driver with a Stilson wrench.

The wreck and fight that day really brought home the drama of stock car racing, and showed everybody there was another kind of racing besides Indy racing, which America had been infatuated with up to that point. Americans all over the country were able to look at the stock cars running around the Daytona track and say, "Hey, I got one of those parked in my driveway. And it looks like Bobby Allison's car." And don't forget, most Americans drive. They can't throw a football, but they can get behind the wheel of a car and mash the gas. So there was a lot of transference. It was a milestone for NASCAR and for America.

CHAPTER 12

Junior Johnson

JUNIOR JOHNSON, ONE OF THE MOST important figures in the history of NASCAR, was a great oak of a man who was always on a diet. He stood an average 5 feet 10 inches, and his weight ranged from 195 to 240 pounds, depending on which diet he was on. He had a Jack Dempsey chin and a lower lip that added to his wonderful mountain drawl, which has been toned down as he's gotten older and more cosmopolitan. He once told Bobby Isaac, who was driving for him, "Boy, you'uns keep runnin' thet car lak thet and ye'll blow a tar." He said of another less-talented driver, "Hit don't matter whut he duz, he ain't never gonna be no driver 'cause he's just skeert."

As the late Dodge public relations expert Frank Wylie once opined when told that Junior's accent was bad for racing's image, "He is probably speaking English the way everybody did in the 1700s."

Junior won 50 races as a driver and more than a 150 more as a car owner. Equally important, there were a couple of times when Junior almost single-handedly saved the racing game. The first time was back in the 1960s when Ford pulled out of NASCAR the year after Chrysler did. Without the car companies, NASCAR was in trouble.

Richard Howard, the track operator at Charlotte and a superb promoter, was trying to get Ford back in, as was Junior because that was the car he ran. Meanwhile, the Atlanta Motor Speedway, which was run by a crony of Bill France by the name of Joe Littlejohn, needed something to attract fans, because Atlanta always had a tough time. Junior convinced Bill France that he could solve the Ford problem by bringing his own Ford to Atlanta for the race. Junior was acting as though the Ford Motor Company had nothing to do with this, but that really wasn't the fact. Ford was in on it, though the car Junior brought looked as much like a Ford as it did a car on the Union Pacific railroad. It was shaped like a banana and painted yellow, and because it was the only Ford in the race, there were no templates for it, and NASCAR let him run it. They could have brought a new Ford into the garage so the inspectors could compare them, but no one dared. They just let Junior run it, and the "yellow banana" helped bring Ford back into the game. A few years later Junior ran a Chevy when Chevy was out of racing, and he literally got Chevy back into it.

The biggest thing that Junior did was help bring R. J. Reynolds into NASCAR as a sponsor. This coincided with the government banning cigarette ads on TV. RJR had a lot of money, and they needed another way to advertise their product.

Junior was a close friend of RJR exec Ralph Seagraves, who also was from Wilkes County. Ralph had been in RJR's Washington, D.C., office for twenty years, putting cigarettes on John Kennedy's and Lyndon Johnson's planes and in the Oval office.

I knew Junior and Richard Howard had been working on getting R. J. Reynolds to sponsor a car, because Richard told me Junior was going up to Winston-Salem to make them a proposal. As a result I painted three cars—a Winston car, a Camel car, and a Salem car—so RJR could see what the cars would look like. RJR liked the idea of racing, but wisely they decided rather than sponsor one car, they would sponsor the entire sport. After they talked to Bill France about it, they spent millions in prize money to be given to those drivers competing for the racing championship. As part of the deal made in 1970, France changed the name of the circuit from Grand National to the Winston Cup, and for many years Winston was NASCAR's primary sponsor. The deal also prompted other companies to begin sponsoring individual race cars. Then, in 1972, Winston pushed Bill France to do away with the hundred mile races. It was the start of a heady new era of NASCAR, and Junior had as much to do with this as anyone.

I first got to know Junior when I was a college student working at Darlington and he was just out of prison. I later got to know him really well when I was working for Firestone. He was still driving, doing some tire testing for us, and he was becoming quite a businessman. This was 1964, and I could tell he wanted to get out of the driver role and become a car owner. I just had a feeling. Not that he wasn't still driving the wheels off the car.

Fireball Robert's wreck at Charlotte in May 1964 had a tremendous impact on everybody in the sport, but in particular on Junior, Fred Lorenzen, and Ned Jarrett, because they all retired not long afterwards. Those three had been close to Fireball and had come up with him. And it wasn't just Fireball's death. Jimmy Pardue and Billy Wade had died in crashes, and then there were the Indy debacles. It wasn't a real happy time.

The transition was very difficult for Junior. He and Banjo Matthews were always close. They were cut out of the same cloth, mechanically and physically. They both had come up through the Modified division. And Banjo had retired and was running his own car.

I remember Junior was driving at the Asheville-Weaverville Speedway, which could get extremely hot even though it was up in the mountains. It was a half-mile track right at the top of a mountain, and very hard to drive. Junior had gained a little weight, and for thirty-five laps he drove the wheels off the car, but you could tell the heat was getting to him. He started slowing down, and finally he pulled in and managed to get out of the car through the side window, which he was outgrowing. Curtis Turner had to take over. I could tell then that Junior was near the end as a driver. His problem was that he didn't know exactly when to quit. The great fear of race drivers is: What am I going to do with the rest of my life? With Junior you knew. He was going to stay in racing.

Junior finally retired in 1966. I thought to myself, *My God, who is crazy enough to be his race driver? Nobody deserves that.* Because I knew Junior would be very hard on him.

That first year Junior put a bunch of different drivers in the car: Gordon Johncock, Fred Lorenzen, Darel Dieringer, Curtis Turner, Bobby Isaac, and A. J. Foyt.

The first driver Junior declared would be driving for him was Bobby Isaac. I thought to myself, *Bobby is going to be toast because nothing will please Junior. How do you follow yourself in the race car?* Junior was very demanding, and Bobby drove but eight races for him. He had a second and a third but I could tell their partnership was going nowhere. I also could tell that Junior would eventually get his act together as far being a car owner and a crew chief. But it wasn't easy.

§

I was at Bristol for the August race in 1966. It was gosh-awful hot, not a breath of air blowing in that bowl. Junior was the crew chief and also the jack man. He was a superb jack man.

As the crew chief, he was supposed to be out on pit road. Instead he sat in his car with the front hood open about three inches so air would get in there because he had the air conditioning running in the car. I sat with him, and we sat in comfort while the cars went around and around the racetrack.

In those days Bristol was a survival race. There weren't a lot of caution flags. All of a sudden, Herb Nab came banging on the window, telling Junior to get out of the car, that it was time for a pit stop. Junior jumped out, grabbed his jack, changed tires in no time flat, and got back into his air-conditioned car. That went on all afternoon. That was his answer to the heat problem up in Bristol.

Junior always wore a white T-shirt, white pants, a black belt, white socks, and black shoes. He had no other uniform. No "Junior Johnson" or "Holly Farms" or anything else on him. His favorite pose was his foot up on the wall, knee bent, elbow on the knee, and his head in his hand. I always thought, *All we need of Junior is his brain. We could put it in a jar, and if it could talk, we'd have all the strategy we needed for a race.* Because even though he was a master strategist, if you sat down with him and said, "Junior, let's talk racing strategy," it would be like talking to Ralph Earnhardt. You might get three sentences, or three words. Nothing more would come out of his mouth, but he just had the knack of being able to figure out when to pit, when to make the right move, and when to stay out. He did it in a way that seemed as though he wasn't thinking about anything. His brain was that good.

The funny thing about Junior, though, was that if he got on the telephone, he could outtalk anybody. If he was trying to make a point, you didn't get a whole lot of words in edgewise. He was constantly politicking Bill France for something. It was incessant.

The other thing that made him so good, like the Pettys and the Wood brothers, was that he and his team worked in a cloistered environment. He always said he was from Ronda, North Carolina, but I never did figure out where Ronda was. Ronda's just a community, but there is no Main Street. Or if there is, it's in a diabolical place, because I've never been able to find it, and I've been there a thousand times. There's a country store down the road. Junior's shop is behind his house, so after a breakfast of huge biscuits and country ham and eggs, he'd wander down the hill to the shop and start working.

His team was interesting because for all his winning I doubt if he ever employed more than eleven or twelve people.

In the middle of the garage was a little room that was strictly off-limits to anybody but Junior. A big night for Junior in those days was for him to spend three or four hours alone in there tinkering with a Holly carburetor. He, like Smokey Yunick, was genetically attuned to carburetors. They both loved carbs. Jack Roush is the same way today. Jack Roush has been known to take a carburetor back to the Holiday Inn and spend an entire evening working on it. Carburetors disappeared from road-going cars in the 1980s. Today, most certified mechanics at a car dealership don't even know what a carburetor is.

Junior loved that whole inner world of the carburetor. Junior was a master of the butterfly, the choke, and jets. After working on one for hours, he would then walk up to his house and eat some more of his wife Flossie's biscuits.

So there was Junior. The second big character on Junior's race team was Herb Nab. You always knew where Herb was by the sound of the five-pound hammer he carried with him. Herb thought you could fix anything with that hammer. He was as good with chassis as Junior was, and the two of them made a pretty formidable combination.

Junior and Herb were a little bit Holman-and-Moodyish due to the fact that I don't know if they ever got along. Tolerated each other would be more like it. I know they respected each other.

Herb looked like a Roman gladiator who had been beaten up a lot. He was a character of characters. He had worked for John Holman for a long time, and then he went to work for Junior. Junior was about the only person who could control Herb.

PROBABLY THE WORST THING that happened to a race driver working for Junior was the two-way radio, because Junior then could actually talk to him during the race. Junior didn't talk much, but when he did, he could put the fear of God into a driver. For long stretches there would be silence, and then came this voice in his slow drawl that said, "They started the race 200 laps ago." Or something like, "That boy in front of you is going about a 150 feet down into that corner farther than you." That's all he'd say, which was like rattling the driver's cage. Junior knew how to do that impeccably and at the right moment.

I don't think Junior ever called his driver by his name. He called his drivers, "Boy," as in, "Boy, you better get going," and the driver had to get used to it. The guys who drove well for Junior could do that and suffer through it because they knew he was putting a great car underneath them that could get the job done. He could make a car handle. And the other thing he obviously could do was fudge the rules.

I never ever could get Junior to tell me how many grades he completed in school, but I always said if he had gone to Duke, he'd have ended up running Chase Manhattan. Thank goodness he didn't. Junior, who was like Smokey Yunick, always kept up with the latest technology.

I can remember when Junior discovered carbon fiber and introduced it to NASCAR. Carbon fiber is a composite material used in Indy racing and Formula 1. It is extremely lightweight. It weighs less than aluminum by about sixty percent and steel by a hundred percent. It was totally, completely illegal in NASCAR. Junior actually had a guy go to North Carolina State, find out about it, and report back to him. He got somebody (he never would tell me who) to make him a set of carbon fiber brakes. Carbon fiber is pretty easy to police because metal magnetizes and carbon fiber doesn't, so it's easy to pick up if you know what you're looking for even though it can be painted to look like metal.

I have to think someone ratted him out. I don't know how else NASCAR could have found it. How long he ran them I don't know, but he ran them for some time before NASCAR finally caught him. If NASCAR hadn't come out with its edict prohibiting carbon fiber in any shape or form, if I know Junior, he would have had his entire car made of carbon fiber.

Junior also had a superb ability to pick talent. I don't think he ever made a mistake with a driver. You can't say he made a mistake with Bobby Isaac, who went on to win thirty-seven Cup races and had a very successful career.

In 1967 Junior hired driver Darel Dieringer, who won one race that year. Darel was an interesting character. He was a midwesterner from Indianapolis. He had driven USAC races, and he had come to Charlotte to work as a tire changer for Goodyear. After a while he decided to drive again. He knew Junior, and Junior put him in the car because he felt he could do the job. I don't think Junior thought he'd be a Cale Yarborough or a Bill Elliott, but it was someone to drive for him, and Darel ended up winning a few races in his career.

Over the next thirty years Junior Johnson had spectacular success with Lee Roy Yarbrough, Cale Yarborough, Darrell Waltrip, Neil Bonnett, Terry Labonte, and Bill Elliott. He walked away from the sport after the 1995 season.

WHY DID JUNIOR GET OUT? He got to the point where he saw the handwriting on the wall. Car owners like Rick Hendrick and Jack Roush began spending massive amounts of money on machines to make their cars run faster. Hendrick bought one cam-grinding machine that cost three-quarters of a million dollars. This offended some of the old guys like Junior, the Wood brothers, Bud Moore, and the Pettys, who had come up through an age where they really didn't have any money to work with. It was ingenuity and hard work, and you did it with few people, and you really had to pick the right driver.

The influx of money changed all that. The new owners began paying their drivers millions of dollars, and they would hire fifty-man crews. The old guys never accepted doing that. They had come up through the Depression, and it was just very, very difficult to turn away from a lifetime of frugality. Not that they were frugal compared to a lot of people, but as we say in the South they were used to "making do." So rather than compete, the old guys, including Junior, closed up shop.

Junior had money, and there were other things he could do. He loved to tinker with food. He raised chickens. You can buy Junior Johnson's ham and Junior Johnson's biscuits.

He and Flossie divorced, and late in life Junior remarried and had kids, which he never had with Flossie. Those who knew Flossie and Junior well were very depressed over their breakup because Flossie is a dear woman. But Junior had his reasons, and you can't trespass on that.

When Junior got out of racing, he really got out. It was hard to get him to come to a race. I used to phone him: "Junior, come on to Charlotte."

He'd come down and stay for fifteen minutes, and he was ready to go back home. He actually comes around more now because his son is beginning to race. But Junior is an extraordinary human being. When I think of that cover story in *Esquire* where Tom Wolfe called him "the last American hero," to a certain extent he is that. Junior is the last remnant of the bootleg days, the last link stock car racing has to its storied past.

§

ONE OF THE STRANGEST DAYS I ever experienced came on the day the state of North Carolina was going to name a highway for Junior. He had been pardoned by Ronald Reagan, thanks in great part to his old friend Ralph Seagraves, who still was well-connected to Washington. Not too many years after he got his pardon, he was invited by the governor of North Carolina to come to a ceremony during which the state was going to rename Highway 421 the Junior Johnson Highway. It was a new stretch of highway of almost interstate standards between North Wilkesboro and Yadkinville.

I was invited to make a few remarks. I arrived at the site on a beautiful day in May. The highway is right in front of Junior's house up on the hill. I drove in there, and when I saw the cars lined up, I thought to myself, *The Apocalypse is upon me.*

On my left were dozens of Highway Patrol cars, plus the governor's limousine, and expensive cars of other elected officials. On my right were '39 Fords and other cars owned by the old bootleggers, friends of Junior who had come out in droves to see his new highway. I thought, *This could only happen in the old South.* It was funny to me, and I mentioned it in my remarks. I said, "This is the strangest assortment of vehicles I have ever seen outside of a racetrack." It got a good laugh.

As I stood at the dais, I looked over at the old Highway 421 (an old two-lane curvy road) that was slumbering off South of the new highway, and I thought, *How many times did Junior go down that highway hauling moonshine to Charlotte, Kannapolis, Gastonia, and other points, as well as his friends here?* I thought, *This is surreal.* And down the road not too far and perched in the valley you could see the old North Wilkesboro Speedway sitting there decaying, returning to the earth.

It was quite a day.

CHAPTER 13

Driving for Junior

JUNIOR JOHNSON DIDN'T HAVE real success as a car owner until 1969 when he teamed up with Lee Roy Yarbrough. I knew Lee Roy as well as I did any driver of that era, because he was one of Firestone's test drivers. He was also an Indy driver.

Lee Roy came from a very rough background in Jacksonville, but he was very intelligent. People don't realize that about him. On many occasions he and I would go fishing, and he just had a knack for figuring out where the fish were and how they were biting. He was a terrific driver on dirt who raced against very formidable competition. He really reached his peak driving for Junior.

The great mystery of Lee Roy Yarbrough is what happened to him. He died an alcoholic after spending time in an insane asylum, but that doesn't explain Lee Roy in that all the years I knew him he didn't take a drink. He didn't take drugs. He was sober and serious.

He was sent to a mental institution after he tried to kill his mother, but I believe there were circumstances that must have led to that. In 1972 he had three really bad accidents that occurred very close to one another. During a race in Atlanta, he had very, very bad carbon monoxide poisoning. Then in practice at Charlotte four cars were coming off the second turn, and he slammed into the inside wall so hard it cut his car in half. From the firewall back was all that was left of his car. The motor and front end were completely knocked off. He was sitting there exposed, but he was luckier than Don MacTavish. No one piled into him. I wasn't there, but not too long afterwards at Indianapolis in an IndyCar, he had the worst wreck anyone had ever seen where no one was killed.

After that things started going downhill for him. I heard that he had contracted Rocky Mountain Spotted Fever, a very debilitating virus that affects you like Lyme disease. And then this strong, powerful guy deteriorated very fast over a very short period of time. There were rumors of fights, drugs, and alcohol use. And that he was suffering from mental illness.

After he tried to kill his mother with a knife, which occurred during the running of the Daytona 500, I got a call from Junior who said he was going to go to Florida to try to get Lee Roy out of prison. He wanted me to go with him, but I couldn't, so he went by himself and got him out. It was so tragically sad. Lee Roy died in 1984. The only thing more tragic is what happened to another equally talented driver, Tim Richmond.

LEE ROY YARBROUGH left Junior after the 1971 season, and he was replaced by Cale Yarborough (last name spelled differently). Cale has an extra *o* in his name. Cale came from the flat tobacco lands and cotton fields of the hottest part of the South near Florence, South Carolina. His family—solidly middle class—lived out in the country. His father did a number of things, including crop dusting. His mother is still one of the most fabulous people I've ever known. Always smiling, she's as smart as a whip with a tremendous personality. She had a tremendous influence over him.

Cale relished danger. He liked to skydive, box, play football, and, more than anything else, race. He was short, muscular, and stocky—a big-necked kid who was just one of the toughest guys in a race car I have ever known as far as being able to keep going. His stamina was amazing.

In the early days, Cale was not particularly good on the short tracks. I often wondered whether he was going to make it. Where was the talent? But he was determined to drive in NASCAR, so he kept pushing and shoving until John Holman gave him a job sweeping floors at Holman and Moody. He moved his family to Charlotte, and before you knew it, Holman had hooked him up with a car owner by the name of Herman Beam. Herman came from Tennessee and was known as the Turtle because he was one of those guys who made a living at driving by never having to spend money on fixing his car. I never saw Herman crash or even spin out. I don't think he ever ran fast enough to do either one. Herman was an engineer, one of the early ones who raced. He wore wire-rimmed glasses and looked like an engineer.

Cale drove a Ford for him, and the car would only go so fast. Cale then went to drive for Banjo Matthews, and he couldn't have been running for a better coach. Banjo minced no words with anyone about anything. He was on Cale's back all the time.

I remember one day Cale was running at Darlington, his home track, and he was running harder than he should have. He went into the first turn, when he suddenly left the racetrack. He hit the guardrail in the first turn and started flipping. His car landed outside the track. It was one of the greatest highlight photos for about a decade—his car going out into the parking lot.

But Banjo had patience and he toned Cale down, and Cale started doing better and better. Four times he finished second. Then in 1970 Cale was determined to run in the Indy 500, and that's when we had our biggest fight. He was driving for Bruce McLaren, and he was under contract with me to run Firestones. He and McLaren, however, decided to run Goodyears, which made me furious. I wanted to go to war with him, and I told my wife, Pat, a very low-key southern gentlewoman if there ever was one. She got so mad she went right up to his room and gave him the what for. She knocked on his door, and he came out of the shower with a towel around him, and she just ripped him apart. Cale didn't know what to say.

The next day I was standing in the pits with Murray Olderman, the journalist from Los Angeles. The flag dropped, and almost immediately there was a huge crash right in front of us involving twelve or fourteen cars. A. J. Foyt was in it. I remember his car slamming the wall. And Cale made it about 300 feet. I said to Murray, "He didn't even make the length of a football field." That's the story he wrote. Lot of good those Goodyears did for Cale. Thank goodness Cale got out of those cars and came back to NASCAR.

Cale settled down and greatly improved, and in 1974 he joined up with Junior, who really settled him down. Understand that Junior's version of settling down a driver is getting him to throttle to the maximum without wrecking the car.

Junior always put a lot of pressure on his driver, and the driver either made it or he didn't. Curtis Turner had driven three races for Junior. Bobby Isaac, Donnie Allison, and Fred Lorenzen had a ride or two, but Junior's success as a car owner really didn't begin until Cale got behind the wheel and magic struck. They had some absolutely terrific wins.

Junior was always so good with engines, way ahead of everyone else except Smokey Yunick, so Cale had horsepower to work with, and his car handled well. More than anything else Cale was able to handle the pressure coming from the Ford Motor Company, Junior, and Herb Nab's five-pound hammer. That was where his mother's genes came in. She was a master of getting along with people and getting people to do things under pressure and tension. She had to contend with losing her husband in the prime of life, and she got through it with grit and determination and with a wonderful attitude. Cale also was tremendously determined. Cale might have been the most tenacious driver we ever had. For ten years he drove Darlington without power steering, and he was able to drive the entire 500 laps without relief.

Cale was the first driver to win three consecutive championships, which Jimmie Johnson just duplicated in 2008. The highlight of the banquet in New York this year was Cale's surprise appearance to congratulate Jimmie. The people just went crazy when Cale came on stage.

THE DRIVER JUNIOR HIRED to replace Cale was somebody we had never seen before. He came from Tennessee, wore his hair in a ducktail, and if they had given him a guitar and a skinny white suit, you might have thought Elvis had rolled in. And as good-looking as he was, he could drive the wheels off a race car, and he could talk. He had a glibness about him that defied southernness. Southern boys were supposed to be respectful and quiet, but Darrell Waltrip wasn't. He was supposed to respect his peers and other drivers, but Darrell Waltrip didn't.

In 1972 when Darrell came on the scene, a young driver would always compliment Richard Petty for how he drove. He'd say, "I have gained a great deal of experience today in practice riding around on Richard's bumper." Or Cale's bumper or David Pearson's bumper. A young driver would say, "I grew up watching Richard Petty race."

Darrell never acknowledged anyone else—ever. He didn't care about them. He was full of himself and very cocky, lacking humility, and that set him apart.

Some fans loved him. A lot of older fans didn't. I can remember one time when he was driving the Mountain Dew car, he walked off the stage to the accompaniment of boos. When he was asked about it, he said, "They are not saying boo. They are saying dew." Darrell with his mouth could turn the worst negative into a positive.

When Darrell came along, there were some very formidable racers to contend with as well as a group of young drivers, including Dale Earnhardt and Tim Richmond. Among the old guard were Petty, Pearson, Buddy Baker, the Allisons, and Cale Yarborough. Stock car racing was really beginning to pick up steam. The sport needed a fresh new approach from a personality, and Darrell Waltrip sure was it. He provided a significant amount of color that was most welcome.

I can remember when Darrell and Cale got into it. This was right after the movie *Jaws* came out, and after a confrontation in a race, Cale referred to Darrell as Jaws. Cale was sponsored by Holly Farms, the large chicken supplier, and driving for Junior. The hullabaloo generated a huge amount of publicity.

The race at the Charlotte Motor Speedway was coming up, and one night I had an inspiration. I pondered whether to do it because I knew it would tick both of them off. I decided to do it anyway.

I called a guy down in South Carolina named Poo McLaughlin who specialized in shark fishing. I said, "Poo, I need you to go and hook the biggest shark you can catch tomorrow and stick it in the back of a truck and ice it down and bring it to the speedway. I gotta have it up here for Wednesday pole day."

Here he came with a 300-pound shark on the back of a long-bed pickup, covered with ice and a canvas. When he called to say he was on his way, I told him to leave the shark in the infield. I had a wrecker that would come get it.

The wrecker hooked the shark's mouth, a beautiful mouth with white teeth. I brought with me a great, big hen, and I stuck it in the shark's mouth with the feathers filtering down.

I told the wrecker driver, "Don't stop for anybody. I want you to park the wrecker in the middle of the pits in front of the scoreboard where they put the qualifying times. Lock it up and bring the keys to my office."

He did as I asked, and the presence of the big shark with the chicken in its mouth created a firestorm. First of all, everyone wanted to see the shark. And second, it took everyone a nanosecond to figure out what that was all about.

The first phone call was from Cale. He started yelling.

"I was just having a little fun," I said.

"You take that thing down . . . ."

"I'll get it after a while."

About fifteen minutes later Darrell called, and he was raising even more cane. He was really livid. I said, "Darrell, I'll take it down after a while. I'm just having a little fun."

"At my expense."

Nobody from NASCAR ever said a word. They wouldn't. They knew it was hijinks time. A photo of the shark and the chicken made the AP national A wire.

Over the years Darrell and I have had conversations about a lot of things. If I was getting ready to pave the track or part of the track and I wanted an expert opinion, Darrell was always very helpful. You could talk to him about anything.

Darrell came from Nashville, and he really cemented the gap between country music and NASCAR. Everybody in Nashville knew Darrell. He was actually from Owensboro, Kentucky, and he lived in Franklin, but he was in Nashville all the time, so all the country music people knew him. As he got more popular, he ended up on their shows because the Nashville Network was there, and he helped attract the Gatlin Brothers, Alabama, Loretta Lynn, Conway Twitty, and a lot of other country acts to NASCAR. He is still very popular in Nashville.

Early in his career I decided to run a Modified race at Charlotte. Bill France had been running Modified cars at Daytona on the road course, and they had fenders and looked real exotic. I decided to run a 300-lap Modified race on the Saturday before the 600. There was going to be a Modified race that same night at Islip, Long Island. I called the promoter, Larry Mendelsohn, and I asked him if I could use some of his top drivers in my race. I promised to fly them down and fly them back in time for his race. He agreed.

Dick Trickle came from the Midwest to drive his Ford Grenada, and Darrell entered in a Robert Gee Camaro.

The race started at one o'clock with a tornado watch in effect. There were no fans in the grandstands to speak of. I was praying for rain so I wouldn't have to run the race. I had advertised it, so I had to do it, and I'm thinking, *Poor Larry Mendelsohn.*

I had to get 150 miles in to make the race official. After fifty miles, it rained. We dried off the track. It rained again.

To get Mendelsohn's drivers back to Long Island, they had to be on the plane by six o'clock. Here it was six, and we still had another fifty laps to go. Poor Larry. I had all his stars, and he was beside himself. Bill France Jr. and

I were up in the control tower trying to figure out a way to get the race in, because not only was it stormy, but it was dark.

At eight o'clock there were three laps to go, and darkness was falling. Darrell was in the lead. It had rained, and we had to dry off the track to resume. I needed to get in the three laps, otherwise I'd have had to finish it on Monday, and no one was going to come back for it. I said to Darrell, "Would you go out and be a rabbit and see if the track is dry enough to get in three laps? And please don't tell us it isn't."

He went out, ran two laps, and he came back in.

"Is it dry?"

"I don't know," he said. "I can't see the racetrack."

I thought, *Good Lord*. Then I decided to run it anyway. And we did.

At the end Dick Trickle started passing cars, not paying attention to anyone, and when we finished the race it was wet and dark. And Tom Higgins with the *Charlotte Observer* blasted Bill Jr. and me for doing that. I swallowed hard and went on.

"Tom," I said, "did you want to come back on Monday and cover this thing?"

He didn't say anything.

There were a number of tracks, including Bristol, where Darrell was almost invincible. In addition to the brashness and the boldness and the quick wit, he was as smart as a whip. He had a little bit of David Pearson in him in that he figured out early not to win the race right away. He played it cool and calm. With a hundred miles to go, it was, "Where is Darrell?" But with fifty left, he was fifth, and then at the end suddenly he was slipping into first place.

Darrell started out driving a race car "owned" by his wife, Stevie. He then joined Bill Gardner's DiGard race team. He was their driver from 1976 through 1980. In his last four years Darrell won six, six, seven, and five races.

One of the best races I can remember came at the Charlotte Motor Speedway in the Coca-Cola 600 in 1980. It was a day when we had two thunderstorms come through, and both times we had to stop the race. Instead of a 600-mile race, we had three 200-mile races. And with each rainstorm, the rubber was cleaned off the track.

The race came down to a duel between cagey veteran Benny Parsons and Darrell. Benny had never won at Charlotte before. You could tell this was going to be a classic, because they swapped the lead back and forth, and with three laps to go Darrell was in the lead with Benny second. Benny was a very clean driver, and coming off two, nobody thought Benny could get around Darrell, who could make his car seem very wide when he wanted to at the end of a race. Darrell did cut Benny some slack by not forcing him to go someplace he didn't want to go, and then Benny reached down deep and made an un-Benny-like daring pass. Benny ended up winning the race, and it brought down the house.

Darrell's tactic of waiting back in the pack ended to a certain extent when in 1981 he began driving for Junior, who was an out-front kind of guy. Junior wasn't interested in his driver sitting back in the pack and waiting for the end. He wanted to be up front all the time, and one of the reasons he did was that he recognized early on that sponsors were really beginning to pay attention to TV. They were looking to see their car, and if you hung back and waited until the end to come to the front, there was no guarantee you'd be around at the end. But if you led the race for 300 miles, your sponsor got a tremendous amount of TV time, probably more than the winner did. Besides, it was also Junior's personality.

Junior had to push Darrell quite a bit. The first Winston All Star race in 1984 was a great example of Darrell Waltrip and Junior at their beginnings. It was 160 miles. Harry Gant was in the Skoal Bandit car, and he was fast that day. Harry told me he thought he had the race won until with thirty laps to go Harry said, "I went into the third corner, and all of a sudden that 17 car came under me, and I felt like I had put my car in park. And I was running as hard as I could."

Harry, knowing Junior, knew it was all over. Darrell took off and had a significant lead, and I was about to fall asleep from boredom when at the start/finish line, as the checkered flag flew, Darrell's engine blew up into a million pieces. Harry Gant knew what kind of horsepower he had confronted, but now there was no way to check the motor. Everyone accused Darrell of clutching the engine when he hit the start/finish line. Junior and Darrell never talked about it, and if they were asked, they denied it. That engine is actually sitting in a museum in Mooresville. It's just the block. You don't get to see the rest of it.

One of the great rivalries was between Darrell Waltrip and Bobby Allison. If you look at the great rivalries, it was strictly a matter of both drivers being in the same place most of the time. Both Darrell and Bobby had the ability to drive certain speedways—mostly the intermediate tracks between one and two miles long as well as the short tracks. I can't say either was super on the high-speed tracks like Daytona and Talladega, but they were magnificent on the shorter racetracks. They both had great equipment, and they both went hard for the wins. Darrell and Bobby each finished their careers with 84 Winston Cup wins, though Bobby really had one more, which he won in a Modified car. Bill France allowed the car to be entered but he only allowed Cup cars to get credit for wins.

Darrell's racing career pretty much ended at Daytona. It was the Friday before the Firecracker race in 1990. Darrell lost it coming off turn four and crashed, and the car ended up perpendicular to the wall. Then Dave Marcis came by and hit him on the passenger door about as hard as I've ever seen a car get hit. If it had been the driver's side, Darrel would have been a dead man. It was so bad the right side of the car was pushed up to the driver's seat.

The car spun several times after Marcis hit him. They had to cut Darrell out of the car, and that's always a bad sign. They took him to Halifax Hospital. I met him there. He was in terrible pain. He suffered a broken femur, the worst injury a driver could suffer. It's the biggest bone in your body, and it takes a long time to heal, and it's agonizing. Bill Elliott broke his in Talladega. Neil Bonnett broke his at Charlotte. Kyle Petty broke his. When they break, it's devastating. I've never seen a driver do really well again after a broken femur. It takes so long to heal, and as A. J. Foyt says, "There's too much sheet time." That effectively ended Darrell's career. He raced until the year 2000, but he never won another race.

His last couple of years he ran his own operation. He had Western Auto as his sponsor, but he lost money. It wasn't a good end to a career. Most of them don't have good endings. Fortunately he rebounded well, and being the smart guy he is, he's had good investments and done quite well.

In 1984 Junior decided to run a two-car race team. In addition to Darrell, he hired Neil Bonnett (who was part of the Alabama Gang) to drive for him. Junior had signed Bobby Allison for a season, but though Allison won ten races with Junior, the two did not get along. Bobby complained that Junior never would talk to him, said Junior would only talk to Herb Nab, who then talked to Bobby. But you have to remember Junior doesn't talk much, period. And besides, what does Junior have to tell him? Bobby's a fantastic driver. He knows what to do. He knows how to make a car handle. It's not like bringing up a young race driver and having to talk to him a whole lot. He's there, and he's going to get the job done. But Bobby has always been somebody who thrives on communication. He's a person who likes to listen. He seems to thrive when people talk to him, sometimes even when he doesn't agree with them. So, at the end of the season, Bobby left Junior and went back to driving his own car.

Neil Bonnett, unlike Bobby, was perfect for Junior. I first got to know Neil when he called me, said he wanted to come race at Charlotte, and asked if I would pay him deal money. Things were pretty tight, and I turned him down, so he didn't come. What impressed me was he never held it against me. We always got along fine.

I always thought Neil was a real good race driver. He was extremely smooth. Coming up, Neil had some pretty good mentors, including Bobby Allison. The two of them traveled together. He learned a lot from Bobby, and he couldn't have had anyone better around him.

Neil went all out, and he knew when to punch the button and when not to. It would have been interesting to see what would have happened if Neil could have stayed with Junior longer than just three years.

There were a couple reasons why he didn't. One was the coming of Warner Hodgdon, who bought into Junior's race team. That was rare then. Jim Stacy was the first, and then Warner. For a guy to come in and spend millions of dollars on a race team in the early 1980s was unusual. Not long afterward, poor Warner went broke. It was not a happy period. It was a time of unrest for Junior. He had never had a partner before. And Warner was an interesting character, very much a general, and Junior was not used to generals. But with Hodgdon, Junior was able to run two cars, and this was the first time anyone had seriously put together a two-car team.

Running in a two-car team wasn't easy for Neil, who didn't like feeling he was second banana to Darrell. But if you think about it, anybody who drove for Junior while Darrell was there was going to have to play second fiddle. Darrell was the Top Gun, and that's just the way it was. And it wasn't easy for Darrell, who was used to being top dog and didn't like the feeling that much of the effort going toward Neil should have been going toward him. Darrell wanted a hundred percent of Junior's attention. Darrell's feeling was, "Hey, I'm the only guy racing here, and I got to look out for myself, because if I don't, nobody else is."

In those days no driver wanted to share with another driver. He just did not want that to happen.

But Junior had always been a visionary. He could see the future better than most anybody else in the sport. He saw, for example, the benefit of having two cars to test. You can try something with one car and do something else with the other, and see which works better. The other thing Junior saw was that with two cars it was cheaper to run the second car. You could buy in bulk, do a little volume, and you could spread out your work force. With one car there were going to be down times, especially if your driver was like Darrell and didn't wreck cars. There were a lot of benefits no one realized until Junior did it. In the past others had done it, but in a different way. Lee Petty and Richard Petty were father and son. Buck Baker did it with lower-powered cars. And Carl Kiekhaefer had six cars, but it was a different time and a different era. Junior's two-car team heralded the beginning of the two-car era.

In 1989 Neil went to drive for the Wood brothers. He was really flying then. He was not only smooth, but he could really drive deep into the corners. Then he had a terrible, terrible wreck at Charlotte. He hit the wall in the fourth turn just about as hard as you can hit it and still live. The car was crushed in the front, and it slid down the front straightaway in front of the crowd and it stopped in the grass near the start/finish line. I was in the control tower when Dr. Petty reached him. Over the radio, Dr. Petty said that Neil had a broken femur and was in terrible pain. As he talked, I could hear Neil moaning in agony. They had to cut him out of the car.

They took him to the hospital. I figured his career was over, but he was one of the few rare drivers who actually came back from a broken femur. It was a tribute to his tenacity and his desire to race.

Later he had another crash in which he suffered amnesia. He wasn't even able to recognize his wife and kids. That should have ended it for him. After he recovered, my daughter, Patti, who was running the sports TV part of the Nashville Network, said to Neil, "You would be excellent in the broadcast booth." She had done a show on him called "Hidden Heroes," and she was able to see that Neil was more than just a race driver—that he had a great ability to tell a story and talk on TV in a way that appealed to people. So Neil had a place to go after retirement. That helped ease things.

The tragedy of Neil Bonnett was that he chose to return to racing during a period of lethal hits among NASCAR drivers. The sport had made the change to using radial tires and shorter wheel bases, and cars had become more rigid. It was harder to save a car if you found yourself in trouble.

I was in my office when I received a call from Daytona saying that Neil had been killed in a crash during practice.

I couldn't believe it. He was always the one who said, "When you lose it, don't try to save it." But this time he must have tried to save it, because coming off the fourth turn at Daytona his car had gone to the inside, and then it shot right back up the racetrack. He hit the wall with the right front of the car, one of those twenty-five- to thirty-degree hits that killed him, Kenny Irwin, and later Dale Earnhardt. I don't know if anyone has ever measured the distance between where Neil hit and where Dale hit, but they couldn't have been very far apart. It was a terrible ending for a guy who had retired, and who we all thought had gotten it out of his system, though obviously he hadn't.

Both Darrell and Neil left Junior after the 1986 season. Junior's choice of driver in 1987 was Terry Labonte, a Texan who ten years later would win the NASCAR racing championship.

To me, Terry is an enigma. I have always pictured Terry as a Western gunfighter—the Gary Cooper of NASCAR—the quiet man who walks into a bar and orders a drink, and who wouldn't think of stirring anything up, but if you started something, watch his right hand because he'd outdraw you every time.

Terry came from a strange place: Corpus Christi, Texas. Indy drivers A. J. Foyt and Johnny Rutherford came from Texas, but stock car drivers didn't. He was very, very young (21) when he ran his first NASCAR race. He was a nice-looking kid, but he didn't have anything to say.

As a promoter, I was trying to figure out what to do with this kid. I could see he was going to be a good race car driver, but he was all but invisible. I figured he could stand to have a moniker of some kind.

It was a brutally hot July day in Charlotte, about a hundred degrees. Terry was driving for a guy named Skip Manning who had made a deal with a new sponsor called Buck Stoves at a time when wood stoves were the rage. The company was out of Asheville, and it's still making them today.

I was sitting in my office. I had the job of promoting the car being sponsored by Buck Stoves. Terry Labonte, the driver who wouldn't say anything, was in the garage area. What in the world was I going to do?

I brought some people in for a brainstorming session, and all of a sudden the light went on. I thought, *It's hot. We're not going to run fast, because you can't run fast in the heat. The track is too slick. What can I do?* I called the owner of the Concord Ice and Fuel Company, one of the last places where you could buy a 500-pound block of ice. I told him I wanted him to bring it to the Charlotte Motor Speedway and set it down on the start/finish line. Everyone was saying to me, "It's going to tie up the track. How are the cars going to get around it?"

"Don't worry about it," I said.

He rolled in with this huge block of ice on his truck, and he set it on the start/finish line. Everyone in the garage area was wondering what the hell was going on. They knew I was up to something.

When the temperature goes over a hundred degrees, nothing goes on. Everything slows to a crawl. There's no news. All the media wants to talk about is frying eggs on the sidewalk. I alerted the media about this block of ice. Only one media outlet bit, the AP, but one was all I needed.

I went and found Terry, and I told him, "You're a good, young, up-and-coming driver. You need some big publicity. How about coming out and sitting on this block of ice, and let's get a shot of you?"

Terry thought I was crazy, but he agreed to do it. He sat on top of the block of ice, which was maybe 5 feet tall, and made a pose like Rodin's *The Thinker*. The AP photographer took a shot, and we made the A wire and got a lot of good publicity. And this is where Terry Labonte got his nickname, the Iceman. It was a moniker that fit.

Terry and his younger brother, Bobby, are alike in that they are unflappable. If you walked up to any other driver right before a race and slapped him, he would go insane. If you did it to Terry or Bobby, they would say, "When is the race going to start?" They would not let anything emotional get in their way. And that has served them quite well.

Terry was never spectacular like Fireball Roberts or Dale Earnhardt. He wasn't quotable at all. He never said anything. He was just there. He and Bobby were very nice. Terry's appeal to Junior was that he was almost robotic in a race car. He would just clip off lap after lap after lap at the same speed. He could hit his mark and run 31.20, 31.22, 31.33, and 31.25. He was uncanny, and Junior just loved that.

Junior also loved that Terry never complained, and if he did, it was always in the most southern way. His car might be absolutely awful, so loose it looked like it was on ice, and Junior would say, "The car is pretty loose, isn't it?" And Terry would say, "Sorta." That meant it was really loose. Or he'd say,

"You might want to tighten it up a little." Just little, teeny words. No adjectives. They didn't exist. And Junior could translate what Terry was saying better than anyone because, although Terry is from Texas, that's also the way people from Wilkes County talk. And both were Scotch-Irish. Labonte might be a French name, but he certainly didn't act French.

There's an interesting connection: The boys from Wilkes County and from Texas sound the same and understand the same language because after the Civil War, thousands and thousands of soldiers who came back to the Carolinas, Georgia, and East Tennessee and saw the ruins went to Texas to start a new life and to look for adventure. These guys were used to adventure. They didn't want to come back to desolate farms and rundown, burned-out houses and twenty-five years of boredom. Texas was cowboys. It was fighting Indians, and who knew when the Mexicans would come back across the border? So you had this great migration to Texas. That's why you have these similar accents that are so uncanny at times.

During his career, Terry won twenty-one Winston Cup races. He was another racer you had to watch out for because in a 500-mile race, you didn't know where he was for the first 350 miles. It was David Pearson all over again.

THE LAST OF JUNIOR's successful drivers was Bill Elliott, who was one of the most interesting characters of all. If you called Central Casting and said you wanted a veteran stock car driver from the country, he was the guy they'd ship to you. I remember the Elliott brothers—Bill, Ernie, and Dan—showing up at Rockingham when they were first starting out in the late 1970s in their father's Ford that they built themselves back in Dawsonville, Georgia, which no one had ever heard of. You had heard of Dahlonega, but not its next-door neighbor. These were boys from the country if we ever saw them. Bill was always saying "Gawllee." He had good looks, but for a long time he sounded like Gomer Pyle.

In 1982 Bill, who was driving for Harry Melling, was close to breaking through for a victory. Three times he finished second. Before the race at Charlotte, I told him, "We're going to have a press conference, and we're going to talk about finishing second. We're going to try to conduct this about how we can break you from finishing second."

He came to it, and there was talk, and afterward I said to him, "You and I need to sit down and talk about this. Something is wrong here."

We met the next week at Belmont Abbey College, a nice peaceful place. We talked for hours about his finishing second. I said, "Some people finish second on purpose. They are afraid of success." I wanted to rattle his cage. And I did. He was very uncomfortable with that.

I said, "I'm not saying that's what you are doing, but you have to start thinking about it because it's happened over and over. Is there a mental reason for this?"

At least we had it out in the open. It's something that happens in sports many times. I think I reached him, because not too long after that, things started to change for Bill.

He won a race the next year and three races in 1984. The dramatic change came in 1985. Bill was driving a Thunderbird. It was the Thunderbird's first year, and I went down to Daytona, and Bill was flying. Nobody could touch him.

I got a page over the PA system from Darlene Brigance, Buck Brigance's daughter. She was working for me at the time. She took care of the Elliott boys and was friends with them. I said, "Darlene, what's wrong?" She said, "You gotta talk to Bill. He doesn't know what in the world to do. His car is so fast nobody can touch him."

I went over and had a long talk with Bill in his trailer. He said, "This car is flying." He was really trying to figure out how to play the game. All of a sudden he had a car nobody could touch. The Thunderbird was so aerodynamically sound, it was in a class by itself, and there were only a couple other Thunderbirds in the race.

I said, "Bill, you have worked long and hard to get where you are." And I gave him what turned out to be a lousy piece of advice. I said, "Don't back off. If you don't take things as they are, sometimes bad results happen." By not running a hundred percent, he might crash or not be on his game.

Well, Bill ran a hundred percent, and he won the Daytona 500, and he won race after race—eleven in all. That was also the first year of the Winston Million. Any driver who won three of the four top races—Daytona 500, Talladega 500, Charlotte's World 600, and the Southern 500 at Darlington— would win a bonus prize of a million dollars from R. J. Reynolds.

Bill won the Daytona 500 and he won the Talladega 500 in May. At this point the pressure really got to him as the media suddenly descended on this boy from rural Georgia. The press would not let him go. They grabbed his leg, and it became a shackle instead of a caress. It really got to him mentally.

With the World 600 coming up, the Elliotts were so uptight I couldn't even get them to agree to hold a press conference. You just don't come to Charlotte and refuse to have a press conference.

I said, "Bill, this isn't going to work. You've got to have a press conference. It's lunch, and you have to eat anyway. Just come to the media center, we'll have a press conference, and you can leave."

Bill really wasn't happy about it. I thought to myself, *Bill really doesn't understand what's at stake here. He doesn't understand what a million dollars is, and I'm going to show him.*

I called my banker. I said, "I want you to bring a million dollars out to the Speedway." He protested that he couldn't do it.

"Wait a minute, are you guys broke or what?" I asked.

Finally he agreed to do it, and we got Wells Fargo to put the cash in a truck. I didn't tell Bill any of this. When the press conference started, he was staring at the reporters like he didn't want to be there. They started questioning him, when all of a sudden from a back door right behind him, two armed guards walked in carrying a million dollars in hundred dollar bills. They piled the money on the table in front of him. Of course, I had to break a couple of bands to let the money fall out. The Wells Fargo men were going nuts.

Bill took one look at all that money, and I think it blew his mind. The money pile was pretty big, about the size of that 500-pound block of ice. It was spilling all over.

Bill didn't win the World 600, but he won the September race at Darlington, and that's when he won the million dollars. The pressure was off him.

I may well have had a hand in ending the dominance of Bill's Thunderbird. In late July before the Talladega race and anticipating the October race at Charlotte, I put out a news release—the infamous Ducktail release—in which I explained why Bill was winning so many races. Late July and August is a slow time for ticket sales, and I was trying to stir things up.

I had talked to a number of drivers, and they were telling me what happened to them when they tried to draft behind Bill's car. When they got behind his Thunderbird, they said, it was like they were backing up. The reason Bill was winning so many races, my experts said, was that the air coming off the Thunderbird was ducktailing around the back of the quarter panels. Instead of having the effect of no air behind him, the design of the car created a vortex of air that actually stopped the car that was running behind so it was impossible to draft him.

When I sent out my news release explaining the ducktail effect, the Elliotts were really hot as I knew they would be. I took it on the chin. I also sold tickets.

Meanwhile, during that Talladega race, Bill fell two laps behind the leader, and he made up the two laps under green and won the race. You can't do that. That's not done. Never has been, never will be again. And anyone who does it, NASCAR is going to bury that race car because NASCAR is going to do something, and it won't be good.

After the season NASCAR allowed the Chevrolets and the Pontiacs to add that funny-looking rear roof extension to make them aerodynamically similar to the Thunderbird. When NASCAR did that, it effectively ended Bill's stranglehold on the sport. He went on to win forty-eight races, but he never again had a year like that.

You can't take it away from him as a race driver, because other teams had Thunderbirds. It took an exceptional driver to be able to win like that, and Bill Elliott was an exceptional driver.

He proved over and over again he had what it took. He will go down in history as one of the great drivers and also one of the really neat guys in racing. He enjoyed his friendships and has helped a lot of people, and he never talks about it. What he brought was a real shot in the arm for the sport, and when Richard Petty retired at the end of 1992, most of his fans went over to Bill Elliott. When David Pearson retired after 1986, he took a lot of his fans as well. Bill was the Southern face of the sport, and that's why he was continually voted the most popular driver year after year.

CHAPTER 14

Curtis and Bruton Go Bust

O N THE SAME DAY IN 1958, Bruton Smith and Curtis Turner announced the building of superspeedways on opposite ends of Charlotte. This was also the year Bill France was completing Daytona. The fanfare over Daytona was so great that Atlanta also announced the construction of a new superspeedway.

Both Bruton's and Curtis' tracks were announced with great fanfare, but everyone knew only one of them would be built. No one knew where either Bruton or Curtis was going to get the money because frankly, neither one of them had any. Each had great bravado but little green to back it up. When cooler heads prevailed, they decided to join together and build one track. Bruton had been a dirt-track promoter, and Curtis had raced for him many, many times. They had traveled together, so they knew each other very well.

Curtis was a very interesting guy. He was the first race driver I ever saw who wore a suit. One time he was in the hospital after a crash, and Max Muhleman and I went to visit him. He was surrounded by law books; they were all over the place. He said, "I'm getting my legal education. I'm trying to figure all this stuff out." I don't know if Curtis ever finished high school, but he had been a bootlegger up in Virginia around Roanoke. I can remember he usually wore brown suits and brown wingtipped Oxford shoes. He had dark, wavy hair and was a good-looking guy—and a tremendous, tremendous race driver. I don't think I ever saw anyone drive a car as naturally as he did. He had that seat-of-the-pants feel on dirt. The only one close to him was Junior Johnson.

Curtis was flamboyant in a very understated way. He liked to party, but he didn't have a terribly outgoing personality. He did talk a lot. I guess you could say he was an extrovert, but not in a showy way. He dressed conservatively. I always thought he was trying to look like he had just gotten out of Duke University.

Curtis always had an airplane, though I doubt he had a pilot's license. I flew with him one time on a routine flight. He was a great pilot. Race drivers make very good pilots. They know how to make an airplane work. He could fly anything in any kind of condition, and he wouldn't think twice about taking a drink before going up in the air.

Curtis always looked like he had just eaten a very good meal. Not that he was fat, just that he appeared like he was ready to take on the world. He always had schemes. There was always something up his sleeve. What he was, was a promoter. Unfortunately, other than driving a race car, nothing he ever tried to do worked out too well. But he certainly acted like he was successful.

People said he made millions and lost millions, but that's a matter of controversy. We knew he lost a lot. I'm not sure he ever made a lot. He acted like he did, but back in those days and being the top racer he was, he commanded significant appearance fees, so he always had money on him, and he'd flash it around pretty good.

Curtis was quite a character.

Bruton, on the other hand, was what you'd refer to in the South as "slick." That means someone from the country who could outtalk and outmaneuver everyone else. Bruton was born on a farm twenty miles east of Charlotte. He was the youngest of eight kids. Though he was very smart, after graduation from Oakboro High School he went to work in a cotton mill. He detested the environment of the mill, so he took what money he saved and opened a small used car lot in Concord. He bought and sold used cars, and in the evenings started to promote dirt races. He ran a number of dirt tracks, including the half-mile track at the old Charlotte Fairgrounds, which ran every Friday night in the 1950s.

I was a fifteen-year-old student in high school writing a weekly column on racing for the local paper, the *Belmont Banner*, and one of the events I decided I wanted to cover was the stock car races at the Charlotte Fairgrounds.

I arrived at the track, identified myself as a reporter for the *Belmont Banner*, and asked the track promoter, O. Bruton Smith, for credentials. He was dressed all in black with his hair slicked back. He was about ten years older than I was, and I can remember thinking that he was quite a dude.

I had sold papers for Chris Economaki, the editor of the *National Speed Sport News*, at that very track. In my column I had written about many of the tracks in the Carolinas. And yet this guy had the audacity to turn me down.

I was really angry. I thought, *Who in the hell is he to do that?* I thought, *My paper is twelve miles away, and this guy needs all the publicity he can get.* My inclination was to hit him with a left hook. After all, I was on the Belmont Boxing Club, and when I was a teen I had a wicked temper. Many times I thought, *He thinks he's so tough. I should have let him have it.*

But I let it go. To this day, Bruton Smith was the only promoter who ever turned me down for press credentials. I never told him about that incident.

Back then Bruton and Bill France had an interesting battle going. After NASCAR was started by France in 1948, Bruton started a rival sanctioning body. His goal was to make it bigger than NASCAR, which wasn't all that hard because NASCAR wasn't very big at the time. He and France were always slugging it out. When the Korean war broke out, he knew he was going to get drafted, so rather than go into the regular army, he enlisted in the airborne division. He was away a few years, and that ended his sanctioning body. When he came back he resumed his dirt-track promoting, which led to his dreams of building a superspeedway.

When I was promoting at the Robinwood Speedway, I didn't worry too much about Bruton, who was running the Concord Speedway on the other side of town. Bruton had his side of Charlotte, and I had mine. He ran NASCAR races, and I ran my own sanctioning body. We were so far from each other we never had to cross swords.

Later he and Curtis Turner got together to build the Charlotte Motor Speedway. History has been mangled surrounding that whole subject because Curtis died suddenly in a plane crash in October 1970, and he hasn't been around to contradict what was written about him.

THE REAL STORY IS THIS, as best as I could figure out: Curtis was trying to raise money, do everything he could, including selling stock at a dollar a share out of the back of his car. As they got into construction, Curtis and Bruton ran into the same problem Bill France ran into, the same thing most builders of superspeedways ran into—they ran out of money. After only paying $300 an acre for the land, they figured they could build their track for $1.5 million. It came cheap because it was pretty bad land. This has never been written, but the land they bought was on the site of an ancient volcano. There's something called a ring dike, which runs in a seven-mile circle, and the center point is where the speedway sits. As a result, there was a tremendous amount of granite rock, which has plagued everyone who has been involved with the speedway since. It's very tough to work with, plus there are very few level places on it.

Building a high-banked speedway presented an especially tough challenge. Basically, it became a land-moving and grading job. These tracks—Charlotte, Atlanta, Daytona—were just giant earth-moving jobs where enormous quantities of earth had to be moved. The third turn at Charlotte, for instance, when Bruton and Curtis were building it, required 130 feet of vertical fill. At the time it was the highest vertical fill ever done in the state of North Carolina. Since then a dam has beat it, but that gives you an idea of the magnitude of what they were running up against. They were constantly running into rock, and every time they did, the price just kept going up and up and up until they went broke.

The original race was scheduled for the weekend before Memorial Day weekend, a week before the Indy 500, in 1960. I do know it was Bruton who came up with the idea of having the race go 600 miles rather than five hundred. Immediately everyone figured none of the cars would be around at the end.

As March approached, they really ran into problems. It snowed three consecutive Wednesdays in March in Charlotte when they were trying to get the bulk of the work completed. It not only set them back but made them rush going forward, and as a result the quality of the construction was rather poor, particularly at the grandstand as they tried to pour the concrete. The track itself never had a chance to settle like it should have. Bruton and Curtis realized they weren't going to be able to make the May date, so they met with Bill France, who decided to extend it to the third Sunday in June. Meanwhile, the creditors were getting very anxious for their money, particularly the grading contractor. A number of creditors got together and decided to foreclose on the speedway and stop construction. And that's when the shotguns came out.

The speedway people raised their shotguns, and the creditors raised their shotguns, and fortunately for everybody, the police got there and settled things down. Nobody shot anybody, but it was a tense moment. Meanwhile, in the background you could hear the rattle of bankruptcy.

When the cars began practicing for the first time, the conditions were awful because the track started coming apart. The drivers and crew chiefs were very concerned about whether the track would stay together and whether they could finish the race. Some wondered whether the race should be run at all. There was quite a bit of talk about canceling it because of the condition of the track.

Some of the race teams took matters into their own hands. Since the track was so bad, they knew this would not be an ordinary race, so they put skid plates underneath their cars and screens across the front, and they did a lot of things to their cars that had never been done before. It was getting pretty hairy, because after a while the retrofitted cars were beginning to look more like tanks than race cars, particularly the cars belonging to Richard Petty and his father, Lee.

Bruton went up to Roby Combs, the flagman, and he said, "I don't care what you do or how you do it, do not stop this race until after halfway. Make sure we get half the race in." That way, he wouldn't have to return the money to the fans.

Bruton had been up all night, and when the race began, he fell asleep, and I don't think he saw any of it. He just conked out. Everyone was exhausted.

The race wasn't at all pretty. As the day went on the conditions grew worse and worse. The track had holes in it, and a lot of cars got knocked out, but in general it was enough to keep everything together, and they were able to finish the race. Jack Smith had a commanding lead, and with eight laps to go he lost it when debris punched a hole in his gas tank. Joe Lee Johnson won the race, the only major race he ever won.

The drama then moved from the racetrack to the courts as creditors kept screaming for their money, which was nonexistent. Curtis had even gotten to the point where he tried to get the teamsters involved in an attempt to get a loan from them. To get the money Curtis promised the teamsters that he would unionize the race drivers. It wasn't a hard sell, because all the drivers felt that they were getting a raw deal from NASCAR as far as the amount of their purses. Most agreed to join. But Curtis, who was being assisted by Tim Flock, didn't anticipate the strong opposition from Bill France who promptly threw Turner and Flock out of NASCAR, presumably for life. Bill France, feeling that they had betrayed him, didn't want to have anything to do with them anymore. When France told the drivers he would close the tracks before he would allow them to unionize, the union attempt failed.

Cut off from the teamsters, Curtis and Bruton tried every other way to raise money. By then the banks saw how precarious their financial condition was, and they wouldn't lend them anything. Sometimes the concession companies from the North would lend money to tracks at very high interest rates, but they also would take over the concessions forever. Bruton and Turner couldn't even arrange that, and when they got to the point where there was no money, they finally had to cry uncle.

The track was then thrown into Chapter 11 by a judge. When that happens, anyone who has anything to do with the company usually gets tossed out on their ears. The judge tossed out Bruton and Curtis. And Curtis was out of NASCAR as well. Both of them took it very, very hard. It was a tremendous personal blow to both of them.

In the meantime Atlanta managed to open even though they had had a hard time too. In Daytona, Bill France was in his second year, and he had his hands full.

Curtis continued to try to get involved in various businesses and races outside of NASCAR. He raced USAC and anyplace else he could get a ride. Bruton went back to operating dirt tracks. And that's how the first chapter of their story ends.

LATER BRUTON BEGAN SELLING CARS at a Pontiac dealership in Charlotte, and he did that for several years. Then he moved to Denver, Colorado, to go to work for a former Charlotte car dealer by the name of Jeff Davis. Bruton ran the dealership for a while. Ford operated a dealer development program, and when the company wanted to open a new dealership in Rockford, Illinois, they offered it to Bruton. Ford financed it. Bruton began to make money, and he opened another dealership in Houston, and then another one in Dallas, and they went well. By this time the Charlotte track had come out of bankruptcy and had been bought in large part by Richard Howard for twenty-five cents a share.

Richard, a talented promoter from north of Charlotte, had made a lot of money in the furniture business. He was a huge man, an ex-Marine who had fought in the South Pacific. He was 5 feet 10 inches tall and close to 400 pounds. He was very smart, and he took to racing quickly. He brought the Charlotte Motor Speedway back to where it started making money.

Bruton began buying back blocks of stock in the track, and by the early 1970s there was a battle of stockholders between Richard Howard supporters and Bruton Smith backers. The first group did not want Bruton to return, and they fought him vehemently. The board meetings were full of drama. Finally Bruton amassed enough stock to barely control the board.

Bruton bulldogged his way into a smidgen of control of the speedway, but that's like giving him a mile. In May 1975 he ended up buying out Richard Howard. Part of the deal was that Richard would remain for a year and run the track through the October 500 race. It was at that point that I came into the picture.

CHAPTER 15

Hired to Run the Charlotte Motor Speedway

O NCE, WHEN BRUTON SMITH was running the Concord Speedway after he lost Charlotte, he called me on the phone to talk. He was very interested in what I was doing. Though he owned Concord, I could tell that Bruton had a terrible desire to win back the Charlotte track. Losing it had been a massive blow to him. His ego had been badly bruised by failure, plain and simple. In the phone conversation he suggested that there might be something for me to do at Concord, but I really didn't want anything to do with him. I was doing fine where I was, and at the time he wasn't anyone I was interested in doing business with.

Bruton left to go to Illinois to sell cars, and I left to go to Akron to work for Firestone. I ran into him once at the Phoenix track. I had little to do with him until I began hearing that he was buying up stock in the Charlotte Motor Speedway in what would become a royal battle for control of the racetrack.

Richard Howard ran the track, and he had allies who didn't like Bruton and didn't want him taking over. Bruton was coming at them hard as only he could. He always had a phalanx of stockbrokers working for him, and they were identifying the stockholders, and he was offering the stockholders cash money at a time when the stock wasn't worth much and not a lot of cash money was floating around.

I got to know Richard Howard very well while I was working at Firestone. He was very honest, very giving. He could be tough, but he was very generous to people. One time he took me fishing out on Lake Norman, and on the boat with us were two men about my age who had been brain-damaged in terrible automobile accidents. They weren't quite right, and Richard had invited them along for a relaxing afternoon of fishing. I thought that was very nice of him to do.

During the time he was running the Speedway, Richard also sponsored a national championship slow-pitch softball team. The Howard Furniture Company team was one of the best in the country. He had former pro and great ex–college players. These guys would hit twenty home runs a game. He supported this for years, and he even built a softball stadium in the country up in Denver, North Carolina. When Bruton began buying up the Speedway stock, the track had yet to be finished simply because there was no money. But Bruton wanted it, and he could be like a pit bull that gets his jaws into your arm. His tenacity is legendary. He does not stop if he wants to do something badly enough. He kept pushing and pushing, and finally Richard Howard agreed to sell him his stock. And that's what broke it.

After I left Firestone, I missed being involved in big-time racing full-time. I had done little things. I had been involved in a couple of low-buck B movies about racing made in Asheville, and in 1975 and 1976 I was involved in the U.S. Bicentennial. I was vice chairman of the Mecklenburg Bicentennial committee, working for a wonderful man by the name of Grant Whitney, who was chairman. This was all voluntary, but I thought this was a good way to become better entrenched in Charlotte.

It was for the Bicentennial that I came up with one of my most successful publicity stunts. In 1775 Mecklenburg County had come up with its own Declaration of Independence, one year before the more famous one was written. It's called the Meck Dec, and though some historians discount it because the original document was never found, most historians believe it happened. My idea was to dramatize the event by getting President Gerald Ford to visit us and also to hire an actor to play Captain Jack, the original rider who took the Meck Dec on horseback through the Shenandoah Valley up to Philadelphia. We found a man by the name of Jerry Linker, a long-distance horse rider. He was wiry, and he looked very good on a horse. We put him in Revolutionary garb, and he looked like he had slept out in the woods for a year. We got him a motor home, and we started the ride up to Philadelphia. This was to be the very first event of the Bicentennial.

When we got to Lexington, the heart of Virginia horse country, a woman filed a lawsuit against us for abusing the horse. It was the greatest possible thing to happen. She said this long ride was cruel punishment and should be stopped. She was awarded a temporary restraining order, so we had to go to court. We weren't far from Washington, D.C., and we retaliated strongly and said we were doing this in the name of history and that this woman should not belittle the Bicentennial by trying to stop Captain Jack's ride. The story ended up on front pages everywhere.

The courthouse was packed with reporters. We made the CBS evening news. It was great drama. The presiding judge said, "It's a rough trip, but this isn't different from what our ancestors had to go through, and this is a tough country." He allowed the ride to continue. After we won, Captain Jack rode the horse past the White House on the way to Philadelphia.

It was a neat deal, and not long after that Gerald Ford came to Charlotte on the 200th anniversary of the Meck Dec, and we had a great celebration.

I went to Richard Howard and told him I wanted to hold a giant Revolutionary War reenactment on the infield of the Speedway, and he thought that was a great idea. We ended up with 7,000 soldiers in full regalia.

While that was going on, Bruton Smith had taken over the Speedway. I was friends with Max Muhleman, a Charlotte reporter who had gone to California to work for Ford and then the World Football League. The league had folded, and he was returning to Charlotte. He and Bruton Smith were friends, and he suggested Bruton talk to me about running the Speedway for him.

I was in the real estate business at the time, and working for the Ervin Company, which was owned by American Cyanamid of Wayne, New Jersey. I was doing PR, promotion, and government relations. When I went to work for them, they had 4,000 employees. Then interest rates rose to twenty percent, and American Cyanamid called a bunch of us in and told us they were getting out of the real estate business. The Ervin Company made a deal with a dozen of us to stay and liquidate it. It set aside $75 million to pay debts and take care of its people as best it could. I learned a lot in the process.

I had an offer to work for a big hardware distributor in Norfolk and another offer from a power company. Each wanted me as vice president of communications. This was a time when corporate PR was coming into its own as far as decent salaries. I was torn because I wanted to get back into racing, but there still wasn't much money in it. Even Bill France wasn't making any money. His son, Billy, had a seventeen-foot center-console boat he fished out of and a little house.

The Charlotte Motor Speedway had been built in 1960, but even fifteen years later it had never been finished. In fact, when I went to look at it, the only pavement in the whole place was the track itself and the pit road. Everything else was dirt.

Bruton and I kept talking. I could see he had big plans, but no money to fund them. I could see plainly how he operated. Like so many entrepreneurs, if he had two dollars, he used them to borrow eight more from the bank. He never had any cash because he just kept pouring the profits back into buying more improvements for the track. It was the same way with his car business. If he owned a car dealership and was making money, he used his profits to buy another dealership. And then another one and another one. So he was always in huge debt and still is. He didn't accumulate money. He accumulated assets. A lot of wealth can be built that way—if the ice doesn't come in.

My concern was how we would get any appreciable dollars, because there wasn't enough cash being generated by the Speedway to do very much. The banks weren't lending any money, though Bruton had begun to make some headway with Luther Hodges, the head of the North Carolina National Bank. Luther's father had been governor of North Carolina, and had been secretary of commerce under Lyndon Johnson.

Bruton kept telling me all these things he wanted to do, and he told me he was going to let me run the Speedway while he returned to his car business in Rockford, Illinois.

We talked and talked. He started offering me money, and I wouldn't say anything. One time he stopped and said, "Are you interviewing me, or am I interviewing you?" I said, "I just want to make sure this move is the right one." I had a theory that sometime between the age of 36 and 40, you had to make a move that would make you or break you. This was my time. I kept telling myself, *I've got to lay the foundation.*

I had turned down a job with Bill France to run Talladega. On his invitation, I went to Alabama and looked around. I-20 wasn't finished. There weren't any hotel rooms close to the track. It just had so much going against it, though as Bill France told me, "The land was cheap, and George Wallace loves us." I decided not to pursue that. The Frances have had their hands full with that place ever since.

I was also offered a job by Larry Lopatin to run a track he was going to build in Cherry Hill, New Jersey. I felt the Michigan and Texas tracks were too perfect, and this was going to be a track just like it, and I declined that job as well.

What it really came down to was that I didn't want to leave Charlotte. In the end, after looking at it hard, I decided to take a chance and take Bruton Smith's offer to run the Charlotte Motor Speedway. Little did I know what lay in front of me—good and bad.

Part of Richard Howard's deal with Bruton was that he would remain in his office for a year and that he could keep his car. That was the best thing that happened to me, because Richard gave me great, great advice the first year I was there. Even though I was running it, he was available all the time. He was so kind to me. In a family business, you'd go to your father. I went to Richard.

Not long after I took over I brought in a guy named Jack Pentis, who had designed Marineland in Florida. He spent three days walking around the Speedway, and then he walked into my little office, and he said, "Gee, there's not a thing I can do with this place."

I said, "Jack, you have to be kidding." I had never seen anyone turn down a job like this. He said, "I can say one thing about this place: early beer can." That's how he saw the design as it was. It wasn't a pretty sight, and there was very little money. That was my introduction to working there.

The first race I promoted at the Speedway was the 1976 World 600. Everything that could go wrong for me did. The Indianapolis 500 and the World 600 were both scheduled for the Sunday of Memorial Day weekend. Charlotte had been sold out every year since 1965, but this year ticket sales were extremely slow because of the entry in the Indianapolis 500 by Janet Guthrie, the first woman to drive in the race. None of the drivers wanted her there, and as a result all of the media was focused on Indianapolis.

Janet's entry wasn't just making the sports page. She was making the front page. This was the advent of women's liberation, and she was playing things perfectly. She was thirty-eight years old, and every time she drove onto the track it made headlines not only outside the South, but also in the South. The burgeoning Southern racing media was fascinated by her, and consequently, we could not compete. I was even having trouble getting publicity in *The Charlotte Observer*. By the beginning of May, only half the tickets to the

600 were sold, and I was really concerned. In fact, I was beginning to panic. Ticket sales were flat. Nothing was happening. May in Charlotte is hot as the dickens, and that wasn't helping ticket sales because the 600 back then was run in the daytime.

But I had a plan. If Janet Guthrie didn't qualify fast enough to make the Indy 500, I could get her to run in the World 600, and I'd get all the publicity. I kept making phone calls to anyone of any consequence at Indianapolis trying to find out how she was doing in her attempt to qualify. As the time trials approached, I was hearing that her car wasn't up to speed and that she might not make it. There were fifty-five cars trying to qualify, and my sources told me, "If she makes it, it will be by the skin of her teeth. The car just won't get going."

During the second week in May I called Janet at the Speedway Motel where most of the race teams stayed in Indianapolis. I asked her to run in my race instead.

"Why?" she asked. "You represent failure to me."

"This is the longest race—600 miles," I said. "You'll look a whole lot better running in my race than at Indy."

She turned me down. I called her again, and this time I threw around some money. But I also knew it didn't make any sense to get her to race in Charlotte if she wasn't successful. A week before race week at Indy, it appeared that she was about a mile an hour from making the race.

We sent Max Muhleman up to Indy as an envoy to talk to Janet. Max knew everyone, and he was able to keep me abreast of what was going on with her. A week before our race, I still had 30,000 empty seats, and I was beginning to panic. So was Bruton, who needed the money badly.

Janet, of course, had the option of not racing at all, but she finally came back and said, "I will run at Charlotte if you get me the car A. J. Foyt drove when he sat on the pole at Daytona." I didn't think that was such a great idea, because Daytona cars don't usually run that well at Charlotte, but if that's what she wanted, then okay. I agreed to buy her the car. She also wanted a top crew chief, which I had already figured out. I had called Ralph Moody and he agreed. When I told her Ralph would run her car, she was pleased because Ralph had such a great reputation.

I still had a couple of problems. I had to get her into the field, which wasn't easy because there were a lot of cars trying out. Also, I knew the other drivers were going to give me pure hell for buying her the car, so I had to figure out a way around that. I knew David Pearson would be the first to howl. Remember, this was back in the days when real men drove race cars. There was no power steering. These guys had big forearms while the Indy drivers looked like jockeys. Here I was bringing this thirty-eight-year-old woman with thin arms down into the bastion of bull-necked, Popeye-forearmed race drivers who would spit tobacco out of the side of their mouths on occasion. And these guys were not going to like this.

But first I had to get her into the race.

I went to A. J. Foyt and told him, "You have to let her drive your backup car at Indy so she doesn't leave there a failure." He agreed, and she went out and drove it three miles an hour faster than the slowest car entered in the race, and that gave her credibility as a race driver. She then got in a plane and headed for Charlotte.

For the first time in history, I did not have to call a press conference. The press left Indy and flocked down here to cover this saga, and the next six days were among the most interesting in my life because of what happened.

At the press conference, the first thing Janet was asked was, "Is there any possible way you can drive 600 miles?" This was wonderful. I would like to say I planted it, but I didn't. I would have if I had thought about it. Janet didn't like that question at all.

Janet is a nice person, but she didn't take any guff off anybody. She was extremely intelligent. After all, she was an engineer. Then one of the other drivers said she had no place in the race, and that started it. She hadn't even sat in the race car yet.

I really needed to sell tickets, so I decided to *really* get things stirred up. I called a friend of mine, Linda Ferrari, the first vice president of marketing of a major bank on the East Coast. This was right around the time when women were first going into executive jobs. Linda was a nice-looking gal in her thirties, smart as a whip, from New York, and she liked racing. I said, "Linda, how would you like to own a race car with Janet Guthrie as your driver?"

Linda jumped all over that. I knew Linda didn't have the money to pay for the car and Ralph Moody, so I told her I would get her a sponsor.

I had a company in mind. I didn't even know where their offices were. Kelly Girl had begun to emerge as a fast-growing entity, and I got on the phone and called Jim O'Brien of Kelly Girl. He took my call, and I said to him, "I want you to sponsor Janet Guthrie's car in the World 600. We'll paint it kelly green. We'll put 'Kelly Girl' on the side, and it'll be the biggest thing this weekend. All for $30,000." Which covered the car, Ralph, and everything else we needed to do. Over the phone Jim said, "That's a great idea. We'll do it. But to get the money, she has to make the race."

I said, "She's not only going to make the race, she's going to do it in a spectacular way." Hell, I didn't know what that was going to be, but I knew I'd figure out something.

I called Linda back and told her I had the money. I said, "If Janet does well in this race, I know Kelly Girl will sponsor her for the rest of the season." I didn't really know that, but it was too much of a natural. Linda agreed to be the car owner.

On Tuesday, the cars were scheduled to practice on the track. I invited Linda out to the Speedway, and when she went to go to her car, Bill Gazaway (the NASCAR official in charge of the garage area) wouldn't allow her in. Gazaway and I always had a nasty relationship. I said, "Bill, listen, you have a serious problem. You have a woman who you won't allow in this garage area."

"You know our policy," he said. He started giving me crap. Then he said, "Besides, she has a skirt on."

"Okay Bill," I said, "we can handle this one of two ways. If you want to be a defendant in federal court this afternoon, you can, because that is where this is headed. Now when you get to federal court, what do you think a judge will do when he hears you won't allow a woman in the garage area?" As soon as I said that, he fumed and he said, "I have to make a phone call."

He called Bill France. Then he told me, "Under the circumstances, we'll let her in today."

"Today?" I said. "She's going to be there all damn week. She's the car owner, and you better get used to it." I was so mad I wanted to go over there and pop him. He mumbled something, and I knew the issue was settled, because I knew Bill France had ordered him to back off. So Linda was allowed in, and she was the first woman ever allowed in the garage area.

Meanwhile, Janet's car wasn't running right. She couldn't make the car handle as she struggled through Tuesday's practice. The car was running all over the track.

Wednesday was the day when the first twenty cars qualified, and the second twenty went out on Thursday. I said to Ralph, "Let's hold out to Thursday. Don't embarrass her by trying to get her to qualify and not make it Wednesday. She's not running fast enough."

Now Junior Johnson was the last person you would have thought would have helped a woman in those days, but I called him and asked if he and Herb Nab would come over and look at Janet's car. They came and worked on it for two hours and straightened out the front end. On Thursday morning Janet got in it, and she said it was like it was a new race car. And, incredibly, she was the fastest car to qualify on Thursday, giving her the twenty-first spot on the grid.

All the newspapers jumped all over this because it went way beyond sports. Some of them who came didn't know the first thing about racing, and one reporter even wrote she had been the fastest car to qualify for the race, not understanding she was the fastest qualifier on the second day. That got us tremendous publicity.

And when she made the field, our phones were overloaded and shut down completely. I had to have the Concord telephone company come in and put in as many phone lines as they could, as ticket orders came flooding in. We kept the ticket office open all night long, and by the end of Friday we had sold more tickets in one day than we had ever sold in the history of the Speedway, before or since.

THE STORY DOESN'T END THERE. On Friday, I got a call from ABC-TV. They wanted to come down and cover the Janet Guthrie story with an eye toward including it in the Indy 500 telecast. That just wasn't done. You don't take the Masters golf tournament and include footage of the Western Open in the middle of it. I asked for some money, and ABC agreed.

By Friday evening we had the event totally sold out, and I was feeling fantastic. We were in hog heaven. Race day came, and it was hot as the dickens, but fine. I went down to the ticket office, and I noticed there were no single seats available. I had more than 75,000 seats, and it made no sense that there were no singles. Even the seats behind the posts and in the corner were sold. Then I began to see taxicabs show up at the track entrance. Every taxi in Charlotte was at the Speedway. I never saw that before—not ever. I thought it strange. I had clues as to what might happen next, but I didn't pick up on them.

The flag dropped, Janet was in the field, and I was feeling absolutely wonderful. Bruton had pushed me to do something I never did again—I sold standing-room seats. They all stood up and went into the aisles, which made movement impossible. When I saw the flagman cross his flags, I was feeling even better because that meant it was halfway through the race and I wasn't going to have to come back another day and race.

Everyone needs someone to bring them back to earth when they get a swelled head. This has always been my brother David's role. And when he delivers the bad news, he calls me "Buster."

"Buster," he said, "you got a real problem." And whenever it's a *real bad* problem, he throws an elbow into my side. I was up in the control tower when he elbowed me in the side. I couldn't imagine what could have gone wrong.

"You're sucking air," he said.

The only thing worse could have been a death in the family.

We weren't on city water at the time, so we had set up a series of Rube Goldberg–type wells all over the Speedway. We had 500,000 gallons of water available. Except the tanks were dry. All of the water had run out, and the ground water could not keep up with the replenishment demands of the tanks for the people going to the bathroom. The commodes had no water in them. I thought, *Oh shit*.

How could this have happened? Richard Howard said he had never run out of water before, even though it took an army of plumbers and well people to keep this contraption going. I figured something was leaking.

As fast as we could, we checked everything. There were no leaks. The water was coming out of the ground. We just couldn't get it into the tanks. All that was coming into the tanks was air.

What was causing this? Then the light bulb went off in my head. No single tickets. Taxicabs. Of course. Thousands of women had streamed into the Speedway to watch Janet Guthrie take on the men. They could have cared less about the race, but they wanted to see the race to see history being made. They had flown to Charlotte or driven to Charlotte by themselves, and many were standing. And all of them had to go to the bathroom at one time or other.

Fortunately for us, Harvey Walters, who was in charge of operations, had formulated a plan just in case something like this happened. Now don't forget this was my very first race at the Speedway.

"Harvey, what should we do?" I wanted to know. He told me.

We got on the phone to every volunteer fire department within fifty miles of the Speedway. And there were many, because it's such a rural area. Every fire department had a tanker carrying water. I called each one, and I said, "I will give you $500 for the water in your tanker if you can be at the Speedway within 30 minutes." What fire department isn't looking for money? And $500 was good money in those days. Within minutes, the fire trucks were hurtling themselves to the Speedway to put water in our tanks.

Here they came, and it was a sight—all those fire trucks running wide open with their red lights on and sirens in full blast. A lot of spectators thought there had been a nuclear attack or a plane crash. From 360 points they flooded into the track with enough water to get through the race, and that saved the day for us.

Janet ran the entire 600 miles in the extreme heat and finished fifteenth. That night turned into one of the most fun nights of my life when I turned on my TV to watch the Indy 500, only to see the cameras going back to Charlotte with everyone acting like it all was happening live. They didn't pay much attention to the 500. The show was all about the World 600, and it made me feel great. That was my first race, and it was quite a day.

CHAPTER 16

Bruton and I

B RUTON AND I DIDN'T HAVE a boss/employee relationship even though that's what he tried to promote. When I'm pushed around I can be one mean son of a bitch, and Bruton truly knew that. He would push everyone else around, but for years we had a pretty close relationship, because he knew he couldn't elbow me without my knocking his teeth out. Also, I really liked many of his ideas, and I was grateful he pretty much gave me license to do whatever I wanted.

We were two intense, creative, aggressive men in a business loaded with violence, intrigue, mystery, and two-fisted testosterone—where the Wild, Wild West met the Scotch-Irish toughness of the Southeast.

From the start, Bruton was absolutely crazed by the idea of expanding the Speedway, making it bigger and better. Even though we had no money to work with, we were always meeting with architects trying to figure out what we could do to expand the place.

This was 1976, a time when racing was considered a blight on the community. In 1974 a rock concert had been held there. It went on for four days, and it was said that more people were there than were at Woodstock. It plagued the Speedway for years afterward. The place was completely over-whelmed. This was the era of Vietnam and drugs, and a huge number of people ended up in the hospital. I rode my bicycle out there while it was going on, and as I drove by I thought, *I'm glad I'm not running this place.* It was wild. Nobody ever did know how many people were there because they tore the fences down, flooded in, and mobbed the place. The reputation of the Speedway hadn't been very good before that, but after that it was very bad. Law enforcement got angry with the Speedway for holding the concert. It was forty years ago, and the joke remains that there are still people who haven't left yet.

Then in 1976 the Speedway's board of directors declared a small dividend, and we sent the dividend checks from the Bank of Concord. The bank screwed up, and they all bounced. My phone rang off the hook from calls by small investors who weren't getting their $23.50. It was embarrassing, and the bank was very apologetic, but even after their checks cleared we weren't looked upon too kindly by the city fathers.

Shortly after the incident with the bounced dividend checks, the Charlotte Chamber of Commerce invited me down to make a speech on the future of the Speedway. I thought I had made a pretty good speech when Luther Hodges, the chairman of the chamber, got up to thank me. I had presented him with a gold flying eagle dollar from the Carson City mint. In return Luther said, "Humpy, it's befitting we give you this," and he handed me a pair of white socks and a six-pack of Blue Ribbon beer.

That's what the chamber thought of the race fans. I thought, *The only thing missing here is Sur-lay hair tonic.* That's an oil all the mill workers used to put on their hair. As I was riding back out to the Speedway, I thought to myself, *Boy, you got a long, long way to go.*

BRUTON, WHOSE OFFICE was in Rockford, Illinois, would call me almost every night at about seven thirty or eight and we would talk, sometimes for two or three hours, about what he wanted to do. He was always pushy and aggressive. He was beginning to make my life very miserable. He was second-guessing and micromanaging, and I was beginning to wonder if I had made a mistake taking the job. This was particularly true on Saturdays, because Bruton works seven days a week. If you're in the automobile business, as Bruton was, you worked all day Saturday. During the week, if I was in a meeting and he called, he insisted I leave the meeting and talk to him. It was constant as he pushed me to expand the grandstand.

Finally, toward the fall of 1976, we got a $2.2 million loan from the North Carolina National Bank, which to my knowledge was the first significant loan to a speedway in U.S. history. To get the money, we had to make our improvements before our next race in May. The expansion called for 10,000 new seats and 17 VIP suites, plus a new press box, which was greatly needed. We had less than six months to complete a job that normally would have taken eighteen months. It was a real booger to get done.

I almost quit one day during the construction project. In addition to the seats, we had to put in a small walkway from our office to the main entryway so when it rained the fans could get around without having to walk in the mud. It was a three-foot-wide asphalt path. I hired a guy from Lincolnton who did it cheap because I didn't have much money to work with. Bruton had come down from Rockford, and when he saw it, he just went berserk. I'll admit it wasn't the greatest job in the world, but he thought it was awful, and he ordered me to rip it up and do it over again.

I'm not sure why, but I held my tongue and kept on. Meanwhile, Bruton and I fought over how many seats to add. Bill France Sr. had a theory on seats. He said to me, "You don't ever want to add more than 5,000 seats at a time. And after you add them, you wait a year and sell them out, and if you sell them out a second year, then you can build 5,000 more."

I always thought that was very smart, because you never wanted supply to outrun demand. You kept the fans needing to buy the tickets in advance. Because if people knew there were seats, they could wait until race day to buy them and you didn't want that.

Well, Bruton threw all of that out the window. Bruton was always over-building. My argument didn't make any difference to him. So we put in the 10,000 seats, and here's what happened: When you do that, you put 3,300 more cars on the road, and you need to have 33 more acres for parking. You can park a hundred cars on an acre. If you pave and line the area, you can fit 125.

Because the 3,300 added cars created a traffic jam, 20 percent of our fans didn't get to see the start of the race. Traffic was backed up for twelve miles at a dead stop, and it just infuriated people—all because we were building seats without incorporating the proper planning. I finally had to bring in a traffic engineer.

The next year, Bruton wanted to add even more seats. We ordered steel seats from a Tampa company. He called me on the phone asking, "What size bolts are you putting on those seats?" I didn't know. Who would? But he would ask me questions like that to get me befuddled. It was his nature. He was always pushing, pushing. I have a friend who worked for one of his car dealerships who told me that if he sold 100 cars in a month, Bruton would order 200 more cars from Ford and have them shipped down, and my friend wouldn't know about the order until the cars landed on the lot.

Bruton is absolutely the most aggressive human being I have ever known or could even imagine. He seemed to want it all, so in order to get it I worked all the time—days, nights, and weekends.

We argued constantly. Bruton wanted more, more, more, bigger, bigger, bigger, and I wanted the races to be better, better, better because I knew instinctively that no matter what we did or how gorgeous we made the track, if we didn't have the product when the green flag dropped, we wouldn't sell tickets. Of course all this massive expansion has come back to haunt him as many tracks today fill less than seventy percent of their seats. I felt that we weren't selling a race ticket—we were selling drama. I argued this with everybody, including Bruton and Bill France, Les Richter, Mike Helton, Tony George, and anyone else I encountered in races I was promoting. I wanted color and excitement. I didn't like black race cars, even as great as Dale Earnhardt's car was. You just couldn't see it because it blended in with the track.

I also was constantly pushing to slow down the cars. I had a theory I kept pounding to Bruton and to Bill France that when the cars run more than 200 miles an hour, you're not going to have much of a race, because it's all the driver can do to just hold on to the race car. How is he going to race somebody? He can do it, but it's going to be tough.

I also thought race fans wanted to see more races, and one of the first things I wanted to do when I came to the Speedway was build a quarter-mile track on the front straightaway so we could have Modified and short-track races before the Cup races. It would have only cost $100,000. Bruton just would not do it. Years later, after we talked R. J. Reynolds into sponsoring Legends races for the retired drivers, Bruton let me build it.

Often if it was my idea, he said no. If it was Bruton's idea, that was a different ballgame. And when he wanted to do something, oftentimes it was so overdone it got crazy. It was that way with adding seats. And it was also about adding glitter and glitz. Bruton was enthralled by the bigness of Texas and also with the glamour of Las Vegas, his favorite town. There is no place on earth he would rather spend his time, and he doesn't gamble. He likes the glitter and the fashion of the place. He likes the over-the-top billboards. If I wanted to put up a forty-foot sign for the Speedway, he wanted a hundred-foot sign.

"It violates the sign ordinance," I'd say.

He'd reply, "Get the ordinance changed." Because to him, rules don't count. Bruton makes the rules. And this was a constant battle because I preferred propriety and I hated ostentation. I wanted things that regular, working race fans could use: clean bathrooms, paved parking areas, places where they would feel comfortable, and better and wider seats. I wanted to spend money on traffic control so the fans could get in and out of the track easily and quickly. Not that he was against that, but when he would build a press box, for instance, he ordered mahogany walls. The writers don't care about mahogany walls. And when we would decorate suites, there was no limit to the spending. Bruton loved suites. I hated them. That was because everyone wanted to get in them free. It cost a great deal to build them, and you were taking so much away from the race fan. Bruton's own personal suite has leather seats, gold-gilded ceiling entrances, $5,000 doors, and the finest carpeting you could install. I never thought you needed to do that. Bruton was the Ritz Carlton, and I was the Holiday Inn. From the beginning, I could not understand the conspicuous way he spent money.

We got into it with the condos we built at the track. I get a tremendous amount of credit for them, mainly because I had to sell them. The job was dumped in my lap. But I was against the condos for one reason: Bill France warned me against selling off a piece of property on the track site, and he turned out to be right. At the same time, I understand the need for France to have an Eiffel Tower and India to have a Taj Mahal. But this was a philosophical difference between Bruton and me that never was resolved, and in recent years it only got worse until I finally had to leave.

BUT THAT WAS A LONG WAY OFF. When I first took the job running the Speedway, one of my most important tasks was trying to bring up the image of racing. Part of the problem was that the residents of the south side of Charlotte (the hoity-toity, old-time Charlotteans) simply would not come out to the races. These were hunkered-down Presbyterian men who wore gray suits and women who wore tweed. They worked in banks and clipped coupons to augment the money they made in the textile business. I wanted to attract these people, and I also wanted racing to become a national sport, so I was all the time trying to figure out a way to create wider interest.

In 1977, a few months before the May race in Charlotte, I was sitting around having a meeting with my staff, and I began by asking, "Who would be the last person in the world who would come to the Charlotte Motor Speedway?"

The answer came back, "The Pope," and second choice was the Queen of England. I knew getting them might be tough. "Who's the third choice?" I asked, and the answer came back, "Elizabeth Taylor," a woman I've personally been fascinated with because she has sustained herself from girlhood through her days as a movie star. "How do we get Elizabeth Taylor?" I asked. At the time she was married to John Warner, who was running for the U.S. Senate from Virginia. I got on the phone and spoke to Warner.

"Look," I said, "if you can get your wife to come down here for the race, we will put you front and center before all of these race fans," and doggone if he didn't think that was a great idea. He was scheduled to come to Charlotte for some other reason, and I picked him up at the airport and took him for a meeting so he could see we were legitimate. We passed the litmus test, and Warner agreed that he and Elizabeth Taylor would attend the 600.

When it was announced that Elizabeth Taylor would be coming to our race, people were amazed and skeptical, especially those blue-hairs from the south side of Charlotte. The media began to pooh-pooh the announcement, so I had a race car driven up to her home in Virginia somewhere in hunt country. I had a driver's uniform custom-made for her, and we took some great publicity shots of her in the car. When they were published, everybody shut up.

Come race day, John Warner and Elizabeth Taylor arrived at the Speedway and, for the very first time, the drivers' wives wanted to meet someone other than racing people. Flossie Johnson, Junior's wife, called to say she wanted to meet Elizabeth Taylor. So did Linda Petty, Richard's wife. Back then, not a lot of celebrities came around. I put up a picket fence in the grass in the infield by the start/finish line, put up an umbrella for Elizabeth to sit under, and I invited the drivers' wives to walk over and meet her. They had a big time.

The Speedway was absolutely packed, a total sellout. We introduced Elizabeth on the pre-race stand, and she turned to me and said, "I've been to a lot of places in my life, done a lot of things, but I have never been in front of such a massive crowd of people." She waved and got a rousing cheer. The fans got a real charge over the fact she came down. They had seen her in so many movies, and they wanted to honor her.

Richard Petty won the race, so here was this good-looking guy in the winner's circle, and here's the most famous movie actress of all time. She smooches him, and the picture of that went around the world. That was the magic photo, and hundreds of local newspapers ran that picture on either the sports page or the front page of the paper.

Elizabeth had a lot of class and grace. We had a small private dinner for her that night. I thought that was pretty neat. To me, having Elizabeth Taylor there that day was as much of a breakthrough as the 1979 Daytona 500 when Bobby Allison and Cale Yarborough got in a fight at the end of the race on national television.

ONE OF THE THINGS I DID in the 1970s was break up the NASCAR TV package. Bill France and I argued a lot about it. I didn't think he was attacking the TV situation the right way. His package included Daytona, Talladega, Darlington, and Charlotte, the perceived big tracks at the time. In 1978 I told Bill we were going to break away and do our own thing.

I signed with the old Mizlou network in a deal that called for the World 600 to be broadcast on a one-week delay. I got some rights money, but not a lot. While France was making his deal with CBS to televise the Daytona 500 live, I was in New York trying to make a deal with CBS for the 1979 World 600. I was negotiating with Neil Pilson and Eddie Einhorn. I knew they wanted the 600, but they wanted something else to go along with it. I tried to sell them the 300-mile Saturday race, but they said no; they wanted something more interesting.

I knew I had to come up with something. I was dealing with a New York mentality. I thought, *What's more New York than taxicabs*, and so I suggested to them the Great American Taxicab Race. They were negotiators who usually didn't show their cards, but when I said that, I thought their eyes were going to pop out of their heads.

"How would you do this?" Einhorn asked.

I made up something on the spot. I said, "We'll take the cab drivers from the top twenty markets in the United States, bring them to Charlotte, lay out a special course, and let them race. We'll use pit road as the back straightaway, and we'll take them down the end of pit road and make them make a sharp turn and come back down the front straightaway." And I said, "When they get down the backstretch, they'll have to stop and pay a toll. We'll set up a tollbooth."

I could see they were excited. They asked a million questions. I said, "We'll have tryouts and figure out a way to do this."

"What kind of cabs?"

"I'll get cars that look like cabs, and we'll put roll bars in them." In another half an hour, we had a deal. I remember getting on the elevator thinking, *Where am I going to get the cars*? I had no idea, but the Great American Taxicab Race was on.

I first went to the International Taxicab Association in Washington, a consortium of all the cab companies in the United States. They loved the idea. We didn't get any money from them, but we did get a lot of help. I went to the Checker Cab Company to see if I could get some cabs from them, but even though they wanted to help, they were going out of business. I then thought, *Dummy, buy big old four-door cars and paint them to look like taxicabs.*

There was a gas crisis, and everybody who had big cars wanted to sell them. I put an ad in the paper: Cash Paid for Crown Victorias, Lincolns, Mercurys, or big four-door Chevys. I gave my brother, David, some money, and he waited in the parking lot near my office as the car owners drove in with their cars for sale. I was up on the second floor, and I'd look down and signal with my hand: zero meant forget it, one meant $250, and two fingers meant $500. One car was so good we paid $700 for it. We took the cars to DK Ulrich's shop and painted some of them yellow and some of them checkered. When they got through, they looked just like cabs. We put the name of the driver on each car and where he was from.

I went to Sears and sold them on the idea of having qualifying at the parking lots of Sears stores across the country on a Sunday afternoon. Most Sears stores were closed Sunday. They thought it was a great idea. We set up a slalom course, and we put ads in the papers. Through the taxicab association we were able to contact cab companies in cities such as New York, Boston, Chicago, and Los Angeles. Whoever had the fastest time at the Sears parking lot qualified for a trip to Charlotte with his wife.

The New York contestants competed at the Islip Speedway. Two hundred cars showed up. The winner went to Charlotte to compete in the race.

As I said, in 1979 we had a gas crisis, and one of the big problems we had was that people stopped buying tickets because they didn't know whether they could get the gas to get home once they arrived in Charlotte. This was April, and we were fifty percent down in ticket sales. So I had an idea. George

Brain had just retired from the Union Oil Company. He had been there when it was Pure Oil, the predecessor to Union Oil. George was an ordained Lutheran minister but he had made his living working with filling station operators during a time when you had full-service gas stations.

I gave George $60,000 in cash, and I told him to go up to every gas station that would be open race weekend on I-85, I-95, I-77, and I-81, and make a deal with the owner that if a customer came in with a ticket to the Coca-Cola 600 he would be guaranteed a tank of gas. The race fan had to pay for it, but we guaranteed his gas. We gave any cooperating owner $500 on the spot plus a certificate that allowed him and a friend or date to come to the October race. We would put them up at a hotel, and they'd be our guests.

We signed up forty gas stations going all the way to Massachusetts and to Ohio, so the people coming to the race would have access to gas. We made a big deal about it in the papers, and we sold out the race. The *Washington Post* later said the people who run the Charlotte Motor Speedway should run the energy department in Washington, D.C., because they solved the problem.

The Great American Taxicab Race was held on Saturday. I built a fake hotel lobby in the first turn where the cabs had to stop as though they were delivering something, and we had a tollbooth at the backstretch. Each cab had to stop two times per lap. I didn't want anyone going too fast and getting hurt.

I also threw in a neat ringer to spice the field. I bought a police car with a hemi engine and I got the Flying Indian, Roy Tyner, to drive it. Roy was one of the only full-blooded American Indians ever to drive in NASCAR from the 1960s to the 1980s. Later he was murdered.

I had a two-way radio with Roy, who was dressed as a policeman, and if anyone didn't stop at the tollbooth or the hotel, he would run them down with blue lights flashing. He could pull a car off the road with his ramming bumpers and penalize him. One other thing no one knew we were going to do: I had installed a pipe ramp, the kind that they install in a movie when you want to flip a car. I knew by the last lap that the police car would be the most hated car on the track, and at the end of the race I had Roy drive over that pipe ramp, lose control, and do a couple of flips.

Ken Squier was the announcer for CBS. As soon as the race started, there was complete mayhem. On the first lap three cars ran right through the tollbooth sideways and totally demolished it. By the fourth lap cars had destroyed the lobby and most of the hotel. Guys were crashing and going sideways, and it was all Ken Squier could do to keep from breaking a rib laughing. It made for great TV and was totally hilarious.

One thing is true: You cannot account for every eventuality. The Great American Taxicab Race was tape-delayed, and it went opposite one of the great cultural events of sports history when "ABC's Wide World of Sports" presented the World Belly Flop Championship. Big, fat elephantine guys were jumping off a diving board to see who could slam into the water the hardest.

Sports Illustrated, in all its prissiness, came out with a blistering editorial blasting "trash sports," taking off on the World Belly Flop Championship. We were fine until the very last paragraph when it said, "Not only is ABC doing this, but at the same time CBS had something called the Great American Taxicab Race." It went off on it for a paragraph.

Because of that the Big Wigs at CBS, the so-called Tiffany network, decided they didn't want to risk their fine reputation with events like that. Thus the beginning of reality TV got off to a bumpy start.

The network did carry the Coca-Cola 600. We even got the president of CBS to come down and watch it. We didn't have the ending that the Daytona 500 had, but we were live on TV, and that's all that mattered.

DURING THE 1960s there were some lean times at the racetrack. Ford, Chrysler, and Firestone all pulled out of racing at one time or another. There was no money, and it showed on the track. A lot of car owners were just trying to escape their creditors.

Things began to change by the 1970s. R. J. Reynolds had begun to pour money into the points fund. We were also beginning to see sponsors come onboard. One of the first was Coca-Cola. It sponsored Bobby Allison's car, which was called the Coke machine. They paid maybe $200,000.

There was no money because there had been very little television exposure. Drivers made hardly any money compared to today. Some drove for as little as twenty percent of the purse. The top drivers like Cale Yarborough and Darrell Waltrip got fifty percent. It was still a sport like the PGA where what you did that day is what you earned.

To my knowledge, the first driver contract was between DiGard and Darrell Waltrip. Bill Gardner, DiGard's president, called me one day and asked me to recommend a lawyer to draw it up. I recommended a friend of mine, Ray Farris, an ex-quarterback from the University of North Carolina.

It was the first time a driver had a guaranteed income. They signed it in 1976, but it was a long-term contract, and in time Darrell came to hate Bill Gardner, so it was very messy when Darrell wanted out of there.

I could sense change was coming. Going into the 1980s, everyone was starving for financial sustenance. Even a small company has a financial base, something to fall back on in hard times. Not so for the race teams before the 1980s. They had a shop, equipment, and parts, but they did not have cash. And when a team decided to get out, a lot of what it had couldn't be sold for much. There was no franchise system. In the past, car owners looked to Ford or Chrysler for help, and sometimes a rich guy like Carl Kiekhaefer came along, but usually, if you wanted to race, you were pretty much on your own.

Until R. J. Reynolds came along, almost all the sponsors were connected with automotive services and parts. STP sponsored Richard Petty, for example. But after RJR came into racing, there was a consumer revolution in racing. You began seeing nonautomotive sponsors like Hanes, Coca-Cola, Texas Jeans, Hardees, Gatorade, and Busch beer.

Hanes had a brilliant marketing guy by the name of Jack Watson. It was Watson who put Wrangler together with Dale Earnhardt, a great move. When Hanes got into it, it was this old-time Southern textile company acknowledging the fact that a stock car race was a way to sell product. They didn't have to go to the ACC college basketball tournament or the Masters golf tournament. They could go racing.

We had a Jewish car owner by the name of Danny Schaefer. Buddy Baker was driving for him, and they were looking for a sponsor. We brought in a representative from Crisco to try to sell him on becoming the sponsor. He said, "But we don't have a big enough market share. We're at eighty percent and we're looking to do better, and we figure the best way to do it is to get into NASCAR."

I said, "Everyone around here has been brought up on Crisco." He signed on as the sponsor.

And thus did groceries begin to replace automobile parts in NASCAR sponsorship.

Something else important started to happen. In the past Gatorade or Coca-Cola might buy a suite, but there were few smaller companies. I can remember sitting in my office in 1983. A man with a Bronx accent called me and said, "I don't know anything about NASCAR, but I just moved here. I'm the general manager of a plumbing company, and I distribute supplies to plumbing companies. My customers don't care about football or basketball. They want to go to races. Tell me what I need to do."

My first thought was, *Hey, this may really be the start of something.* I said, "Here's what you need to do," and I sold him thirty-six tickets. I got him special parking. And that's when smaller operators began buying eight, ten, twelve tickets in order to entertain their customers. Instead of, "Let's go to Yankee Stadium and see the Yankees play tonight," for the Southern companies it became, "Let's take our best customers to the Charlotte Motor Speedway and see the race." And while they sat there, they did business.

There was another distinct reason why so many sponsors were now nonautomotive, and that was the influx of women coming to the races. In 1976 I did a survey of fans coming to the Coca-Cola 600, and fifteen percent were women. I felt we were in trouble because that was far too low.

I came across a very interesting study in *Fortune* magazine about what oil companies did during World War II to get women to come to their filling stations. Before then, it was their fathers or husbands who went to service stations. Women felt out of place there.

What the oil companies did was install beautiful new restrooms, and they cleaned their places up. I remember as a kid working at a gas station. The guy in charge would be on me all the time asking, "Is the women's room clean?" He never once asked me about the men's room.

I decided, "Let's build some really nice restrooms." Bruton agreed. I did one other thing. I started changing the sort of people we had at the gates of the Speedway. We used to have prison guards, gruff people who would bark at the customers. I began hiring teachers, coaches, salesmen, and saleswomen—people used to handling the public and putting them at ease. We stopped barking at them like we used to. We planted flowers and began treating everyone with great respect. We started to get a lot more women, and then an amazing thing happened: The security problems dropped drastically to the point where we hardly ever had an altercation at a racetrack. That's because she's just not going to let you do it.

By 1980, ten years after R. J. Reynolds injected its much-needed money into the sport, I could see that the crowds were becoming larger and more sophisticated. I could also see that the sponsor money was making for much better racing. I have always had a theory that to make a great race you have to have seven great cars in the field. Before 1980 we rarely, if ever, had that.

Usually it was Richard Petty and David Pearson and a couple of others, but almost never seven. If the race is over three hours long, you need seven great cars to ensure a great finish. Why seven? Because two or three will go out, and one might have a problem with a pit stop, leaving three cars that will be on the same lap running fairly close together. If you're really lucky, out of that seven, two will be there at the end battling for the lead. Starting in the 1980s we had a lot of great racing because finally the race teams had the money to make the cars run great.

We also had a good old boy from the Carolinas who became the new face of NASCAR. His name was Dale Earnhardt.

CHAPTER 17

Dirt Poor Dale

WHEN I LEASED THE CONCORD SPEEDWAY and started running it in 1971, I felt I had to have Ralph Earnhardt run there on Saturday nights. In addition, Ralph built his son, Dale, a car, and he started racing there too. I didn't pay much attention to Dale then because he was all over the racetrack. I was sure he wasn't going anywhere.

Dale was wild in the early days. I'm sure his dad told him to calm down, but Dale drove every lap like there was no tomorrow. It's what the next generation of racers did because the cars held together so much better than the cars of the past. But one thing Ralph didn't do was run on asphalt, and that presented a real problem for Dale. Dale had a very, very difficult time when he first got on asphalt, because on dirt if you have a fifth-place car, you can win if you're a good enough driver. You can't do that on asphalt. After his father died, Dale had to figure out for himself how to drive on asphalt, and obviously he ended up figuring it out very well.

Dale started racing around 1973, running a '55 Chevy, which was exactly what his father ran. As I said, I was not impressed with him at all. He was a little, stringy-haired kid, and back then it seemed that every racer was trying to get his kid into racing. They do the same thing today, though only a few of them amount to much. It was so typical of what racers did that I didn't pay a lot of attention to Dale in that he didn't run anywhere close to the front. He was a back marker. After I came to the Charlotte Motor Speedway in 1975 I began paying more attention to him.

I gave Dale his first big break in May 1978. My job was to promote the Speedway and sell tickets, and I thought I might create some controversy by finding a black driver to race at Charlotte. I made a deal with a car owner by the name of Will Cronkite for the use of his car.

I just couldn't find a black race car driver in the South. There was a guy named Randy Bethea who had tried to become another Wendell Scott, but he hadn't had very good luck, and I kept hearing about a nineteen-year-old road racer from California by the name of Willie T. Ribbs. I loved the name, and I started talking to him on the phone. He had the gift of gab, and I could tell he was going to stir up the pot big-time. He flew in, and we tried him in a car, and I was really impressed with the job he did.

The Talladega race was that weekend, and Ned Jarrett was going to take the pace car down there. We had construction going on at our track, so I couldn't go. I asked Ned if he'd take Willie down there. They stopped in Atlanta and had a press conference, and everyone was all stirred up, some good and some not so good. It was the Deep South, and despite the Civil Rights Act, there was still a lot of racism.

That night, while Ned was sleeping, Willie "borrowed" the pace car, and he went out on the freeway and took a 120-mile-an-hour joyride. He didn't get caught, thank heaven.

The next stop was Talladega. Don Naman was running the track. We were friends but we were also very competitive, and he knew my sending Willie to Talladega was an invasion of his territory. Our race was three weeks away. Ned took Willie to the drivers' meeting to introduce him. Les Richter talked about the perils of Talladega, and what not to do. After he finished, he asked if there were any questions. And Willie (who was not really supposed to open his mouth since he wasn't driving at Talladega) raised his hand and said, "I have one question. Can you pass on the grass?" He just wanted to let everyone know he was there, I guess.

He was a little too much, and I was becoming concerned about him. At the same time, by bringing in this black driver, I was walking on the edge of a cliff, and that's what I liked to do. Willie was getting a tremendous amount of publicity.

The following week Willie returned to Charlotte. We had him staying at a motel downtown, and we had loaned him the pace car. About two thirty one afternoon, I got a call from someone at the police station. "We have a guy here by the name of Willie T. Ribbs. You need to get down and get him out of here."

"What did he do?" I asked.

"When you get here, you'll find out."

I said, "Come on. What did he do?"

Well, Willie was speeding the wrong way down a one-way street at high speed in downtown Charlotte, and then he tried to elude capture. The police had chased him down an alley when they finally caught him.

I got down there and got him out. Willie was kind of laughing. He wasn't drunk, wasn't on drugs. He said he did it because he thought I'd like the publicity.

I said, "Willie, you just can't do this." By that time the press was all over it. I got back to my office, and my secretary told me to pick up the phone, and a guy at the other end said, "If you let that nigger race, you're going to die."

"Who is this?" I asked. Of course, he slammed down the phone. I didn't really pay much attention because those kinds of threats never amount to anything.

Nevertheless, I felt it was time to end the experiment. My brother was with me, and I told him, "We have to tell Willie the timing is not right." It wasn't the death threat. The thing had gotten too far out of hand.

I told him, "Willie, this ain't working out. We have too much bad press."

In those days, racing had a rough enough image. One of the things I was trying to do was bring it up a notch, and this wasn't doing it. Willie was very disturbed by the whole thing. He knew he had blown it, but he didn't want to admit it, and he tried to blame it on me.

I had my brother take him to the airport and put him on the plane, and back to California he went.

But now I had a race car and no driver. Will Cronkite was going to be all over me, because I had made a deal to put someone in it. I said to Will, "How would you feel about my putting Dale Earnhardt in that car?"

"That's okay," he said. I couldn't tell if he was enthused about it or not. So I called Dale and asked him if he wanted to drive Will Cronkite's car, and he just about jumped through the phone. NASCAR was okay with it. Back then there were few qualifications. It wouldn't have mattered to them if Dale had never driven in a Winston Cup race before. It would be different today.

§

I WAS IMPRESSED with the way Dale got the car around the racetrack. The car was a Ford, a good car, but it had its limits. It wasn't a top-ten car by any means. But he performed well in practice, and he listened to Will. Dale finished seventeenth in the race, eighteen laps back, and he didn't wreck the car. Not bad for only his fifth Winston Cup race.

From that point on, Dale and I really began working together. He'd come by my office, and we'd start talking about what he wanted to do. I'd give him my suggestions. I told him, "You have to learn to smooth down." And Dale began to get more rides. Johnny Ray, a former racer who owned a trucking company, had taken an interest in him. Johnny put Dale in a car, and Dale went to Atlanta and he flipped about eight times in the third turn. It was really spectacular.

He wasn't racing full time, though, and I told him, "The one thing you've got to do is race on asphalt. Sell that dirt car of yours and buy some asphalt equipment." Which he did—grudgingly.

Dale's head was about ten inches thick, and he and I had some very hard times. On one side, I knew his hardheadedness was going to make him a great racer. On the other side, he had to learn to listen to people who were trying to help him. One time in my office we almost came to blows.

He was driving wild with reckless abandon. There's a time for that, but you can't do it all the time and be successful. I said, "You've got to learn to settle down." He just mouthed off, and I told him, "I'll whip your butt right now." I was really mad, and he got mad, and he stomped out of there.

About a week later he came back. He said, "I have something I want to show you."

He had bought a Chevy Vega (about the worst car Chevy ever made) for his passenger car, and he had pulled out its four-cylinder aluminum engine and put in a V-8, which was about the most useless thing you could possibly do because the car wasn't any good to begin with. But he was really proud of what he had done.

"How are you going to change the spark plugs?" I asked, because there was so much engine in that little car that there was no way to get to them.

"Well, aah."

"You're going to have to put it up on a lift to do it," I said.

Dale started running on asphalt, and he really didn't do very well. And at the time he was having marital troubles. He had married his first wife, Latane, in 1968 when he was 17. They had a son, Kerry, and were divorced two years later. He wasn't but twenty-two, and already his second wife, Brenda, had left him. Brenda, who was car fabricator Robert Gee's daughter and Kelley and Dale Junior's mother, had worked for me in the Speedway ticket office.

I was home one Friday night, and I had gone to bed, and about one thirty in the morning the phone rang. It was Dale. He said he had hit the wall at Asheville, had torn up his car, and was totally destitute. His whole demeanor was awful. I could tell he was at his wits' end. He said, "There ain't nothing left of this car. I just don't know what to do."

I could tell that everything in his life was affecting him—his father's death, his divorces, and now he had wrecked his race car and he didn't have any money left. He had no car, no money, no nothing.

I said, "Load up what you can, and come and see me on Monday."

I called Robert Gee whose shop was right next door to the Speedway. Robert was basically a body man, and he always had a race car for the race at Charlotte. I had always helped Robert deal with one problem or another, but this time *I* was calling *him*. And, not only was I asking for help, I was asking for help for his ex–son-in-law. I said, "Robert, won't you hire Earnhardt to do some bodywork?" Dale was real good working with Bondo.

Robert said, "All right, but I won't pay him a lot."

I didn't tell Dale any of this when he came to see me in my office. I told him, "Racing is one thing where you can go backwards in and make forward progress. You can't go back to asphalt because it costs too much money. You don't have any money. Here's the only thing you can do. Now hear me out and don't backtalk me. Go to work for Robert Gee. He'll put you to work if you talk to him right." I could see him buck up a little.

"Listen to me," I said. "He has an old dirt car sitting up there under a canvas. It doesn't have a motor in it. Get back on dirt because if Robert is behind you, you can figure out a way to get that tarp off that car and how to get a motor in it, and you can win some races. That's what you need to do now—win. You don't need to be finishing eighth or ninth."

Dale went up to Robert's place, and he talked to Robert, and Robert gave him a job. I sent a water truck up there to get painted.

"What color do you want me to paint it?" Robert asked.

"I don't care," I said. "It just needs to look decent." Of course he painted it orange, and I was all upset because that's Clemson's color and I had graduated from the University of South Carolina.

I would go to Robert Gee's once a week to have lunch with him. He was another one who had eaten those Ralph Earnhardt slick-meat lunches. Robert and I would go into his living room—which did or didn't have furniture depending on whether his wife had left him that week or not. His wife came and went, and when she went she took the living room furniture. So if there was no furniture in the living room, I knew she wasn't there either.

This one time, though, I really went to check on Dale. They had the water truck in the shop, and I opened the door about an inch, and I looked at Dale—and he was totally covered in orange, as was Robert. The three of us went into Robert's house, and they took paint thinner to their hands so they could eat lunch. I sat there looking at Dale; his entire body was covered in orange paint. His face was orange. Even his eyebrows were orange.

IT TOOK DALE ABOUT THREE WEEKS to get the tarp off that race car. He never said a word to Robert, never asked him about it. Just took the tarp off and started working on it. That's the Southern culture. And Robert let him do it. He knew what Dale was up to.

How Dale got the engine is totally beyond me. I never got a correct explanation. I don't know if he borrowed one from Geoff Bodine, or what happened, but all of a sudden the car had an engine in it, and it was ready to go.

Dale started out running the Metrolina Speedway Friday nights and the Concord Speedway Saturday nights, and once in a while he'd race at Myrtle Beach or somewhere else, but he started on a succession of wins that was just unbelievable. This was when dirt racing was very competitive. It had gotten expensive too. There were a lot of great dirt track racers at the time.

I went down to Darlington, and I saw Rod Osterlund, a car owner who I knew was dissatisfied with his driver, Dave Marcis. Dave had been a good race driver in his day, but things weren't working. Rod had brought in a crew chief, Roland Wlodyka, from California to run the operation, and he and Marcus didn't get along. The Darlington race was on Sunday, and Osterlund said, "I have a late-night flight to L.A. this evening."

I said, "Why don't you come back with me to Charlotte, and we'll go by the Metrolina Speedway. I want to show you this kid. They're having a hundred-lapper tonight, and we'll watch part of it, and then I'll take you to the airport." He agreed.

We got over there, and I introduced him to Dale. Dale just tore them up that night. He hadn't qualified too well for some reason so he had to start at the back of the field, and it was really tough to pass at Metrolina, a half-mile track that was narrow in the corners.

Osterlund was really impressed with him. He said, "I'm going to run one of my cars at Charlotte in the 300. Do you reckon we could really pull this off?" I said, "Yes."

I made a deal with him to run the car with Dale as the driver. I told Dale, and he was thrilled. He finished third behind Darrell Waltrip and Richard Petty and won a purse of close to $30,000. He did so well that Rod put him in the same car for the 500 at Atlanta a few weeks later, and after the race, he fired Dave Marcis and put Dale in the car for good.

CHAPTER 18

Dale and Richard Childress

I F EVER THERE WAS a marriage made in racing heaven, it was between Richard Childress and Dale Earnhardt, although it didn't seem that way at first. Richard Childress was the poster boy for how you got into NASCAR racing. He came from a rural area in North Carolina, up near Winston-Salem, and he was the good old boy of good old boys. He had been a pretty good short-track racer who moved into the big time when you could do it if you had a lot of brass—and brass in the South is not like brass anywhere else. In the South, brass means determination. Richard had no real money, but he had talent, brass, and loyal friends who would help him work on his race car.

I got to know Richard pretty well when he was racing back in the 1960s. I always thought he was a good driver and that if he ever had money to build a really good car, he could win races. That was the Catch-22 that detoured many careers. But once in a while he would finish well. When I was at Firestone, I would give him tires because he was one of my guys. I had him on a free-tire deal because I thought he was an up-and-coming driver, and I was sure that if he didn't make it as a driver, he would eventually be a successful car owner, because Richard is very smart. He was one of those guys who would fool you because he had that North Carolina accent, which equates with "He don't know much about anything," but the truth was he knew a lot about a lot of things.

Richard and I used to talk about race drivers because, at the time, I was trying to find the best drivers I could find for Firestone, and he had a real knack for determining that. He finally got to a point where he knew that he needed to position himself to get ready for the next quarter of a century. He always seemed to have a good penchant for anticipating the future, knowing what was going to happen.

When Richard raced, he suffered through the Factory Wars when money was extremely tight. He was on the fringe as a driver, and never could get quite the right equipment, but one reason he did as well as he did was because he struck up a friendship with Junior Johnson. Junior liked Richard, and Junior helped Richard out a whole lot. When the factories got out, we went through terrible lean years between 1970 and 1975, and that's when Richard decided to become a car owner.

Dale Earnhardt was driving for Rod Osterlund at the time. I never could figure out whether Ron Osterlund ran out of money or whether he just wanted to go back to California and build shopping centers. He found out how excruciatingly expensive stock car racing could be, and also what a pain in the butt it was. You had to put up with crew chiefs, drivers, fabricators—all the things that aren't difficult in a normal business, like if you're running a car dealership. But you take those same people who are back in the service department, put them in the racing business, and put another zero at the end of their paycheck, and it just becomes a whole new ballgame. The egos get inflated, and all of a sudden the guy isn't playing Class A ball, he's playing for the Yankees and he becomes a different person.

I don't think Rod was having a lot of fun—that's the main thing—and if a guy isn't having any fun, he's going to get out of it even if he's been successful. So Jim Stacy came along and bought his race team, and we knew that was the end of that. Dale just wasn't going to drive for Jim Stacy. He didn't trust him. Dale left and finished the rest of the 1981 season driving for Richard Childress. He finished seventh in the points standings even though he didn't win any races. He then spent two years with Bud Moore.

Bud was running what was left of his old Ford factory stuff, and he was doing okay, but it wasn't the kind of equipment Dale needed to race. In 1982 Dale struggled badly. The equipment kept failing, and as a result he didn't finish most of his races. The next year he won two races, and he finished eighth in the points standings.

§

AT THIS JUNCTURE, everybody in the business was certain Dale Earnhardt would end up with Junior Johnson. If ever there was a driver made for Junior, it was Dale. I mean, they were both cut out of the same cloth. They both came from North Carolina. They both were great on dirt. And Junior used to talk about Dale all the time. I also know that Dale Earnhardt thought Junior Johnson spun the world.

Well, what happened was, the stars weren't lined up right. There was a meeting down in Talladega between Dale Earnhardt, Junior Johnson, Richard Childress, and Wayne Robertson of R. J. Reynolds. Wayne brokered Dale's move from Bud Moore back to Richard Childress. Wayne had a big influence on Junior, and Junior had a big influence on Richard, and when Wayne suggested to Junior that Dale drive for Richard, Junior was the one who actually suggested it to Richard. And because Richard Childress had never won any races, what everyone was thinking was "Is this going to work?" But I knew that Junior Johnson was feeding Richard information and helping him with his motors. I also knew that Wayne Robertson (a very, very smart guy who really understood racing) engineered the deal, so I figured it *was* going to work.

And when Earnhardt went with Childress, it was a great combination, because they totally, totally understood each other. And Richard knew that what Dale needed most was to be around at the end of a race.

We all said that if the races were a hundred miles long, Dale would never lose a race. But they were 400 miles or longer, and before he hooked up with Richard, he didn't win many because he would run his car into the ground or blow a motor. Richard knew how to stay up front but also how to conserve the race car, and he instilled in Dale the ability to do that—which is the hardest thing for a young driver to learn, particularly one with the competitive drive that Dale had.

In his own quiet, Southern way, Richard instilled in Dale all he knew. Richard knew what to say and when to say it, and he knew how to get the best out of his driver. Richard was a brilliant, brilliant coach, something most race car drivers never really get.

Richard was different from Junior Johnson. Junior could get heavy-handed at times with his driver. Junior would say, "Boy, are you driving the car, or are you just going to sit out there and let everyone whip your butt?" Junior wouldn't hold anything back. Richard was different. He came across more subtly.

Junior would say, "Boy, you go down in that corner about three or four hundred more feet, and you'll get around the racetrack a whole lot faster, and you might win this race."

Richard would say, "You know, if you went down there and hit the second mark where the Coca-Cola billboard is, you might pick up a little speed." They both said basically the same thing. Richard just did it in a subtler, kinder way.

Usually when you've got a car owner/driver relationship like Richard and Dale did, it can sour because the car owner gets jealous of the driver's fame or the driver gets angry because he thinks the car owner is making too much money. Dale and Richard never had that problem. And during the years Dale drove for Richard, Junior Johnson changed drivers two or three times, and every time he did, I know that what went through his mind was how much he would have liked to have hired the driver of that No. 3 car. But Junior never would go and try to steal him away from Richard, because Junior is a very honorable person.

ONE OF THE OTHER FACTORS that seasoned Dale a great deal was Teresa Houston, who became his third wife. Teresa today is a very controversial figure, but at the time he met her, she was what he needed.

I've said this many times: I have not known too many really great race car drivers who didn't have a strong woman behind them, because if you think about it, even a prolific winner like Dale Earnhardt lost most of the time. So on Monday, the car owner is not happy with him. The boys at the shop aren't happy with him, particularly if he wrecked and the fabricators had to fix it. And when he comes home, his clothes are dirty, and he's three or four days behind everything because he's been away, and she's been left there by herself. Back then, race drivers weren't known for having servants. They may have had someone to cut the grass for them, but they wouldn't have a group of people in their employ like some do today.

One other thing that happens to a race driver: A lot of them won't admit it, and there's controversy to what I say, but the day after a race most drivers have symptoms of a mildly depressed person. That comes from the tremendous concentration that driving takes, and the fact that a driver has to focus for three and a half hours. The stick and ball guys get a break— halftime, a time-out, a change of teams on the field—but race car drivers never get a break. They cannot think of anything but what's happening at the present moment for that entire time. Their minds cannot wander to anything else.

And for all but one of them, they will have lost the race the day before. A couple might have had what they call a "good finish," second or third, but they still didn't win, and that's the object—to win every race. So the next day is a letdown, and who's around to pick them up?

Teresa had the ability to pick Dale up when he was down, and she organized him in a way no one else had ever been able to do. For instance, Dale never knew how to dress. He was very conscious of that. She solved that problem. She took him down to Charlotte to a guy who knew how to dress people, and had clothes made for him. Now when he needed to be in Brooks Brothers suits he could be. When he needed Wranglers, he had that.

Teresa had an inborn sense of class. She just picked it up from observation. In the South, a lot of people who don't have the opportunity to go to college pick up a lot of this stuff through the movies and television. She helped him become much more comfortable in social settings where he had typically been very uncomfortable. He began to come out of his shell, and as he matured, he began to relate to people a lot better. Dale's confidence in himself grew, and as it grew, he became a better person.

NOW SOME PEOPLE, when their confidence grows, they become obnoxious and arrogant. That didn't happen to Dale, and Teresa's influence helped there, but I think it was also because there isn't an arrogant bone in Richard Childress' body. Dale was looking to Richard for guidance as well, and Richard is just wonderful with people. Richard can go into any social setting. He led the way for a lot of guys. He was the first racer to go to the SEMA show. SEMA is the Special Equipment Manufacturer's Association—all the people who make and sell performance equipment for cars and trucks. The SEMA show is one of the biggest tradeshows in the world today. By going there, Richard picked up a lot of sponsors other guys couldn't get.

Over the years, Richard and Dale used to have a ritual, one that took place two or three nights a week. Richard had a great love for wine, and, consequently, Dale developed a love of wine. So when Dale and Teresa had dinner, they'd always have a bottle of wine. Richard and his wife, Judy, would be doing the same thing fifty miles away. Richard would wait until he knew Dale had finished dinner, about eight thirty, and then he'd call him on the phone. They'd sit there drinking wine and talking on the phone about what they needed to do to make the race car better. This went on and on through six championships and is one reason Dale Earnhardt's death hit Richard Childress so hard. No one except Judy knows just how tough that was.

Dale could have died in a crash at Talladega in 1996. Talladega is a place where you are on edge all the time. You don't know what's going to happen, and all of a sudden there was a big crash right in front of the pits. Ernie Irvan lost control of his car, and he collided with Dale, and the No. 3 car started flipping and flipping. This was not that many years after the terrible wreck Bobby Allison had down there that could have shut us all down forever had his car gotten up into the grandstand.

Dale ended up perpendicular to the track, upside down. We had always ragged him about his seat. He had the worst seat in racing. He would lean over to the left—like he was driving a cab the last hour on a Friday afternoon in New York City—trying to feel the beads in the back of the seat. It was the worst way you could sit in a race car. Dale told me when his car stopped, he looked out the corner of the windshield, and he saw a car coming straight at him. He said, "I thought then that this might be it." These accidents happen so fast. When the car hit his roof and windshield, it was apparent to everybody in the garage area that this was possibly a lethal blow because Dale's car was hit right square into the top. I didn't think anyone could take a hit in the top of the car and survive. The week before I had even talked to Gary Nelson, who was running NASCAR's competition, about this. He said, "I don't think it's possible either."

Looking back on it, the fact that Dale's seat was positioned like it was no doubt saved his life. After the impact, Dale's car hit the wall and finally came to a stop. Dale told me, "I was determined to get out of the car. I was hurting bad, and I was also in shock." He had a broken sternum—which outside your femur is the toughest bone in your body—and the fact he could stand up and walk to the ambulance was one of the great feats in the history of any kind of sport. And, of course, the fans went crazy when they saw him emerge from that car. They didn't think it possible. But he was hurt a lot worse than people realized. Despite his injuries, Dale went up to Indianapolis the next week, which was pretty incredible, and he started the race, only to exit after the first caution to allow Mike Skinner to take over. Then a couple weeks later he went to Watkins Glen, and he won the pole, led most of the race, and should have won, but he tired and finished sixth. I went to visit him in his motor home, but Teresa said, "He's so beat up. He's sleeping."

I said, "Don't bother him. Don't wake him up. I don't want to do that." I knew how bad he was hurting.

THE ACCIDENT AT TALLADEGA took steam out of Dale, and started a decline in his fortunes that lasted a couple of years. A lot of people thought he was washed up. Finally, we saw the man was human after all. He didn't win a race in all of 1997.

As we know, he did come back. I remember going out to Sears Point, which can be terribly hot, and this was one of those days when it was a hundred degrees. It was a Saturday afternoon. Nothing was going on there, and everyone was working on their cars out in the open. This was before the garage area was covered. Dale's car was sitting in the hot California sun up on jacks, and he was in the car sweating like a hog working on his seat. Drivers didn't normally work on their cars anymore, but Dale didn't like anybody screwing with his seat. He wanted to get it right. I handed him a tool, and while he was working, he and I talked. I knew he was feeling bad. I knew his lack of success was really getting to him mentally.

He said, "Humpy, I'm coming back. Everybody thinks it's over for me. It's not. I'm going to make it back." I felt then that he might do it even though he was in his forties, and racers don't usually return to what they had been at that age. Harry Gant had run well for a while at that age, but generally by then life as a competitive driver is over.

I just kept thinking to myself, *Tell him to quit.* He had already made the Hall of Fame. He had won seven racing championships. He was the Intimidator. He had more money than he could ever spend. He had a wife and a family and time to be with them. He had already done all the things he wanted to do. I wanted to tell him, "Get out." But I didn't, and I have always felt a little guilty about that. Would he have listened to me? Hell, no. So he did come back, and after twenty years of trying, he finally won the Daytona 500 in 1998. But what really got him back, in my opinion, was that his son, Dale Jr., was coming along and was being successful.

I remember Dale calling me one day. He said, "I want to start Dale Jr. off. He needs to get started in something right, so I'm going to buy a Legends car for him." Legends cars were cut-down versions of stock cars with motorcycle engines in them that I had created. They raced at the Charlotte Motor

Speedway. I made a deal to sell him a car, and I remember going down to the garage area for a Tuesday night race, and Dale and Neil Bonnett were trying to work on the carburetors of that car. Because it had a motorcycle engine, they didn't have a clue as to what they were doing. I got someone who knew about those engines, and they looked pretty relieved.

Dale Jr. started racing well, and winning some races. Dale moved him from Legends into Late Models, and then he got him into the Busch series, and it was hard to look good in the Busch series. But Junior won some races, and I could tell Dale was mentally coming back.

One day Dale called me and he said, "I'm going to build a shop." He said he was going to get the man who had designed Bobby Allison's shop. And when Dale built it, it was the race shop of race shops. When I saw that thing going up between Mooresville and Kannapolis, out in the middle of nowhere, I couldn't believe it. For racers, it *was* the Taj Mahal.

When I wanted to talk to Dale, I would go over to the little house he had where he kept all his trophies and souvenirs. He'd get up at five o'clock in the morning or some awful hour, and he'd eat breakfast, and then he'd go over to this little house and sign autographs. He'd be sitting at a desk, and someone would be feeding him the souvenirs to sign. He'd be signing and talking to you, and he wouldn't even be looking at the items. He'd sign every one, one after the other for three hours.

I said, "Dale, this thing you're building does not look like a race shop. It looks more like the CIA headquarters at Langley. You are going to do more for Alcoholics Anonymous than anybody since the two guys who started it."

Dale laughed. He said, "What are you talking about, Alcoholics Anonymous?"

I said, "Some drunk in Mooresville on a Saturday night is going to ride out here on this highway, and he'll go past these old dairy farms and see all these cows and come upon this place, and he won't believe what he is seeing, and he'll never have another drink again." Because his shop was so out of place and still is. It's so weird to see it out in the middle of nowhere. It's just crazy. But he got it done, and he was real proud of it. After it was finished, I went over and blessed it.

CHAPTER 19

Rick Hendrick
Changes the Game

I KNEW OF RICK HENDRICK before I ever met him. He came from southern Virginia. He and his father, a drag racer, were very close, and so Rick had started out as a drag racer. He also raced big boats. He started selling cars up in Raleigh back in the days when automobile companies were looking for young guys to come in and sell a lot of cars. Rick got into Chevy's dealer development program, and he ended up with a dealership in Bennettsville, South Carolina. That's where he was when I first heard about his boat racing.

City Chevrolet in Charlotte for years had been one of the premier Chevy dealers in the state of North Carolina, and when it came up for sale Rick bought it. I remember the shockwaves that went through the business community that a guy as young as he was—Rick was about twenty-eight—and someone not from Charlotte was buying it. Charlotte was a traditional, conservative Southern town where most of the businesses were owned by Charlotteans. And here was a young guy from Virginia coming in and buying one of the most successful franchises around Charlotte.

I became aware Rick had moved to Lake Norman because one day I noticed a cigar boat running very fast on the lake, and when I asked who owned it, I was told it was Rick's. We ran into each other somewhere, and he said, "I'd like to talk to you about NASCAR. I'd like to get into it."

That was in 1983, a time when single-car owners without a whole lot of money could still get into racing. That's not possible today. Rick came to my office, and little did I know that sitting across from me was one of the most interesting, engaging, complex characters I would ever get involved with. I was embarking on a friendship with an extraordinarily bright and intelligent person and also one of the most caring and giving people I've ever known.

Rick wanted some information from me. I have learned that Rick is very good at asking people's opinions on purpose. He wasn't just looking to get my opinion so I could feel good. He actually wanted my opinion. I told him the pitfalls of getting involved in racing. I talked about getting in bed with the wrong driver or the wrong employees. We talked about playing the NASCAR game. Usually I'm not so frank with strangers, but I just felt so good around him I figured I'd tell him everything I possibly could.

"You don't jump in with both feet flying," I said. "You don't tell NASCAR what to do. You have to come along slowly and gain everyone's confidence. It takes time for people to even talk to a rank stranger. People have to get to know you, and you have to prove yourself. There are no open arms in NASCAR." My guess is he realized this anyway.

We talked about drivers and crew chiefs and about finding a place to operate.

Rick started his race team, and he did everything just right. He is the most forceful unforceful person I know. He never acts aggressively. He never acts like he wants it all, needs it all, and he's going to get it no matter what. He is kind to a tee, just a person you enjoy being around.

For me this was really refreshing, because I had been around so many people who were the other way, who felt they had to steamroll you to get their way. Rick was so good-natured, I started to ask myself, *How in the world is he going to get results*? Little did I know how brilliant his approach would be—putting together the right chemistry to have the most phenomenal operation in the history of NASCAR.

Rick's first driver was Geoff Bodine, who was from Chemung, New York. Geoff's father had run a racetrack up there. Geoff was a complete Yankee. He had a snarly attitude. A lot of people didn't like him, but he was a hell of a race driver. He had had a phenomenal record in the Modified division. When Rick signed him, I didn't think Geoff would be successful, because I thought it was too hard to make the jump from the wide tires of the Modified division to the narrower tires of Winston Cup where the cars drove on loose, slick racetracks. I was wrong, of course. Geoff would go on to win eighteen races in a stellar career. And when Geoff signed with Hendrick, he became General Grant of the Union army fighting Dale Earnhardt, a private in the Confederate States of America. It became the North against the South.

Geoff became controversial while driving for Rick during the third running of the Winston in 1987 when he, Bill Elliott, and Dale Earnhardt got together. Elliott was put out of the race, and Earnhardt went on to win.

ONE OF RICK'S MOST IMPORTANT HIRES was crew chief Harry Hyde. No one had been able to handle Harry, who was cantankerous and had all the diplomacy of 80-grit sandpaper. (That's a grinding sandpaper.) Harry was really tough on drivers. He was a tobacco-chewing guy, a World War II veteran who came out of Kentucky. His brother was police chief of Louisville. Harry didn't put up with anything or anyone.

Before Harry went to work for Rick, Harry and I didn't get along. He had had a huge run-in with J. D. Stacy, which led to all kinds of allegations. J. D. owned a coal mine, and Harry had once worked in the mines. Stacy was from West Virginia, and Harry was from Kentucky, and the two weren't but a sixteenth of an inch from being the Hatfields and the McCoys. The final end was that they parted ways, but Harry, the guy in the fight who didn't have any money, ended up losing most of what he had. Stacy even had the garage padlocked so Harry couldn't get to his tools.

What saved him was that Harry was a close friend of Nord Krauskopf, who owned K&K Insurance, one of the three major companies that insured racetracks. Harry had been Nord's crew chief when Bobby Isaac won the championship in 1970, and when Nord was dying, he called Harry and several other friends to his death bed and bequeathed them each a substantial amount of money.

During the row with Stacy, I defended Harry in the press, and that's how Harry and I got to be friends. I didn't believe what Stacy was saying about Harry. I knew he was honest, and I defended him. One day he walked up to me and told me how much he appreciated my support. He was very gracious.

Of course, that didn't stop Harry from being Harry. After Rick came into racing, he and Harry had set up shop in a building owned by the Speedway. They were renting it from the Speedway and when their lease was up, the Speedway needed it back and asked Rick and Harry to move. Harry had put a wall up inside without asking my permission, typical of Harry. I said something to Harry about the wall that ticked him off. He didn't like having to leave anyway, so he took a front-end loader and knocked the wall down.

I confronted him on the phone.

He said, "I ain't taking crap from you."

"Well, I'm not taking it from you either," I said. "You're off base, and I ought to . . . . "

We decided we'd meet out on Highway 29 and duke it out. That's the way people up in the mountains like to fight, by the side of the road. But something happened, I don't remember what, and the Duel of Highway 29 never did happen.

Harry and I resumed our friendship, and then one day I got a call from him. "I gotta see ya," he said. The Speedway had owned a house that we had been using as our ticket office, and we were going to tear it down. There was some controversy over this because George Washington supposedly had eaten dinner in the house once. He didn't sleep in it. He slept in every other house in the South. The historical society ruled it really had no historical interest and that we could demolish it, and so a few days before it was to come down Harry said to me, "I want to be there when you tear the house down. There is gold buried underneath there."

I asked him how he knew that. "I've done some research," he said.

The demolition crew moved in and while they ripped it down, Harry sat on a millstone watching and waiting. After the debris was cleared, Harry took a shovel, and he dug for hours. He found nothing and was extremely disappointed.

At the time Rick was thinking about hiring Harry, he and his nephew, Tommy Turner, were building race cars for whoever hired them. Harry had bought a piece of property about a mile away just off Highway 29. He put up a mobile home and a garage, and he moved in. That led to Rick Hendrick buying land from Harry and locating where he did. A lot of people don't know that.

When Rick asked me about Harry, I said, "I think Harry will get the most out of a driver. He's going to make sure things are done right." I'm sure Rick asked quite a few others for their opinions, and then he hired Harry.

With Harry, Rick began to have success. He hired Tim Richmond to drive for him, and in 1986 Tim won seven races and came in second four times.

§

Tim Richmond was the new James Dean. He looked like him. He acted like him. He was handsome and debonair, and the girls loved him. He was completely reckless, a total daredevil in everything he did. Tim was the only son of a wealthy Ohio industrialist. He went to prep school. In short, Tim did none of the things a stock car driver did in those days did. He even went to college for a while. He was quite an athlete—a football player and a track man.

Tim's father didn't bring him up on road courses. Rather, he started him out on oval courses in Ohio running their weird kind of race car called a Super Modified, one of the most powerful oval race cars ever built. It was very lightweight and had loads of horsepower. And right from the start, everyone knew Tim Richmond had it. Guys who were there say that very few people who ever got behind the wheel of a car were as good as he was. We have a standing joke that Curtis Turner must have been floating around Ohio somewhere back in the 1960s because Curtis and Tim drove so much alike it was incredible.

I didn't know him when he was running Sandusky and made the jump to Sprint cars where he was so prolific on the track. People who saw him said he was Curtis Turner, A. J. Foyt, Mario Andretti, and Parnelli Jones all wadded into one. He was a rebel, a James Dean rebel.

He showed up at the Indianapolis Speedway, and he astonished everyone his first year by finishing high. He was the IndyCar rookie of the year. His car conked out on the last lap, and he jumped on top of Johnny Rutherford's car and rode around the track sitting on top of the car, and of course the photographers ate it up. I can remember seeing four different angles of it.

The next thing I knew, people kept telling me, "You gotta meet Tim Richmond. He's just what stock car racing needs." We had Harry Gant, Cale Yarborough, and Darrell Waltrip, but none of those guys were going to play Hollywood.

Meeting him turned out to be one of the best and the worst decisions of my life.

I first met him when he came to Charlotte looking for a ride. I knew right away Tim was just what NASCAR needed, though I felt like someone had thrown me a K-bar knife, and both sides were razor sharp. He was something else. He dressed Mod—like no one in stock car racing had ever seen. He looked like he had just come from a store on Rodeo Drive. He reminded me of Jackie Stewart on steroids.

We talked and talked. I explained to him how different NASCAR was from Indy racing and said these cars weren't easy to drive. He acted like he was paying attention but he probably wasn't. It wasn't long before he got a ride, and right off the bat he was something else.

Tim Richmond was really the first Indy driver to come in from the outside and challenge the "boys." He had left Indianapolis to come to stock car racing full tilt, and that had not been done before. He got in the cars and he took off. He impressed everyone from his first ride.

He began racing for Raymond Beadle, a drag racer from Texas who also liked to have a good time. Tim drove like the dickens. In fact, he drove exactly like Dale Earnhardt—and those were two of the most opposite people in NASCAR at the time. Sooner or later you knew those two would be getting into it.

I started working with Tim in every way possible. I could tell, number one, that he was spoiled rotten. Every time he messed up, his mother came to the rescue. His mother really loved him dearly, but she kept him from god knows what. And although his father, Al, was a tough-looking guy, he wasn't tough on Tim.

That needed to be corrected. I knew if I didn't straighten him out, he was headed for a big oak tree. Like James Dean, I had the feeling that something was going to happen to this guy. And it was not going to be good. Because he was so reckless in the way he acted, the way he drove a car, and the way he drove a motorboat.

One time we had a party at my lake house with just the guys. The only non-racer I invited was a tough-guy game warden from the state of North Carolina who I liked. I noticed during the party that Tim was sitting out at the entrance to my cove in his boat with another guy. I couldn't figure out why he wasn't coming back to my party. I sent my brother-in-law, Joe Williams—who in 1943 had been blown out of a Liberator and ended up in a POW camp for several years—to go and get him. When Tim returned, he was three sheets to the wind, to put it mildly. I don't know how he got that way. I was never any good at mixology.

As soon as Tim saw the game warden, he went ballistic and acted like he was going to attack him. Tim couldn't lick a postage stamp so I'm quite certain the game warden would have beaten him to a bloody pulp. Joe grabbed Tim, and I led him back to the boat. We sat him down, and I proceeded to chew his butt out. Fortunately, the game warden showed tremendous patience and restraint.

"That son of a bitch," said Tim. "He pulled me over." Tim owned a cigarette boat. Many a night after a race I could hear Tim crank that thing up. He didn't care what time of night it was. He'd crank it up and take it out into the main channel. It sounded like something out of the bowels of hell. I thought I was at the Bonneville Salt Flats again. Over and over I told him not to take it out on Lake Norman. I told him, "That boat is for Miami Beach, not Lake Norman." Tim said, "I was just going down the lake minding my own business and he pulled me over." I asked him, "How fast were you going?"

"About a hundred."

"He should have given you eight tickets," I said. He started letting me have it, and I just blistered him. He left in a huff.

Two days later he called me. He wanted to meet. I told him to come over to the Speedway where we had a father-son-type talk. Now he was playing the role of the penitent. I said, "Tim, you can't act like that. You have to get rid of that damn boat." Of course, he didn't get rid of the boat. Tim only did what Tim wanted to do.

About three weeks later, on a Saturday morning, he called me in a panic. He said, "Humpy, you have to come over here. My boat is ruined." I went over there, and as soon as I got there, I knew what had happened. He had the boat on a lift, and someone had snuck over there and poured sulfuric acid into the hatch. It melted the fiberglass and got down into the manifold and heads. Tim's boat was pretty much ruined, and he was livid.

"Tim, I hate to tell you this, but I knew this was going to happen," I said. "They are just not going to put up with this bullshit." Tim got really mad.

Tim wasn't intimidating as far as banging people around, but he could just drive the heck out of a loose race car. That's what really makes them go fast. Dale Earnhardt was never particularly good at qualifying, and at Charlotte one time he went out first and ran fairly well, and Tim said, "I'm going to beat that by a half second." He went out, and he came off that fourth turn, and I've never seen a car as loose as his coming off that turn. His right rear quarter panel just barely touched the outside wall. Anyone else would have wrecked big time, but he didn't. It was a fabulous run, and with that run he got the pole.

That was the year I put up a new Thunderbird as the prize for the pole sitter. It had 5,000 miles on it, and Tim raised holy hell. He said, "This isn't no damn new car. It's a used car." Which it was, but I never said it had zero miles on it. He started raising hell and talking about me, and when he did that I had enough. I went over to the garage area, and I said to him, "What the hell are you doing talking about my damn car?" He said, "It's a blankety-blank used car." I didn't like the way he said it, so I grabbed him by the collar and shoved him against the back of the rig. Along came Eddie Thrap and his other crew guys. They were running to protect their driver. I said, "He doesn't need any protection. He can handle himself." They were trying to grab my arms, and we had this brouhaha. I started to think, *What the hell am I doing here? I'm the promoter of this race, and I'm grappling with some damn driver over a friggin' car?* I decided that valor was the better part of discretion so I threw him back against the truck and let him go. He said, "I want a new car." I said, "Fuck you. You ain't getting a new car." It really ticked me off that he would have that kind of attitude after all the work I had done with him. I thought, *Okay, that's just Tim.*

The next day Bill Gazaway, who was running NASCAR, decided that Tim and I needed to meet. We met in his trailer, and of course Bill was well aware of my temper and Tim's tantrums. He said, "You guys are too good of friends to do this," and he walked out of the room. I said, "He's right. We shouldn't be barking over a stupid car." Tim said, "You're right," and we made up, and that ended it.

At that point Tim decided that he needed to learn how to box. I said, "Okay, I'll teach you." I could tell right away that even if he had had Angelo Dundee teaching him, he was not going to learn how to box. He didn't have the temperament. But he kept wanting to. We had been working for about two weeks, and we were getting nowhere. My son, Trip, was a senior in high school, and a real good athlete, so I said to Tim, "I can't box you. I want you to box Trip." Trip hit him right in the nose and knocked him cold as a cucumber.

"Tim," I said, "you really need to be doing something else." He finally agreed.

BY THIS TIME TIM HAD DONE SO WELL in racing that he was being acclaimed as the next great race driver. The media loved him because he had that gleam in his eye. The women loved him. There were rumors floating around about some unsavory habits off the track—staying up all night, partying with prostitutes. At the same time Rick Hendrick, who had a wonderful eye for talent, started talking to me about Tim. Sooner or later he said, "It would be great if we could get Tim and Harry Hyde together."

I said, "Rick, if you could pull that off, we'll put an eighty-foot bronze statue of you on Highway 29, because that will never work."

Harry Hyde, who was from Kentucky, was the most cantankerous human being who ever has been in the garage area. On his best day Harry was in a terrible mood. He put up with nothing from race drivers. Absolutely zero. He would have been better off if he had remote control equipment and a transmitter and a receiver rather than a race car driver. And he was totally old school. He wore stiff collars and high-topped brogans. If you had gone to Central Casting and said, "Give me a man from Kentucky in 1918," Harry would have showed up. He still used Brylcreem.

Rick, being much smarter than me and everyone else, put that deal together to everybody's astonishment. No one in the industry believed they could work together. But they did. Harry gave Tim a whole lot more room than I thought he would. All of a sudden under Harry Tim blossomed and began to finish races, began to stop knocking walls down, and started to lead races.

Around this time, Tim got into it at Daytona with David Pearson, who was long in the tooth by then. It happened after the race when Tim got too close to David and bumped him. I heard people talking about what happened. David, being from a mill village, wasn't going to take crap off anybody, especially a "long-haired Yankee," as he would say. Tim walked up to him and said something nasty and called him an old man. The next thing you know, Tim was laying flat on his back in the garage area. David dusted off his hands and walked away. Tim learned not to mess with David Pearson any more.

Tim continued driving great, and by this time he was driving for Folger's coffee for Rick Hendrick. He was winning races, but the dark rumors kept circulating. Tim called me one day and said, "I'm so damn tired of the Charlotte airport. You have to do something about those people out there."

I said, "What's wrong?" He said, "Every time I go out there, I get hassled. Damn cops hassle me. Everybody hassles me. I can't get through the gate."

I said, "Tim, you've been going to Miami, haven't you?" "Yes." I said, "I want you to think about this for a minute. You walk in the airport. You're on a flight from Miami; you have gold chains around your neck. You've got a gold watch on, a gold bracelet. You're wearing a silk shirt. You got tight blue jeans. You got a big old Rolex. It's the height of drug traffic. What the heck do you think they're going to do?"

He said, "What do you suggest?"

I said, "Number one, throw all that gold away. Dress normally. Wear a

T-shirt, and you won't get hassled."

"They should know who I am," he said.

"Get a haircut," I said. But he didn't want to hear any of that. Looking back on it, he didn't want to hear much of anything I had to say about his behavior. But when he'd get in trouble, he'd always come around.

As good as he was doing, I could tell something wasn't right. I went to the banquet in New York in 1986 and saw him at a reception. He looked absolutely awful. Two weeks before that he looked terrible. He told me he had the flu. I said, "You have to go to the doctor." I got him an appointment with a doctor in Charlotte. He went to my doctor, and then he absolutely disappeared off the face of the earth. No one knew where he was. No one heard from him, so I began to worry. I called his mother, and she wasn't saying anything. I began to suspect the worst. I suspected he had AIDS.

He wasn't gay, but he had described his symptoms to me so extensively, and I was a guy who read everything medical I could read. I'm a nut about that. His symptoms shouted AIDS. This was when it was rampant. I thought, *How could he have AIDS?* He was dating a girl who used to work for me—a gorgeous girl by the name of LaGina Lookabill. She had been in and out of Little Theater in Charlotte and had left for Hollywood where she was a young actress. She flew back and forth to Charlotte, because she knew a lot of people in racing and a lot of people knew her.

Rick didn't know anything and neither did Harry Hyde. His mother wouldn't tell me anything. But they thought he had pneumonia—pneumocystis pneumonia—that's what you get when you get AIDS. He was from Ashland, Ohio, and I figured that if he was getting medical help it would be at the Cleveland Clinic. I called there and asked for Tim, and after they gave me the runaround, I figured he was there. I was flabbergasted. I came very close to flying up there.

Carolyn Rudd (Ricky Rudd's sister) who once worked for me, had her own business, and Folger's was one of her accounts. She had married D. K. Ulrich, a former race driver. I called her and asked her if she knew anything about Tim. Carolyn is smart as a whip, and she said she was beginning to suspect the same thing I did. But she didn't know either.

I told her, "I can't find him. I keep calling Rick and Harry. A lot of people are looking for him, and nobody can find him. Nobody. This is a mystery. We know he's sick and has pneumonia."

Then one day out of the blue Tim called me. He said he was in Ohio and said he felt okay, but I could tell he wasn't.

"What's wrong with you?" I asked. He repeated that he was okay.

He then called Rick Hendrick and told him the illness was going to keep him from racing at Daytona. He didn't run for several months, and then in May he called me again. He said he wanted to come down and watch the World 600 at Charlotte with me.

Around seven o'clock the morning of the race he showed up at my house, and we rode to the track together. He didn't look good, but he was okay. He acted very nicely. I got him a pass so he could go wherever he wanted at the track. I told him if he got tired, he should come up to my office. After the race he said he was going to hang around the Speedway Club.

"How are you going to get home?" I asked. He said he'd find a way. I had left the keys to Tim's truck in the ignition at my home. When I got up the next morning, Tim and the truck were gone.

I didn't hear from him again. By this time rumors were really flying around, especially the one that he had AIDS. Then one day he called Rick and told him he was ready to go racing again.

"I want to go to Darlington and test," he said. He ran like he had never been out of the race car. And he won the race, which was incredible.

I needed to ask him point-blank what was going on with him because I was baffled by how well he was running. And he ran again and won another race. But Watkins Glen wasn't a pretty scene. Before the race he fell asleep. The other drivers were very concerned about him. And just like before, Tim disappeared again. Nobody knew where he went.

I found out he was in Miami. But I couldn't locate him. I called a buddy of his in Miami, and he didn't know where Tim was. When the Daytona 500 came up, Tim decided he wanted to run it. Because AIDS had become so rampant, NASCAR was concerned about what would happen to the rescue workers if he got hurt and was bleeding. Bill France Jr. told Les Richter that Tim couldn't run unless he took a blood test.

Tim and I were staying at the Hilton on Daytona Beach. Bill France Jr. invited Pat and me to dinner Saturday night with him and Les Richter. The whole conversation centered on Tim Richmond. Tim wouldn't submit to a blood test, and he threatened to take NASCAR to court if he couldn't run the race.

I told the others that I had talked to Tim a couple of times but that Tim wasn't talking. Then Sunday night, after the Busch Clash, Tim called me.

He said he needed to talk to me. I went up to his room. Visiting him were the weirdest bunch of people I had ever seen in my whole life, including his girlfriend and a far-out motorcycle guy.

He said, "I'm going to race. I'm going to do whatever it takes to get this done. I'm going to have a press conference."

"Are you going to take the blood test?" I asked.

"No," he said. "I'll take one only if everyone else takes one."

He held his press conference. I attended. He announced he would either race or go to court. There was a showdown. NASCAR replied by saying he couldn't race without a blood test.

Then as fast as he had arrived, he left, and that was the last I ever saw of him. Not long afterward I got a call from Carolyn Rudd who told me that one of the girls Tim had been dating had died of AIDS.

He called me on the phone one time from Miami. When I asked him how he was, he was evasive. A month later, I received a call he had died.

It was a tragic story that didn't end there. A few months later I got a call that LaGina Lookabill was coming out with a story on the front page of the *Charlotte Observer* that said Tim had infected her with HIV. It had happened in New York, and she was telling her story because she wanted everyone to know.

60 Minutes picked it up, and LaGina called me and asked if I would be on the show. People were very reluctant to talk about it, mostly because at the time it was regarded as a strictly homosexual disease. But LaGina had recently gotten married to Danny Green, an actor I knew, and out of respect for her, I went on the show. And that was the end of the chapter on Tim Richmond.

Looking back, I often thought of what might have been had Tim not contracted AIDS. He would have lasted up until the early 1990s when racers started getting killed again, starting with Kenny Irwin and Adam Petty and ending up with Dale Earnhardt himself. Could he have made it that long? I don't know. Frankly, I don't think Tim would have raced that long. What he really wanted to do was try Hollywood. He had been out there, and he was enough of a ham and an actor that I believe he could have pulled it off. But we'll never know.

Chapter 20

Days of Thunder

I ALWAYS USED TO LET Rick Hendrick use the Charlotte track for what he called "play days." He'd bring friends in, usually sponsors of people he knew well, and he'd let them drive his cars. It was dangerous, but he did it anyway. I let him do it and waived all expenses, because anything I could do for him, I did. The reason: Anytime I wanted something from him, he never refused me. If I needed an engine for a young driver, or whatever—didn't matter—he always came through.

Rick would have five of these play dates a year, and they would be a couple days each. One time Keith Crane, who owned *Auto Week, Advertising Age*, and other magazines, called me and asked if his seventy-five-year-old mother could ride in a race car around the track. Rick said she could come to his next play date, and we got Tim Richmond to drive her around. Tim was being nice that day, and he drove her at around 150. She said she wanted to go faster, and he clicked off a lap at about 175 and fishtailed on purpose, but it didn't bother her at all. After that was over, I was walking down through the garage area where Rick's cars were, and I saw a familiar face behind the wheel of one of the cars. It was Tom Cruise. I could see his belts weren't on tightly enough, and I told him so.

Tom went out and ran, and before the day was over he had cut a lap at about 160, which wasn't bad for a guy who wasn't a race driver. Then he began coming down to the track on a regular basis.

Rick had called and asked for a half day. This wasn't easy to schedule, because the Speedway rented out a lot, but I managed to find a time for him. Tom drove, and finally I asked him what he was doing. I had shown him how to get to my office through a back stairs, and he came to see me. He was wearing an old T-shirt, blue jeans, sneakers, a hat, and sunglasses. None of the girls in my office recognized him.

"I'm seriously thinking about doing a racing movie," he said. He had done *Top Gun*, a huge box office hit. He said, "I don't like to do a movie unless I really know about the subject, and I really want to learn what racing is all about." He added, "Besides, I have really gotten to like Rick Hendrick a lot." Cruise said the next time he came he was going to bring the writer of the movie with him. He asked if I would read the script. Yakety Yak.

I made a couple of suggestions. They didn't know who was going to play the female lead, but the character was supposed to be a neurosurgeon. I said, "A neurosurgeon studies so long she would be a middle-aged woman before she got out of medical school. Why not make her a nurse? As for the romantic entanglement, what difference does it make?"

Tom said he thought they were pretty good ideas.

It was through *Days of Thunder* that I learned how movie-making worked. The original script was pretty good, but by the time they started shooting producer Robert Towne put in his two cents along with director Tony Scott (two Brits), and all of a sudden Nicole Kidman is the leading lady, and she's still a neurosurgeon. In the movie Tom crashes his car in the middle of the Daytona 500 and still wins the race. Before it was over, what would have been a wonderful movie wasn't. It was saved only by the performance of Robert Duvall, a brilliant actor, who kept the picture from being one of the worst ever made.

Meanwhile, during the filming of the movie Tom Cruise, this Catholic boy, was going through a divorce from his first wife. They kept that under wraps. He brought his sister to stay with him, and until the picture was done no one on the set—not one person—knew that Tom and Nicole had something going on between them.

The majority of the movie was shot at Charlotte even though it was made up to look like Daytona. I spent a lot of time with Tom during the filming, and I could tell Tom was mailing it in. I had been told that during *Top Gun* he would often yell, "Cut," and he'd make a suggestion to improve the film, but during *Days of Thunder*, he just went through the motions. Had he been more involved, maybe he could have taken out his wrecking at Daytona and then winning. Again, Robert Duvall salvaged the movie, which did quite well overseas.

Rick Hendrick had played a vital part in getting the movie made in Charlotte. It was a period when Rick was having great success. The movie came out in 1990. Everyone knew it was based on the characters of Tim Richmond, Harry Hyde, and Rick Hendrick, which gave Hendrick Motorsports a great deal of prestige. The year before Darrell Waltrip had won six races driving for Rick, and so he was on top of the world. Then I got a call one day saying that Rick had contracted leukemia, which was a great shock to all of us.

When I talked to him about it, he was matter of fact, said he would try to beat it, and thought he could. He went to Seattle for a bone marrow transplant. The way he described it to me it sounded like the bowels of hell to go through. And while all this was going on, he was indicted in federal court— charged with paying off Honda executives so they would give him more cars for his dealerships.

The federal prosecutor really went after him. When you go after high-profile individuals, you make a name for yourself—like what Eliot Spitzer made a career doing. It was full-blown warfare, and Rick's name was plastered everywhere. He was indicted first in New Hampshire and then in North Carolina.

They moved the trial to Asheville, and all the while he was fighting leukemia. Ultimately he was sentenced to house arrest. He wasn't allowed to leave his house. But when he won the racing championship with Jeff Gordon in 1997 and 1998, he went to the banquet in New York anyway, which I found astonishing. He came with his wife, Linda, held his head high, maintaining his dignity and his good spirits as best he could. Underneath I could tell he was seething about the prosecution. But he was there, showing up despite so many things going against him. It was one of the more outstanding acts of courage I have seen.

I went to visit him at his home while he was under house arrest. I couldn't believe the positive attitude he had. I realized it was that attitude that made him different from the rest of us.

What got him through wasn't the car dealerships and the money. It was the racing, the competition, beating the best. It took a while, but eventually he was pardoned by Bill Clinton. His leukemia is in remission. Recently another friend of mine, Ken Ragan (David's father), called me petrified to say he had contracted leukemia. He wanted to know who to see. I called Rick. I said, "Rick, Ken has leukemia. I really need him to get to see Dr. Lemontadi." Dr. Lemontadi is Rick's doctor. Five minutes later Rick called back and said, "Tell him to be down there at ten in the morning."

Then after you think nothing else bad could happen, I got a call from Felix Sabates telling me that Rick's plane had gone down in Martinsville. Nobody knew who was on it. Felix was supposed to be on the plane, but he had begged off because of bad weather. Rick wasn't on the flight, but his brother John, his son Ricky, his engine builder Randy Dorton, and a number of other crew members all were killed.

I went over to see Rick the next day. You could see the terrible sorrow, but he continued to display that positive attitude. And little did we know that son Ricky's girlfriend was pregnant with Rick's granddaughter. Rick found out a month later. Again, Rick bore up under terrible strain.

So many of your tremendously successful people are narcissists who have no emotion attached to anything, who have no feeling for others. Rick is the complete opposite—a caring, feeling person who has given millions of dollars to charity and to individuals without anyone finding out about it. He's given millions to people in need, but the public knows none of this. He is an extraordinary human being.

Rick Hendrick was the one who developed and perfected the two-car race team. Junior Johnson had done it first, but Rick Hendrick made it work. After Tim Richmond died, Rick signed Darrell Waltrip to be the marquee star. Darrell had the credentials, but there wasn't anything earthshattering about their time together. In 1989 Darrell won those six races, but after that he didn't do a whole lot. Ricky Rudd, Ken Schrader, and Terry Labonte also drove for Rick with only fair success.

All this time Rick was picking my brain in an attempt to sign the best young driver he could find. Looking for young talent wasn't what owners did back then. It was rare for a driver in his twenties to race in the Winston Cup series. But Rick and I used to talk about young talent a lot. "Who's the best young driver?" "Who's coming up?" For several years I told him the same thing: "Jeff Gordon. No question in my mind. That kid has got that something that's going to be incredible."

I had been following Jeff since he was a ten-year-old kid racing in California. Except for the Kart program, racing didn't have a program for pre-teen drivers. But Jeff had been part of a race training program his whole life. His stepfather, John Bickford, set up the program for him.

Bickford was from Vallejo, California. He made his living modifying vehicles for the disabled. If you had no legs, he moved all of the controls onto the dashboard. He also made vehicles that transported the disabled. Jeff's mother, Carol, is a sweet, wonderful woman of tremendous character.

John Bickford started Jeff in racing, and by the time Jeff was thirteen, he was winning about every race at the Kart level, and John was sure Jeff was ready to start racing full-blown midgets. The problem was that California would not give a thirteen-year-old boy a license so he could race. One reason was that midget racing is second in danger only to Sprint car racing. Instead of waiting, John moved his entire family to Indianapolis, Indiana, so Jeff could start running midgets at Raceway Park. When I read about that I thought John Bickford was out of his mind. I said to myself, *Giving a thirteen-year-old kid a full-blown midget race car is like giving him a .357 magnum with a hair trigger.* Years later when I said that to him, we both had a good laugh. At age thirteen Jeff Gordon started winning races against the hardened veterans. By the time Jeff was sixteen, he was turning his attention to NASCAR, which I thought amazing because just twenty years earlier NASCAR would have been the last place a top driver would have wanted to go. Indy would have been the place, and Jeff was in Indy's backyard. My, times had changed.

When Jeff came to Charlotte for the first time to meet me, I couldn't believe how small he was. Bill Davis had beaten Rick Hendrick to the draw, signing Gordon to drive in the Busch series on Saturdays.

In the meantime Rick continued to build his race team. He put up a building and stocked it with the most expensive equipment. He spent three-quarters of a million dollars alone on a machine that bored engines unlike the Wood brothers, Bud Moore, and the Pettys, who often would go to an auction and buy used equipment from failed race teams to make ends meet.

I can remember one time going to Bud's race shop in Spartanburg. It was one time when Bud actually spent some money for equipment, though he did tell me he got a good deal on it. Bud never bought anything he didn't get a deal on. That was typical of the owners like Bud back then who were brought up during the Depression. I could tell he was agitated. I said, "What's wrong?" He said, "I just bought a dyno from Japan, and it doesn't work."

While I was there, this Japanese gentleman, who looked like an agent from MCA, walked into the shop. He wore a nice black suit with a white shirt and black tie. He had a beautiful attaché case with him, but instead of papers in it he had a pair of overalls and tools. He was the salesman of the dyno and also the mechanic, and he had flown from Jacksonville, Florida, to Spartanburg to fix it. Two hours later it was fixed. I knew then that the American economy would soon be in trouble. No American dyno salesman would know how to fix a dyno.

So when Rick came into racing, everything changed for the mom-and-pop car owner. It became very difficult for them to compete against Rick's money and his ability to win races.

Rick also began to impress everyone with his ability to get big money from sponsors and to keep his sponsors, to whom he paid a great deal of personal attention. Another thing he did was to treat his employees remark-ably well—even those who didn't work out. There was never a "get the cops and have him removed," or "Take his toolbox and march him out the door to his car," which is what you saw owners do all the time. Such treatment made their employees hate them, because if their co-worker could be treated like that, were they going to be next?

Rick was always giving his employees second chances, something else most owners didn't do. I learned a tremendous amount about being a manager from him. He would have an employee go to alcohol or drug rehab. If someone is having a problem, and you help him, work with him and turn him around, not only do you have a friend for life, but you have an employee embedded into the concrete of your business.

He also continued to buy up dealerships, and he kept adding more and more people to his race shop.

Racing is a cauldron of gossip. I never heard anyone say one negative word about Rick. Still haven't. Not one. Oh, there are plenty of people you don't say bad things about, but they usually are off in a corner not doing anything. Rick is out beating people on the racetrack. And his competitors don't seem to resent him for doing so.

Jeff Gordon won only one Busch race running for Bill Davis, and one of the reasons for that is that the Busch cars had a nine-to-one engine ratio, far less powerful than the fifteen-to-one ratio of the Cup cars. The more compression, the more problems. The tremendous advantage of these less powerful Busch engines was that you could run an entire year on two engines, rebuilding them a few times. But though it's money-saving, it also produces a lot of parity. The engine makes it difficult for one driver to win a lot of races.

It was also clear that Gordon needed to be on a better-funded race team. Bill Davis had a perfectly acceptable race team, but Gordon had to be on a team capable of helping him win ten races a year. Jeff's stepfather knew that too, and so Jeff ended up signing with Rick Hendrick some time in 1992. No one noticed, but Jeff entered his first Winston Cup race in the last race of the season in Atlanta. It was a historic day, to put it mildly. It was Richard Petty's final race, and it was the race that would determine the racing championship in a fight among Bill Elliott, Alan Kulwicki, and Davey Allison. Allison would crash, and Elliott would win the race, but Kulwicki would win the championship.

Jeff didn't win any races driving for Hendrick in 1993, and I'll tell you why. It was one of the major reasons why NASCAR got rid of the nine-to-one compression Busch engines and made the specifications more like the Cup engines.

When you drove the nine-to-one compression engines, you could run wide open around the track. But when you got into a Cup car with an added 200 horsepower, you couldn't do that, and it took quite a while to get used to the different handling of the car. It was like going from a goat to a bull, and it took a full season to discover the difference.

But you could tell Jeff was learning. He was very consistent with his times, and he was coming along just fine. He still was very immature, which was normal. One day he and his friend Bob Lutz came to visit me for lunch at the Speedway. John and Carol had asked me to keep an eye on Jeff, who was born in 1971. He was twenty-one, just a kid.

During the conversation Jeff and Bob started talking about "our snake."

"You guys have a snake?"

"Yeah, we have a boa constrictor," said Jeff. They told me its length. Ten feet. "It's a pet. We like him," Bob said.

I asked whether it was in a cage. It wasn't. It had free run of their house.

"This is a very conservative neighborhood you are living in," I said. "Those people are not going to put up with a damn huge snake."

I gave them so much hell that they finally got rid of it.

Otherwise, Jeff was behaving himself. He had had a girlfriend back home in Indiana, but he was discovering the racing girls—not the tawdry ones—the good-looking ones. I would say to Rick, "The thing is about Jeff, a guy has to mature a certain amount before he can start winning races. He's got to be mature in the car and out of the car. I don't know how you can expect a twenty-one-year-old to have any maturity.

"You know what we have here, don't you? We have a programmed driver." That was the first time I had used the phrase. I told Rick about how his father kept putting him in faster cars as he mastered the ones he was in.

"Has he even had a childhood?" I asked Rick. "Is this going to cause problems down the road?"

It might have had it not been for his wonderful mother, as well as his stepfather, and also for a fabulous mentor in Rick Hendrick, who spent a lot of time with him. Whenever Rick flew, Jeff flew with him.

Rick also recognized the genius of car builder and crew chief Ray Evernham, and when Rick got those two together, it was that sweet spot in time. In 1996 Jeff won ten races, and then he won ten again in 1997, and he won thirteen in 1998. He won seven in 1999 and three more in 2000. All the while he challenged Dale Earnhardt for racing supremacy.

As a promoter, since Jeff's first ride at Atlanta in 1992, I looked forward to the rivalry between Jeff and Dale—the bumping and banging and the unkind words, and the headlines that would sell tickets. This rivalry seemed inevitable. I would lick my lips thinking, *This is going to be incredible—the old gunslinger and Billy the Kid—and we're going to have the Gunfight at the O. K. Corral because they are going to go after each other tooth and nail.*

It never happened. There was a hint of bad blood when Dale started calling him the Boy Wonder, and he wasn't being kind about it. In self-defense Jeff grew a mustache, but it was the most pathetic-looking mustache in the history of mustaches, and he finally shaved it off.

No bad blood was shed after that. Why? Dale Earnhardt was certainly capable of it. But Jeff Gordon was not a conflict race driver. Had he been a combat pilot, he never would have mounted a frontal attack. He'd have very carefully circled, come around, and come out of the blinding sun with guns blazing. Had he been a boxer, he would have been a Sandy Sadler who would have jabbed you to death.

I'm not saying Jeff isn't capable of a bump and run, but his brain isn't wired to do that. He wins purely by outrunning everybody. And after awhile if a guy like Dale Earnhardt taunts long enough and there's no reaction back, he stops. And the next thing I knew, someone was calling me on the phone telling me that Dale and Jeff had gone into the real estate business together! I wanted to throw up. But I couldn't so I almost crushed the phone.

The Earnhardt fans were rough on Jeff, calling him names like "pretty boy." But like Jeff, his fans rarely say anything. They just cheer like crazy after he takes the checkered flag. And little kids began liking Jeff because the kids loved the color scheme and they would buy the models of his car. Other than the Petty blue and the Earnhardt black, it's one of the best color schemes.

As a result of his youth, his good looks, and his success, Jeff Gordon has become one of the most popular drivers on the NASCAR circuit. Jeff has always been cooperative with the media, giving his time to the fans as well. A few years ago, at the height of Jeff's popularity, I was down at Atlanta in the lobby of the hotel I was staying in during the afternoon before the race. A man, woman, and their daughter—a fifteen-year-old girl in a wheelchair—apparently had been waiting for me. The father grabbed me and said, "We've come all the way from Chattanooga because my daughter supposedly has won a contest to meet Jeff Gordon. We drove all the way down here. We paid money to enter the contest, and she won, only to find out the whole thing was a scam."

It was obvious these people had no money. They had no tickets to the race. Could I do something? The Saturday afternoon before the race is absolutely the worst time for something like this. I told them I'd talk to the general manager of the Atlanta track. I went upstairs for a meeting, and when I returned, they were still sitting there. The little girl was crying.

Meanwhile, it was Happy Hour in the garage area. I had an important meeting at seven with a sponsor. If it was going to get done, it had to be done now. I said to the father, "Pick her up, and I'll see what I can do."

The father picked up his daughter, who had cerebral palsy, and put her in my car. I drove over to the garage. Gordon's race car was up on blocks. I figured they were having a team meeting in the back of their trailer.

I pulled up behind the trailer, got out, and went inside. I interrupted their team meeting. "Jeff, I hate to . . . ." I explained as briefly as I could what had happened. "Can you spare three minutes and meet this girl?"

"Absolutely," he said. How many drivers would have done that? Not during a team meeting. He got up, sat in my car, and he talked with the girl like they were best friends. He signed everything she handed to him, and I can remember as we sat there race cars went flying by on the track. After twenty minutes, he graciously said he had to go, and he went back into his trailer.

The next day I saw him at the drivers' meeting. I said, "I really appreci-ated your doing that. I hated to impose on you at a time like that."

"It helped me as much as it did her," he said. I thought to myself, *If only race fans could have seen Jeff Gordon yesterday.*

What hurt Jeff more than anything else were his marital problems. He had started dating a woman who was Miss Winston, which was a no-no. Ralph Seagraves had established a policy that Miss Winston should never be seen romantically with anyone associated with racing. Ralph wanted to keep Miss Winston neutral. One time a Miss Winston was sitting and playing cards with someone in racing, and he raked her over the coals.

After a while everyone realized that Jeff and Brooke were an item, and when the talk grew loud enough, wisely she quit.

I remember getting an invitation to the wedding. I thought someone in the House of Windsor was getting married. This wasn't Jeff's doing, believe me. He'd have printed the invitation using off-set. And it was as Scotch-Irish a wedding as you could possibly have had. It was very formal, in grand style. I don't remember anyone cracking a smile. They held it downtown at the First Baptist Church, and moved it over to the Adams Mark hotel, where they had a grand reception, and it was grand all right.

Jeff and Brooke moved to Lake Norman, near my house. They installed all kinds of security. And then came the buzz when Mr. and Mrs. Bickford were cast out, made persona non grata. John left Charlotte and went to work for Action Performance, the souvenir company. He ended up exiling himself to London. Everyone in racing loved John and Carol, and their banishment was met with a lot of gnashing of teeth. Brooke began to go everywhere with Jeff, and she was seen arm and arm with him at all times, so much that they soon became known as Ken and Barbie.

We weren't surprised that it all ended in divorce. Brooke left with many millions of dollars. But after she left, Jeff was able to reunite with his parents, and his father is now running Jeff's enterprises. His mother once again is her normal sweet self.

Jeff met his new wife in New York, and they have a child. They are living happily ever after.

As the 2009 season is about to begin, Jeff has won eighty-one races, three fewer than Darrell, and four fewer than Bobby Allison. He won six races in 2007, finishing second in the chase to Jimmie Johnson. He didn't win any last year, but I have a feeling he's not done winning, though I must say I do ask myself at times, *Why is he still racing?*

CHAPTER 21

Alan Kulwicki's
Too Short Journey

I KNEW ALAN KULWICKI probably as well as I knew any race driver. He had been running in the American Speed Association (ASA) circuit in the Midwest when he first came to see me, and I readily agreed to talk with him because I had known his father, Jerry, a mechanic and engine builder from the old USAC stock car racing days.

When we first met, I wasn't sure Alan would make it in NASCAR because he was so lacking in personality. He had Bobby Allison's pragmatism, but was totally lacking in flair. He had exactly zero personality and charisma.

We discussed this all the time. I said, "The good thing is you're smart as a whip and a hell of a race driver. But you gotta come up with a shtick, something that makes you different. You need to be the independent guy. You need to continue driving for yourself and not driving for Junior Johnson or Bud Moore or someone else.

"And you have one other strike against you: You're Polish." Now I have devastated this man. I said, "Something else you want to do. When you win a race you need to celebrate in a different manner. You need to do something no one else has ever done before, and you want it to be funny."

As I'm talking, Alan, a man with zero sense of humor, was looking at me as though I was about to tell him he was going to have to start driving nude.

I said, "When you win a race, you should drive in the opposite direction around the racetrack to the winner's circle."

"Why?" he asked. "What are you talking about?"

"Because you're Polish, and you're going the wrong way. Race fans will get a bigger charge out of that than anything they've ever seen."

Well, I must have told that to Alan twenty times, and I didn't know whether he bought it or not. I was not at Phoenix when he won, but I was absolutely overjoyed when I saw that he did exactly what I told him to do. He became famous for his Polish victory lap, and it's something drivers still do today.

One day Alan came to me and he said, "You want me to be an independent race driver. I'm going to have to build a building." I had just put in an industrial park behind the Speedway, and I told him I would sell him a lot for $80,000. He had signed Zerex antifreeze as a sponsor, so he had some money to spend. We sat and negotiated, and he said he would buy it for $75,000. We sat there, and he wouldn't budge until finally I said, "Alan, why don't you go over to your shop and get a drill."

"Why?" he asked.

"Because I want to drill into your skull and see where your brain lies because your skull is so thick you can't make a deal."

Nevertheless, he held his ground, and I sold him the lot for $75,000 because I needed the money.

He had one reservation. He said, "I think there is rock under there."

"There isn't any rock," I said. "The lot next to you doesn't have any rock. There's no reason there would be rock on yours."

Well, there is a lot of rock around the Speedway. If you remember, the discovery of rock was what caused Bruton Smith and Curtis Turner to go bankrupt and lose the Speedway.

Alan said, "If you're so sure there's no rock, then if I run into rock, will you pay to remove it?"

"That's not a very good deal," I said. But Alan wouldn't budge, and so I went ahead and signed the contract with a clause that I'd pay to have any rock removed.

Everything went great during the first day workmen dug the foundation. They went down three feet, and it was all nice, rich clay. On the second day they hit solid granite, and $80,000 later the building started to go up. So it ended up costing me $5,000 to sell Alan that building.

Alan loved Merlot, and he sent me a bottle of Merlot. He said, "I got the cheapest bottle I could find. It was $4.99, and the tax made it five-something, so we're even."

AFTER I GOT TO KNOW HIM, I was constantly trying to fix him up on dates. His problem was that he hadn't a clue as to how to get along with women. We were having dinner one night, and Alan said, "Why don't we go by Trip's house?" Trip is my son, but Alan didn't really want to see Trip. He wanted to see my daughter, Tracy, who was living there too. It was about quarter past nine at night.

I went with Trip into the living room and left Alan and Tracy to talk in the kitchen. After forty-five minutes, I told Alan, "It's late. I gotta go home." After we got in the car, I said to Alan, "How did it go?"

"She didn't talk much," he said. "I couldn't get her talking," which I found odd because Tracy is a very outgoing person. I said, "Wait a minute. What did you talk about?"

"I was talking about my car, my shop," he said.

"Alan, you don't talk to girls like that. They don't want to know about your car. Talk to her about her."

Alan tried, but he couldn't get it to work with Tracy. He got nowhere with her. The stoplight had gone up.

A couple of things about Alan—he was smart and determined, and he hated to lose. Later, Alan and I were in the garage area when this absolutely gorgeous woman, a television reporter by the name of Hanna Storm, who was working at Channel 36 in Charlotte, came up to me. She said she wanted someone new to interview. I suggested she interview Alan.

When I introduced them, I could see immediately that Alan was taken with her.

After the interview Alan called me. He wanted to know how he could get a hold of Hanna. I said, "Hell, she won't date you. She's not your type."

Alan said, "I asked her, and she said she isn't married and isn't going with anyone."

"She's certainly not going to go out with you," I said.

Alan kept insisting she would, until finally I said to him, "Okay, I will bet you one hundred dollars that by the morning of the Rockingham race you haven't had a date with her."

The Rockingham race was about a month away.

"You got it," he said.

It was a bet I intended to win, and so I called Hanna, who later was the lead on the CBS "Early Morning Show," and I said, "Dear, you've only been in Charlotte about six months. You're the same age as my daughter, and some of these race drivers are people you don't want to fool with. And one of them definitely is Alan Kulwicki."

"What's wrong with him?" she wanted to know.

"Oh my God, he's fast and furious," I said. "You just don't want anything to do with him."

A couple weeks went by, and I asked Alan how he and Hanna were getting along.

"Not too good," he said.

I couldn't wait for the Rockingham race because we had arranged for the winner to pay the loser at the drivers' introduction. I said, "In cash. I don't want a check. I want cash." I wanted to embarrass him in front of all the other race drivers.

The day of the Rockingham race I went over to Alan's truck. Paul Andrews was his crew chief, and I asked Paul where Alan was. Paul said he was around somewhere, but he hadn't seen him.

He and Rusty Wallace were pals, so I went over to Rusty's trailer. Rusty said he hadn't seen him either. I was getting the runaround by his friends. I had no choice but to wait for the drivers' introduction to see him because if a driver misses that, he has to go to the back of the field.

I looked everywhere. No Alan. And then with five minutes to go before the drivers' introductions, in walked Alan—with Hanna.

I was so sure I was going to win the bet that I didn't have any money on me. Alan walked up to me, and in front of all the other drivers, who apparently were in on it, he said, "I'd like my hundred dollars please."

"Wait a minute," I said, "just because you're with her doesn't mean you've dated her."

Hanna looked at me and said, "It certainly does. We went out last night, and not only last night, but we went out Wednesday night too." Alan beamed.

I wasn't going to wait four and a half hours for the race to end to pay up, so I borrowed a hundred dollars from a guy named Red Robinson (who billed himself as The World's Number One Race Fan), and I paid Alan off right then and there in front of everyone.

§

Alan hit the big time when he was signed by Hooters, the restaurant chain that featured chicken wings and waitresses with ample breasts in skimpy attire. Alan was a very devout Catholic, as I am, and he pondered the appropriateness of having Hooters as his sponsor. It also bothered him that it wasn't a traditional sponsor like Coca-Cola or McDonalds.

"Well, you will get to see girls," I said.

"Not those kind of girls," he said. He was funny that way, almost prudish. He showed me the Hooters contract, and it looked rather good. And with Hooters as his sponsor, he then had the money to go on and win a championship in 1992.

A few years earlier, Junior Johnson decided that the driver he wanted was Alan. He offered Alan many hundreds of thousands of guaranteed money to drive for him. When Alan asked me what I thought, I told him it was up to him. I said, "You're independence is at stake. You're the only one who can make that decision."

Ultimately he turned Junior down, becoming the only driver that I know of to ever do that. It would have been interesting to see what would have happened if Junior and Alan had joined forces.

Alan won the championship in 1992 at Atlanta in the final race of the season. The battle was among Bill Elliott, Davey Allison, and Alan. Any one of the three could have won it. Alan went into the race with enough of a lead that even if Elliott won, Alan would still be champion if he could finish sixth or better. Ernie Irvan blew a tire and crashed into Davey halfway through, leaving Alan and Bill to battle it out. For most of the rest of the race Bill ran first, and Alan ran right behind him.

I told Ed Clark, the GM of the Atlanta track (who used to work for me), "You take the championship winner's circle, and I'll take the winner's circle for the race."

Winner's circles aren't fun. People can get very cantankerous. It's high emotion, and you have to let certain people in and keep others out. The media is pushy, especially with the drama this race brought.

Bill won the race, but Alan won the championship. I've been to hundreds of winner's circles, and this was the most morose I had ever seen. It was like the wake scene in *Coal Miner's Daughter* in Butcher Holler when Loretta's dad, a coal miner, died. Everyone was grumpy because Bill had lost the racing championship to Alan.

Alan was as overjoyed as Alan Kulwicki could be about anything. I called him the next day and I said, "You're obviously celebrating." Actually he was working in his race shop, not celebrating anything. I said, "Let's go out to dinner and celebrate." He didn't even think that was a good idea. I told him, "You have officially merged the cultures of the Polish and Scotch-Irish into your celebration." We didn't go out.

The next day I was riding to the Speedway in my Chevy Suburban minding my own business on this two-lane road where there's never any traffic when all of a sudden I felt a whack on my back bumper. I thought it might have been Dale Earnhardt. It was something he did occasionally. I'd look in the mirror and see that mustache over a big shit-eating grin. This time I looked up into the mouth of Alan's great big Lincoln, the car he loved to drive. Hitting me in the bumper was his way of celebrating.

ALAN WAS ONLY WITH US for eight full seasons and five races of a ninth. In the spring of 1993 he was flying from Knoxville—where he was signing autographs at a local Hooters—to Bristol where he was to race. Tommy Roberts, the PR director of Hooters, was supposed to be on the plane, but he decided not to board. I don't think he has ever figured out why. The twin-engine Hooters plane took off, and as it approached the airport at Bristol something went wrong—the consensus was pilot error—and the plane plunged to the ground. Everyone on board was killed.

They had two memorial services for Alan: one in Milwaukee and one at St. Thomas Aquinas Church in Charlotte. I knew the priest, and he told me Alan had been to the little chapel the morning of the crash. That chapel is now the Alan Kulwicki Chapel. Up until a year or two ago Alan's grave was the most visited of all the graves in that big cemetery in Milwaukee.

I got the call at five o'clock in the morning that Alan had died. I was crushed. When Davey Allison heard that Alan had died, he was happy that Alan had beaten him out for the championship. Davey figured he would have plenty of time to win one for himself. Davey didn't know it, but he didn't have a whole lot of time left himself.

CHAPTER 22

The All Star Race

JERRY LONG, THE PRESIDENT of R. J. Reynolds and a guy from Brooklyn, of all places, was the one who invented the All Star race. The government was doing everything it could to stop the tobacco companies from advertising on TV and in magazines, so Long kept coming up with alternative ideas. Some were good and some were not so good.

One thing R. J. Reynolds did was put a lot of money into the point fund. Depending on where a racer finished in a race, he would get points, and the racer with the most points at the end of the year would win a pile of money. R. J. Reynolds supplied the money, so Bill France changed the name of the circuit from Grand National racing to Winston Cup racing.

The problem was that finishing high up in the race became more important for some drivers than actually winning the race. We began to have two races on the track instead of just one. As R. J. Reynolds put more and more money into the fund, fans were beginning to see points racing as the most despicable thing you can do on a racetrack. Racers were saying, "Gee, I finished sixth today. I had a great run. I had a great points day." Smokey Yunick, Junior Johnson, and a few other people would have cleaved their driver's head off for saying that.

Bill France was enamored with the whole points deal, which I could understand because the weakness in auto racing in general, when competing with stick and ball sports, is that you don't always have an exciting ending to the season. There's the World Series, the Super Bowl, the Stanley Cup, and NBA playoffs, but too often in stock car racing one driver runs away with the championship and the drama is gone.

But with the points fund, all of a sudden drivers were beginning to think about being satisfied finishing second or third or fourth rather than trying a difficult maneuver to try to win the race. I know for a fact there have been drivers who could have tried to pass to win a race but who just sat back and settled for second and the points lead instead. I can tell you that Curtis Turner, Junior Johnson, and Cale Yarborough never would have considered that. They would have gone for the lead, and the devil may care. Instead, you end up with dull races, and dull races do not sell tickets.

Generally there are no surprises at the end of the year-end banquet. You know who the top ten are. Sometimes there's a surprise winner of the Bill France lifetime achievement award. On this particular night in 1984, there was an announcement that there would be an All Star race. Jerry Long announced that the first one was going to be held at the Charlotte Motor Speedway.

IT'S A MIRACLE that first All Star race was held in Charlotte because I had taken on RJR back in 1979 when nobody else would. I didn't like the way RJR was running the program to begin with, and I hated the fact that the tracks didn't get any of their money. I had had a big fight with Ralph Seagraves. I told him, "Your program isn't worth a damn. You're giving all your money to NASCAR, putting all your money in the points fund, and all you're giving the tracks is red and white paint."

Back in those days RJR was giving the tracks red and white paint—Winston's colors—which the more dilapidated tracks used to spruce up the guardrails and walls.

I felt my track was colorful enough, and so I took the red paint and traded it in for brown, and I mixed the brown and white into a subdued cream color and painted the walls with that, and that really got them ticked off at me.

I said to Ralph, "I don't think you're doing anything for the tracks. You need to give the tracks some money."

Ralph was a diplomat. He didn't say much, but I knew he didn't like it.

I then began talking with Lou Bantle, the chairman of U.S. Tobacco, about sponsoring a race car with U.S. Tobacco on the car. I had gotten to know Hal Needham and Burt Reynolds who were going to sponsor the U.S.

Tobacco race team, and I got to know Lou Bantle well, and I said to him, "Lou, you need to spend some money with the tracks."

"What do you have in mind?" he asked.

"How about putting up $50,000 in lap leader awards for the World 600?"

"I think that's a good idea," he said. "We'll do it."

No one had dared do anything with another tobacco company. I knew RJR was going to react badly. I didn't know how badly. And I didn't know whether NASCAR would try to take away our sanction.

When we made the press announcement that U.S. Tobacco was going to sponsor $50,000 in lap leader awards, which at the time was a fortune, all hell broke loose. The first thing RJR announced was that it was pulling out of the World 600.

The person who saved me was Bill France Sr. I was sure NASCAR was going to have this terrible, terrible reaction. When RJR called Bill to tell him they were pulling out of the World 600, it hit a nerve, harkening back to when the car companies pulled out in the 1960s. Chrysler pulled out first, and Ford was the only factory team, and then the next year Ford pulled out and Chrysler came back in. It just about broke him and everyone else, and France's immediate reaction to RJR's threat was: "We're not going to let any manufacturer tell us what to do."

The rest of NASCAR wasn't thinking that way. Junior Johnson, who had brokered the original deal with RJR, was hot at me. He was on the phone wanting to know, "Why did you do this?" But I stuck to my guns. I was going to do it anyway. I didn't even consult Bruton on this. It got really, really hairy for a while. The drivers and car owners began to talk about it badly— because they liked the points money they got from RJR. I was wondering whether they would strike over this. After all, it hadn't been that long since the drivers went on strike at Talladega in 1969.

I had to wonder whether Lou and U.S. Tobacco would stand tough. I called him in Paris where he was doing business.

"I understand there's quite a stir," he said.

"It's worse than a stir," I said. "We've blown up the teapot."

"You can count on us standing behind you," he said.

That was all I needed to know.

We held the race, and everyone showed up. U.S. Tobacco paid the lap leader money, and no one turned it down.

About six weeks later I got a call from Junior Johnson. He wanted to know if my wife, Pat, and I would come up to his cabin. He had taken an old mountain cabin and rebuilt it up on the Blue Ridge Parkway above North Wilkesboro. He was married to Flossie at the time, and he had bought a beautiful porcelain wood stove for her. Not many people alive today can even cook on a wood stove. Flossie can.

I said, "That's great, Junior. What are we going to do?"

"I want you to come up," he said, "because I've invited Ralph and Ardette and Wayne and his wife, and we're going to spend the day together."

I knew then that Junior was the peacemaker. I agreed to come. And Junior's cabin was really neat. When we got there, Junior said, "I'm going to take the girls and Flossie, and we're going to leave you boys on the front porch."

I hadn't spoken with Ralph Seagraves, RJR's president and Wayne Robertson (who was running the sports marketing department) since early May. I pulled a tin of Skoal out of my pocket. I opened it up, and Wayne said, "I see that."

"Yup, that's right," I said. It ticked them off, which is exactly what I wanted to do. I didn't want them to think this was going to be easy just because it was a multimillion dollar company versus a small racetrack.

Ralph said, "Why, you don't have to do that."

I put a little pinch between my cheek and my gum, and we started talking. We sat there, Ralph smoking Winstons and Wayne chewing gum, and we finally got around to talking about what I had done, and I let them vent their spleen. After that, Ralph being the diplomat that he was from working in Washington, D.C., for twenty years, finally said, "Let's cut all of this out. We're not worried about oral tobacco anymore. Let's just be friends and move on."

So they let Skoal do their thing, and they did their thing. RJR had snuff and chewing tobacco, but it wasn't a big deal to them. It was the principle of the thing. Cooler heads prevailed, and they finally got over it.

After about four hours Junior came back with the girls, and we all went out for dinner. Everything was hunky-dory. And I knew when R. J. Reynolds awarded us that first All Star race the bad blood was genuinely over.

THEY ANNOUNCED the All Star race would be 105 miles, which I knew was a big mistake because that meant two pit stops. It was too long and there would be too much strategy. It didn't strike me as anything that would attract ticket sales. But I went along with it, and we promoted the heck out of it, knowing in the back of my mind it wouldn't be a particularly exciting race.

As it turned out, the only exciting thing about the day was that Harry Gant had a pretty good lead, and somewhere around the middle of the race, Darrell Waltrip went by him like a rocket. The only exciting event after that was that Darrell blew his engine right at the start/finish line as the checkered flag flew. I mean he blew it all to pieces. It looked like a grenade went off inside it. It was a Junior Johnson engine, and there wasn't enough left for NASCAR to do an inspection. Everyone concluded the engine was illegal, of course.

Jerry Long had announced his intention to move the All Star race from track to track, something I opposed, of course, and the next year the race went to Atlanta. Mike Helton, who is now president of NASCAR, ran the Atlanta track. The race was held Mother's Day weekend on a Saturday. Before the race I got into a big scene with Walt Nix, a promoter I never did like.

I was a friend of Sam Belnavis, the director of sports marketing for the Miller Brewing Company. His father was from Jamaica, and Sam was born and raised in Brooklyn. I had known Sam since 1980 when I promoted the USA versus Cuba boxing matches in an event in Charlotte. It was a sellout, and I met Sam then. I got to like and respect him.

Sam was black, and the Atlanta officials were giving Sam a real problem with his credentials. He couldn't even get in to see Walter Nix. Remember, we're in Atlanta in 1986. To me, it seemed racially motivated.

I got mad, and I went in to see Walter, and I asked him point blank why he wasn't taking care of Sam. He said something, and I went across the desk at him, so they threw me out. I was taken out of there by an African-American deputy sheriff who handled me rather gently because he knew exactly what was going on. I decided not to go to the race, along with the vast majority of people who just weren't interested. They announced a crowd of 15,000, but observers said fewer than 8,000 paid to see it.

Even after Atlanta failed so miserably and got so much bad press, I knew that Jerry Long was determined to make the All Star race a success. I went up to Winston-Salem to meet with Ralph Seagraves and Wayne Robertson. I said, "Let's bring it back to Charlotte. That's where it needs to be. But the concept needs to be changed. We need to do something special."

"We're all ears," they said. "What do you propose?"

"Let's make it like a Saturday night shootout," I said. "We'll run some heat races beforehand to get everybody's chassis set up, and we'll have a ten-lap shootout to win."

It was different from anything else they had considered.

"We like the idea," they said, and one thing about those guys: They always made decisions fast. Before I left, we had a deal.

And so the race returned to Charlotte in 1987, again on a Saturday afternoon, and in 1990 a twenty-lap shootout produced controversy among the drivers. The shortest race the drivers were used to running went about two hours and forty-five minutes. This was a race that could be over in five minutes. To have a Cup race on a superspeedway that ended in ten laps was beyond what a lot of them could envision. A lot of them didn't think too much of the idea, though I do remember Dale Earnhardt liked it.

I went down to trackside before the race as the drivers were getting ready to get into their cars. I noticed something. There was a lot of tension. And great tension always happens before great events. You felt like it was a heavy-weight fight. I saw something in their eyes that I didn't see before most races: anticipation, excitement, and uncertainty.

They dropped the flag, and you could tell it wasn't going to be an ordinary race because the drivers were bumping and smacking into each other before they got to the first turn. Geoff Bodine, Bill Elliott, and Dale Earnhardt smacked into each other in the second turn, bouncing all over each other, and that was during the time when Bodine and Earnhardt had a great rivalry going, something akin to the North versus the South. Bodine was from New York state and something of an outsider, and he didn't take any guff from Earnhardt, who represented the South. Bodine was Sherman, and Earnhardt wasn't Lee. He was a private in the Confederate army, but he was still a rebel.

Bodine got knocked out of the picture, and it got down to a battle between Bill Elliott and Dale Earnhardt. It got ferocious, lap after lap. They were on top of each other. Bill, I believe, had a little faster car, but Dale had the lead, and whenever Dale got a lead his bumper got very, very wide. Bill was determined to win and Bill could get very aggressive if he wanted to.

Coming off the fourth turn Bill was on the outside, and he came down low as Dale went up high, and they banged into each other. Dale, with the lead, went down into the grass. Everyone figured there was no way he could keep control of the car on the slippery surface. They waited for him to go sideways or backwards and crash, but Dale somehow kept control, maintained the lead, and won the race. A lot of words have been written about the Pass in the Grass, and there have been paintings made as well.

If you look at Dale Earnhardt's whole career, people talk about his win at Daytona, but the Pass in the Grass is probably the signature landmark event because it epitomized him as a guy who could drive a loose race car and get away with something nobody had ever done before. It was quite an epic moment.

I swear there must have been 750,000 people at that race that day because just about every race fan I ever talked to told me he was there. It went down as a great event, and the ten-lap format was heralded by the press as great theater.

In my opinion it was the best race ever run in NASCAR.

THE 1988 WINSTON ALL STAR race took place in the middle of the tire war between Goodyear and Hoosier, a company that decided to take Goodyear head on. Most of the cars had Hoosier tires, and a lot of those cars blew tires. The winner of the race, Terry Labonte, had Goodyears, and his car held together as he came from a lap back to win.

The Winston of 1989 featured a duel between Rusty Wallace and Darrell Waltrip. Rusty, Mr. Mid-America, was a very popular driver who for twenty years teamed with car owner Roger Penske, one of the smartest businessmen and most successful car owners in the history of racing.

I first met Roger back in 1964 when he was a very good road racer. This was back in the days of Mark Donohue, Bruce McLaren, and the Chaparrals, with Jim Hall and Hap Sharp. Roger drove with moderate success, and then when I was with Firestone, he became a Goodyear tire distributor. He also became an IndyCar owner, with Mark Donohue as his driver.

In those days Penske was a little like Carl Kiekhaefer. He was very detailed and very controlling of everything around him. His employees were Ivy League types who wore button-down shirts, suits, and ties. He insisted that his shops be letter-perfect, eat-off-the-floor places when no one else was like that.

Roger also had the ability to jump from one type of racing to another and have success. He took over the Michigan Speedway when it wasn't doing well, and he negotiated a contract with American Motors to use its track as a test facility. That deal helped Penske finance the track. He later built the track in Fontana, California—a carbon copy of the Michigan track. His tracks were very successful because they were spotless like everything else he did. They were known for their cleanliness and efficiency, and I was very impressed by how he did things. Later he bought the North Carolina Motor Speedway. No question the DeWitt family sold it to Roger because they liked him. They were trying to keep Bruton Smith from getting his hands on it, because they knew Bruton wanted it so he could close it and open another track.

Not too long ago, the rumors were flying that Roger was going to become the chairman of General Motors. That might not have been a bad move because he is very savvy and very good with his people. He's extremely loyal to those who have been around him. He's treated them well, and they've been with him a long time. Walt Czarnecki, the president of Penske, is just one example of this. Walt is one of the smartest people we have in racing, a textbook example of the genius of Roger Penske who knows how to hire the right people, put them in the right positions, and keep them for a long period of time. It's the secret of his success.

Roger Penske is totally into racing. He came to NASCAR in 1972, and he had success with Bobby Allison in 1975 and 1976, but Bobby left him after two years because Bobby was so independent and also wanted to do things his way. He was always looking for a better deal, another team that could win more races. That was just Bobby.

Then, in 1980, Rusty Wallace came aboard, and they combined for one of the longest-running combinations in racing history.

Rusty, who came from Missouri, was one of the first drivers coming out of the Midwest to really hit the big-time in NASCAR without midget experience. He began as a stock car racer because that's what his father drove. He had two brothers, Mike and Kenny, who also raced. Rusty was a Roger Penske kind of guy because he was Hollywood good-looking, very well dressed, and clean-cut. Roger brought him down to Atlanta in 1980 to run one race, and Rusty surprised everyone by finishing second, extraordinary for someone who had no experience on the big tracks.

Rusty ran for Penske for twenty years because Rusty appreciated Roger and felt he was working with the best. I'm sure he had offers to go other places because he was a terrific driver, a guy who could run very hard and not crash a lot, though one time at Daytona he turned his car over at least a dozen times and came out of it okay. In 1993 Rusty won ten races, and he

David Pearson celebrates a 1976 World 600 win with Humpy.

Humpy gives advice to Kevin Harvick prior to the five-hundred-miler at Charlotte in 2006.

Humpy gives encouragement to Brad Keselowski in 2007 before the October three-hundred-miler.

Humpy with friend Morgan Shepherd, NASCAR's oldest driver, in 2007.

Humpy at a big press conference offering his views on safety after Dale Earnhardt's death in 2001.

Humpy converses with Kasey Kahne's pit crew in 2007.

Humpy and wife Pat in Italy in 2007.

Humpy walks the qualifying line prior to the 2004 600.

Humpy addresses another sold-out crowd of 170,000 before the 2003 600. Sellouts have not happened since he left.

Humpy and Pat relax in the Wyoming mountains south of Jackson Hole in 2007.

Humpy and his grandchildren relax in Seabrook Island, South Carolina, in 1999.

On a dare and always the showman, Humpy sticks his head in a tiger's mouth at a press conference in 2001 to promote the 500 race.

won eight in 1994. As a promoter, I saw him as a driver who sold tickets. He just had a great natural ability to drive a race car. And he wasn't afraid of combat if it came to that.

So it was Rusty from the Midwest against Darrell Waltrip, the mouth of the South, in the 1989 All Star race. Darrell had a lot of fans, but there were a lot of fans who didn't like him. When the flag dropped, you could tell they had the two fastest cars.

Charlotte at one-and-a-half miles is one of NASCAR's intermediate tracks. It tends to become a one-groove race track when it gets slick. Charlotte is a quad oval that is fairly narrow, as narrow as forty feet in the corners. It's not an easy track to pass on. And yet, because the cars at Charlotte have engines that are unrestricted, they run at high speeds. You run close to 200 miles an hour going into the first and third corners. It's all a driver can do just to hold onto the car much less think about passing someone. During the 500- or 600-mile races, drivers usually tend not to let it all hang out until the end of the race because it's so easy to wreck.

So at the end of the Winston in 1989, Rusty was running second to Darrell. Rusty now had to make a decision. Did he want to risk wrecking both of them by trying to pass or should he just sit back and be satisfied with finishing second?

No driver will ever admit he settled for second place unless he has the slower car, in which case he has a good excuse, but in a race like the Winston where no points are at stake it makes much more sense to go for it. So when Darrell and Rusty came to the last lap with Darrell leading and Rusty down on his inside, you could see that Rusty was going to make his move.

As they got into the middle of three and four, the cars began inching toward each other. They came to the fourth turn, which is the most dangerous place on the Charlotte track—narrow, bumpy, abrupt, everything that can put you into the wall. Whether Darrell moved down on Rusty as Rusty moved up at the exact same moment was hard to tell, even after watching the video. What is certain was that Rusty got into Darrell's left rear quarter panel and turned him sideways. As Darrell came off the fourth turn sliding in the grass, Rusty passed him and won the race.

The fans in the grandstand immediately determined that Rusty had spun Darrell out, and they began booing him roundly when he came back around the track to make his way to victory circle. I was sitting in the control tower listening to this cacophony of boos when the phone rang. My office was calling to say that an anonymous caller made the statement, "Rusty isn't going to leave the track alive."

After Rusty accepted his trophy, I asked security to bring him to the control tower rather than the press box. I could see he was really shaken by the boos he was getting. Rusty had always been a driver with a squeaky clean reputation. It was the first time he was feeling the wrath of the race fans. What I had to tell him didn't help his mood any. I said, "Rusty, I have assigned you extra security. We got a threat against you. It's probably a kook, but I'm not taking any chances. I'm going to have two Charlotte policemen staked out at your house tonight."

That shook him up even worse. Then the media tore him apart at the press conference. Afterwards Darrell told the press, "He made $200,000, and I hope he chokes on it."

Looking back, it was hard to determine exactly what happened. In the heat of the battle, as hard as those guys were running, with the adrenaline pumping and a lot of money at stake, I just felt it was part of racing. That was the 1989 Winston, quite an eventful event.

THE NEXT TWO WINSTONS were uneventful with Dale Earnhardt going wire to wire in 1990 and Davey Allison doing the same thing in 1991.

When I sat with RJR's Wayne Robertson to discuss the next year's event, he informed me he wanted to move the race to Richmond. I was darned if I was going to let that happen. Wayne said to me, "We have to do something different. We gotta. We don't want to move the race, but we will."

It was August. The race was in May. I thought, *I'm going to think of the most outlandish thing I can think of.* I said, "We'll light the speedway and run the race on Saturday night."

The other executives of the Speedway looked at me as though I had just fallen off the onion truck. I hadn't talked to Bruton, and I didn't have the slightest idea how it was going to be done, but I figured if you could light a half-mile track, you could light a mile-and-a-half track. Even though nobody had ever done it.

Wayne really jumped on the idea. He said, "My God, no one has ever run a superspeedway race at night. That will be fantastic."

"And besides," I said, "a full moon is going to be out, and we'll do a big campaign around the lights and the full moon." I knew then I had him hooked.

I went out to the parking garage with the other two Speedway execs. The three of us hadn't said a word. We got in the car, and they knew not to talk to me until I paid the toll because I needed all my concentration to get out of the parking garage. I needed to get my money out and get going.

Once we got out onto the street both of them at the same time said, "What in the hell were you talking about?"

"We'll light the track," I said.

"How are you going to do that? Who's going to do it?"

"I haven't the slightest idea," I said, "but I'll figure it out."

I called Bruton, and he was okay with it even though I had no idea what it was going to cost or how we were going to do it.

I called together the electricians. May was not that far away. I figured if you can light the fourth turn, you can light anything. I rigged up lights in the fourth turn, and we turned it on, and it looked pretty good. It was September, and it was dark. I had lights on the inside and lights on the outside, and the lights on the inside were kind of low. We needed someone to get in a car and drive it a hundred miles an hour as a test.

I volunteered. I jumped in the pace car and got it up to 110 down the backstretch, and got into the third turn—everything was okay—but when I got to the fourth turn where the lights were, all of a sudden I was completely blinded where I looked to the left side. How I didn't crash and die is beyond me. I thought then, *I better leave this to the experts.*

I called a couple of lighting companies, including one in Europe, and they didn't seem to get it. Then I found a company up in Muscatine, Iowa, called Musco. It was known for its temporary lights—at the Bristol race track and at the Notre Dame football games on Saturday nights for NBC.

When I called Joe Crookam, the company president, I approached him with an angle. I knew this was going to be as expensive as the dickens, and I needed a hook to get him to do it without charging us an arm and leg. I knew the 1996 Olympics were coming in Atlanta, and I said, "Joe, did you ever think you could light a mile-and-a-half speedway?"

"I'd like to try," he said.

"We have the Olympics in '96," I said. "I figure if you can come down here and do this—if we can work out some kind of deal—you might get that contract in Atlanta."

He lit up big time, and it wasn't long before he flew down to Charlotte with Musco's chairman of the board. His name is Myron Gordon, a short, muscular-looking guy who doesn't look like the chairman of anything. He doesn't talk much, but he's a lighting genius. He started wandering around the track.

We went back to my office and we started talking. I said, "Here's the challenge. I don't want any ordinary lighting system. This being the first night race, there is going to be a tremendous amount of publicity. I don't want poles in the infield. We've got to come up with a way to light the track from a low angle so we don't have that picket-fence effect from the grandstand."

I figured that would stop them right there.

Myron said just one thing. "I want to take that Petty driving school course." This was a Thursday, and the Petty Racing School ran about every day. He took the three-day course, and when he returned to my office, he said, "I think I know how to do it."

Meanwhile, Bill France Jr. wasn't too happy about my lighting plans. To him it was just a big pain in the rear end. He said, "Why would you want to do that? Why mess with it?"

"Because I want to do something different," I said. "You know the All Star race is an RJR deal, and it's what I had to do to keep the race in Charlotte."

"NASCAR has got to approve the lighting system," Billy said. "And there has to be a pre-test done, and if we don't approve it, then you have to run the race on Saturday afternoon."

"Okay," I said, "We'll do that."

Then they threw in another monkey wrench. Billy France Jr. said, "You have to come up with an emergency lighting system so if the main transformer goes out, you have enough lights to get the drivers off the track and down pit road."

Everyone had heard about what happened at the Robinwood Speedway the night the driver hit the light pole and knocked out all the lights. People still joke about that.

"Okay, we'll figure that out," I said.

They started working on the lights, and one cold, cold day in January, Joe Crookam called me from Iowa to say he thought he had figured it all out.

"Come up here, and we'll show you what we've got."

Muscatine, Iowa, is grim in January. When I landed, the snow was blowing sideways. I didn't have far to go because Musco had taken over a hangar at the airport and had built a replica of the fourth turn in it. They had set up their lighting system with normal poles on the outside, but on the inside they bounced lights off mirrors. The light would come back in a diagonal across the track so when the driver looked to the left, he was not looking into the lights. It was a brilliant concept, so incredible it ended up winning twenty-seven international illuminating patents. The design won every award the International Illuminating Society gave. Every one of them.

I was buoyed with enthusiasm, and I told everyone. In late April, the installation of the lights was completed, and now it was time for the test. Les Richter and Bill France Jr. came to Charlotte to test the lights. Every driver of every Cup team also attended. This was a period when China was just crushing the United States in manufacturing, wrecking our economic system. I remember standing on the roof looking down thinking, *Boy, every American should see what I see right now.* A bunch of guys from Muscatine, Iowa, had come up with this whole system.

Everything was going fine, and then Richter said, "It's time to test the emergency system." I needed a driver to go out there; it was a risk if the backup lighting system didn't work. When no one volunteered, I said to the drivers, "This isn't the trial for the electric chair." Kenny Schrader, who had literally run every track or note in America, finally agreed to do it.

Richter said, "We'll let Kenny run a few laps, and we'll hit it but we won't tell him when." He told me it would be on the fourth lap, but I did not tell Schrader. He went out and ran well. Then on the fourth lap—bang!—the lights went out, and—bang!—the emergency lights came on. Kenny was supposed to come back down pit road, but the system worked so well he stayed on the track for three more laps. He came in smiling.

"Evidently you didn't have any problems," I said.

Schrader had run every short track in America. "Listen," he said, "the emergency lights you have now are better than most of the short tracks on Saturday nights."

That pretty much cinched it, and NASCAR gave its okay to hold the race at night.

The atmosphere was festive, and I was ecstatic. Even the NASCAR Big Wigs felt a milestone had been crossed. The drivers kept telling me, "We see better than we do in the daylight. There's nothing on the horizon. The cars look faster."

The race was advertised as "One Hot Night." What I was also proud of was that my oldest daughter, Patti, was chosen by TNN as the producer of their live show. Ken Squier was the anchor and Buddy Baker did the color on the broadcast.

As darkness began to fall we ran the Open, a race for the year's non-winners. The first two cars to finish entered the main event. For the pre-race ceremony, I talked NASCAR into letting the cars line up right in front of the main grandstand. The drivers were introduced, and then they walked to their cars and they stood there until told to climb inside. We put up a special stage, and it was magical, and I also noticed that the tension had doubled, telling me that this was going to be a special night. Dale Earnhardt, in particular, was about twenty times twitchier than normal because he knew this was going to be the Gunfight at the O. K. Corral.

The main event was ten laps. I talked NASCAR into allowing a double-file start, so we had all the cars lined up side by side. Or as they say in the South, side by each. The flag dropped, and you knew dynamite was about to explode.

Davey Allison was in Robert Yates' car. Larry McReynolds was his crew chief, and Davey was real, real fast. It was real hot that day, and the track had gotten really slick, and Dale Earnhardt was in seventh heaven. And Kyle Petty was running fast all day.

It came down to the ninth lap. The cars crossed the start/finish line with Earnhardt in the lead, Petty second, and Allison third. As they went into the second turn, I was sure Kyle Petty was going to win. He had had a drought, but he was determined to beat Earnhardt and prove something to himself.

They went down the third turn. Kyle never lifted. He went right down the bottom of the racetrack, and there was nowhere to go except up into the side of Earnhardt's No. 3. Kyle knocked Dale up into the wall where he crashed.

Kyle's car started to go sideways into the fourth turn, and then Davey drove underneath him, and there they were side by side—Petty and Allison—just slamming into each other. They both got sideways before they reached the start/finish line, and both crashed. After crossing the finish line, Davey's car turned completely around and slammed into the wall—driver side first—really, really hard. His car came to a stop on the inside of the first turn. Kyle's car was also torn up.

Davey was declared the winner, but the crowd didn't say a word. It was completely somber because Davey was slumped over lifeless, and everyone could see him. He was right in front of the grandstand. On the radio I heard a Code 3, which meant the driver was unresponsive.

I took off from the flag stand to go to the track hospital. Patti was in the director's booth when Buddy Baker started talking. Patti yelled to him, "Shut up. This is a time when everyone needs to shut up."

All went quiet on TV as they panned to the car. The rescue workers were working to get Davey out. Everyone knew it was big-time trouble because there were three ambulances surrounding the car, and everyone was working on Davey.

As I headed to the hospital, the winner's circle became bedlam. Bruton was over there with Robert Yates, the car owner, but there was no car and no driver. This had never happened before or since. They finally got Davey, who was unconscious, out of the car. And as I entered the track hospital, the place was bedlam because all the Allison clan was there. There are a lot of them—the Allisons seem to be a fertile bunch—and they were all screaming and hollering. It was chaos. I couldn't do anything with them.

It had been three years since Bobby Allison's terrible crash at Pocono. He had suffered a serious brain injury, but on this day I could tell that Bobby eventually was going to recover because it was Bobby who walked in there and ordered everyone to be quiet. He said, "We don't know what's wrong with him, and we can only expect him to be okay. Now everybody be quiet." And the place went silent like a tomb.

They brought Davey in on a gurney. Dr. Jerry Petty, a wonderful neurosurgeon, pulled his eyelids back, and you could see his eyes were dilated but Davey was breathing. His vital signs were okay. But it was clear he had a pretty good concussion.

Dr. Petty looked at me and nodded his head that Davey was going to be all right. I told that to Bobby. "He just has a concussion," I said. Everybody then calmed down.

Meanwhile, his car was terribly wrecked, and when the wrecker came over, they didn't know whether or not to tow it to the winner's circle. There was a big squabble over this. The only other time I can recall this happening was after the 1976 Daytona 500 when Richard Petty and David Pearson crashed into each other right before the finish line. That time they brought the car to the winner's circle, but at least David was still able to drive it. This one was really torn up. They towed it to the winner's circle, but there was no driver. Davey spent the night in the hospital, and he was released the next day.

It was a great race and a great night. There never has been a race like that loaded with all the drama and history that went with it. A lot of other All Star races have had drama, but nothing like that One Hot Night.

CHAPTER 23

Robert Yates
Knows Tragedy

Robert Yates started out working for Holman and Moody in the 1960s. From the start, Robert had an incredible knack for building engines. In 1973, Bill Gardner, who founded the DiGard race team, combined Robert's engine-building talents with Gary Nelson's, a chassis genius. Add to that Darrell Waltrip behind the wheel of the Gatorade car and the combination was terrific. Darrell won twenty-six races for DiGard, and then in 1984 Bobby Allison won six more.

Bill Gardner was an accountant from Connecticut who didn't look like an accountant. He was a short barrel of a man who talked very fast, was full of energy, but who wasn't liked a whole lot because of the way he treated people. He was rough on them. He was a so-called Yankee, but so was Roger Penske. Roger knew how to deal with people in the South. Bill Gardner didn't. Gardner would run over them. One of the messiest fights between a driver and an owner was between Darrell Waltrip and Gardner. Darrell had signed one of the very first driver contracts, and when Darrell decided he wanted to walk out on Gardner, Gardner decided to hold him to the wording of the contract, and the fight became very messy.

If Gardner got mad at a member of his crew, he would call the cops and tell the guy, "Get your toolbox and get out. You have fifteen minutes."

Gardner divorced his first wife and married a beautiful girl named Chris who was sixteen. Her parents ran a short track in the Midwest. I haven't heard from him in years. He was a colorful figure and a successful car owner, but that success primarily lay in the hands of Gary Nelson and Robert Yates.

Robert Yates (who looks like Robert Redford) never appears to be in a hurry, never appears to get flustered, and is not the kind of guy who you'd think could get anything done, but he's worked magic everywhere he's gone in racing. Yates is the epitome of the generation of owners we have in NASCAR who started out as a crew chief. He's in the same line as Bud Moore and Glen Wood.

In 1989 he had the opportunity to buy the Harry Ranier race team that included Davey Allison as its driver and Larry McReynolds as its crew chief. Ordinarily a frugal man, Yates took a big risk borrowing the money to buy the team, but everyone involved—including Texaco, the team's sponsor—was sure he could succeed, and they were right.

I'd been around Davey since he was a little boy. When Davey first started racing regularly in the Busch series in 1985, you could tell the boy really had it. Those genes of Bobby's had been successfully transferred. He drove like his father—smooth, with a strong will to win. He and his father had some stirring battles. He finished second to his father in the 1988 Daytona 500. These are races promoters dream about.

And Davey had a great wife, Liz. I've always said that most of the great drivers had great women behind them. A driver loses more than he wins, so he has to have someone to pick him up off the floor on Monday morning. Plus the driver is out of town a lot, and someone has to keep up with the paperwork and keep his life organized.

I can remember I didn't like it at all in 1992 when Davey showed up at the Speedway in a little helicopter. "Davey," I said, "you need to get rid of that thing. Why do you need it anyway?" I had never been a lover of helicopters. This one didn't look like it was meant to go anywhere and stay up.

He didn't laugh when I said it, which bothered me. I knew he was a good pilot, because his father was, but it was agonizing for me to see him flying around in that thing. And the next year at Talladega he crashed the helicopter trying to land it and died. I really think if Davey had been able to keep racing, he could have won as many races as his father because he certainly had the ability, and he had Robert Yates as his car owner.

§

AFTER DAVEY DIED, Robert signed one of the wildest guys I ever saw behind a race car, Ernie Irvan. Ernie was a short track racer who came to the Carolinas from Modesto, California, and he was broke and trying to find work. When I ran into him, he told me, "I can weld anything."

A light bulb went off. I was expanding the seating of the Charlotte Motor Speedway. Seats were thirty dollars a piece, but I saw that if I bought the components I could have them installed for half the price if I could just get someone to weld them in place. I got a tube bender and set up shop in the infield. All I needed was a welder. That was when Ernie came along, and Ernie literally built 5,000 of those seats for me. And he did a darn good job. After he became a driver of note, I would say to him, "Well, Ernie, if you ever want to give up your night job, I can get you back building seats again."

When he first started out driving the Kodak car for Larry McClure, they called him Swervin' Irvan because he drove hell-bent for leather. He wasn't intimidated by anyone on the track, including Dale Earnhardt.

Ernie and Robert Yates combined to produce the worst race ever held at Lowe's Motor Speedway when he won the 500. He took off, and his car was so strong nobody could touch them. Everyone else seemed to be on either Prozac or Valium because there was no excitement at all. Ernie led, with no one to challenge him, and I couldn't buy a caution flag. I kept going over to the NASCAR officials, saying, "There has to be some debris on the damn racetrack." But there wasn't. Had I been less scrupulous I might have gone down there and dropped something on the track myself. My frustration grew as I watched the fans fall asleep in the stands. Even when Ernie had to pit on the green, no one could catch him. After I made about my tenth trip to the NASCAR booth, a spot of oil was found on the backstretch so the yellow flag went out, closing the field. Ernie to this day swears there was no oil, but it was the only break in the monotony that day. And Ernie won anyway. No one came close to challenging him. He had so much horsepower and the Texaco car was handling so well. It may have been a great victory for them, but it was terrible for me because I had to sell tickets to the next one.

And like Davey Allison, if Ernie hadn't been injured in two terrible crashes, he would have won a lot of races.

Ernie's first crash was up in Michigan, and when they helicoptered him to the hospital, it didn't look like he was going to make it. It was a miracle he survived. He wore an eye patch and lost a great deal of weight, and you could tell he had been in a serious accident. I gave Ernie and his wife, Kim, a ride around the Speedway. At that point he didn't know whether he was going to be able to race again because with head injuries you never know how it's going to turn out. Is the guy all there? Will this end his career? Miraculously, he healed, and he drove again. Ernie was sponsored by M&Ms when he crashed again, almost died, and had to retire for good, no question. If he had one more head injury, he would have been a dead man.

Ernie moved into a beautiful home on the other side of Mooresville where he and his wife started breeding Paso Fino horses. I don't think anyone ever found out why it happened, but his house burned to the ground, and the biggest loss was all of his trophies. Ernie and Kim are now living on Wadmalaw Island, South Carolina. He's a country gentleman raising horses.

DAVEY'S DEATH AND ERNIE'S INJURIES are the dark side of racing. You lose people, and sometimes it's forever, and sometimes they get hurt bad and have to go away. If you get people to tell you what they really think—if you talk to Richard Childress about Dale Earnhardt, or talk to Richard Petty about the loss of his brother-in-law in a pit accident, or the loss of his grandson Adam in a crash—you can see it sears a tattoo on their soul and mind that is always there. They never think the same after that. The fear of it happening again never leaves them. And you know it will. It's inevitable. It shouldn't be part of the business, but it is. And yet they stay in the business.

Robert signed Dale Jarrett away from Joe Gibbs, and they have won races, including the Daytona 500. Robert has since retired, and the operation has been taken over by his son, Doug, and this raises the question: Will Doug Yates, the Wood brothers, and the other one- or two-car owners be able to survive in this business? Or will it be taken over completely by the mega-car owners like Jack Roush, Roger Penske, Joe Gibbs, and Rick Hendrick? Right now Doug Yates can survive because Jack Roush builds his cars.

NASCAR has taken a step by limiting the number of cars of future owners, but the current owners are grandfathered in and can keep their cars going. Had NASCAR not put a limit on it, there's no doubt in my mind that eventually we would have seen one owner owning half the field, literally twenty cars.

NASCAR may thwart the future of the mega-teams through its Car of Tomorrow. The chassis are all going to be the same, which will keep the costs down. And NASCAR also has a sealed-engine program soon to begin in the

Nationwide Series. I expect that one of these days it'll go up to Cup racing as well.

One or two outfits will make all the engines, which will be sealed so no one can work on them other than to adjust the flow of fuel.

As a result, the chassis and engines will be the same for everyone, and teams won't have to hire sixty people to work on one race car anymore. This may also lessen the success of the bigger teams. This may bring about a parity that we haven't seen in a long time. Is that good? In some ways I suppose, but you don't want to get in a situation where you can't produce superstars, and superstars only are produced when they win a lot of races.

CHAPTER 24

Bobby Allison's Nightmare

O N THE DAY BOBBY ALLISON was almost killed in a terrible crash at Pocono in 1988, I was in Charlotte listening to the race on the radio. Pay television had entered the scene, and a pay-per-view company in New York was broadcasting it, but it wasn't available in Charlotte so the only way I could get it was listening to the radio.

When you listen to enough radio broadcasts, anytime there's a wreck, you can sense things by what the announcers don't say. Bobby had been T-boned, the thing you fear most, and as I listened I didn't hear a report on his condition. As time went on and the race wasn't restarted, I knew Bobby was hurt bad.

I got on the phone and called Joe Mattioli, the owner of the Pocono track. I said, "Joe, what's going on?"

"Well, it's bad," he said. "Bobby's still in the car. He's unconscious, and it doesn't look good."

I thought to myself, *What kind of neurosurgeon does the local hospital in Allentown have*? I said to Joe, "Keep me informed. I'm going to see if I can get Dr. Petty on the phone." Jerry Petty is the Charlotte track doctor, a renowned neurosurgeon who had saved Donnie Allison's life after a very bad accident at Charlotte.

Donnie and Dick Brooks hit each other sideways in the corner, and Donnie was badly hurt. He had a terrible headache, but the symptoms mimicked a ruptured aorta. Dr. Petty made a life saving decision. Had he invaded him at that point, it would have killed Donnie because he couldn't have taken it, but Dr. Petty made the diagnosis that it wasn't a ruptured aorta but rather that Donnie was suffering from a serious head injury. As a result Donnie survived.

I called Dr. Petty and told him about Bobby. I said, "It looks bad. Is there any way you can get up to Pennsylvania if I can get a plane?" He said, "Yes." I called Joe Mattioli back. I knew the president of Cessna was up there. Joe got him, and he flew down to Charlotte and picked up Dr. Petty and flew back to the Allentown hospital along with Jerry's associate, Scott McClanahan, who is an expert with shunts. Turned out the neurosurgeon who was already up there was also pretty terrific.

They performed surgery on Bobby. Not long afterward I flew up there to see him. He was still in a coma.

Jocko Maggiacomo was the driver who had T-boned Bobby. Two careers were destroyed that day. Pocono is a very fast racetrack, one that's very difficult to slow down on because it's not banked. Jocko never saw Bobby when he hit him. And for Bobby to survive something like that was pretty incredible. It was one of the worst accidents anybody had ever survived in NASCAR Cup racing.

Fortunately, Bobby is just absolutely one of the most amazing human beings who ever lived. His survival was a miracle. Today people revere him, not just for the races he ran and won, but also for what he went through and how he bore up under it.

Another test for Bobby came in the 1992 All Star race at Charlotte when Davey crashed, won the race, and was knocked unconscious. There was chaos at the track hospital. Though Bobby's brain had been scrambled and he subsequently had a tough time talking and thinking clearly, that day he was forceful, ordering everyone to be quiet. That was the day I thought he had come back and that he would eventually recover his mental faculties, which he has done.

After Bobby's accident, he suffered terribly from depression. To give him something to live for he decided to run a car with his youngest son, Clifford, as the driver. Despite his severe brain damage, which prevented him from doing very much, being Clifford's crew chief made Bobby's life seem worth living. Then one day during practice at Michigan, Clifford, who wasn't used to the radial tires on the car, hit the wall at a terrible angle and he was killed instantly. Bobby was the first one to get to the scene even before the rescue crew. Clifford was lifeless as he sat slumped in the car.

Then in 1993, only a year after Clifford's death, Davey died in a helicopter accident. Davey's death put a tremendous pall over racing, especially for those of us who had been around the carnage of the 1960s when Joe Weatherly and Fireball Roberts were killed. It's very difficult to promote anything after you have a tragedy like that. It takes all the starch out of you, and even if you make an attempt, people don't respond anyway. All they want to do is talk about the tragedy, what happened at the track, and why he died. They don't usually find out, but it doesn't stop them from wanting to keep talking about it. As I said, it puts a real pall over things.

Davey was beloved. People really liked him. He was good-looking and a heck of a racer. He was a fighter, a combat racer like his dad. And people knew Davey was a kid who did not grow up with a silver spoon. He had a tin spoon. People knew that and respected that. Bobby knew how hard he had worked to become a success, and he wanted Davey to do the same. He thought that was the best way for his son. I can remember one day having an argument with Richard Petty about his son Kyle. Richard decided to start Kyle out driving in a Cup car rather than have him start at a lower level. I asked him why he would do that.

"If you're going to be flying 727s, why not start him in a 727?" Richard said.

"I would start him in a Piper Cub," I said, and the argument continued. Richard did what he did, and Bobby did the opposite, making Davey work on the car and get dirty. And when Davey and Bobby raced against each other, whether at Birmingham or in a Cup race later on, Bobby gave him no quarter whatsoever. It was like, "I'm going to treat you worse than I ever thought of treating David Pearson." Bobby had done the same thing to Donnie, his younger brother. So to see him do that to his son didn't surprise anyone. Bobby was from the old school. He knew one way, and that was to learn the fundamentals, and learn them and learn them and learn them and never forget them.

The thing about both Bobby and Davey—they would race anytime anywhere at the drop of a hat. They both got exposure all over the country, because the short tracks are where the drivers can get really close to the fans. And so when Davey was killed, all of racing mourned.

After losing their two boys, Bobby and his wife, Judy, became estranged. Bobby spent a lot of time by himself in an airplane hangar with his plane.

Judy was left by herself an awful lot. They had been inseparable, and no one ever thought they'd get divorced, in part because they are Catholic, but one day Judy filed for divorce and moved to North Carolina, leaving Bobby alone with his thoughts back in Hueytown, Alabama.

After a friend's child suffered a tragic death, my mother once said to me, "This is going to be the hardest thing that marriage will ever go through." Divorce commonly is the result of a tragedy like that. And the Allisons lost both their sons. It's incredible they were able to survive at all. I know one time Judy got extremely angry with me. Bobby had some classic cars, and he asked me to sell them for him at an auction we had at the Speedway. She didn't like the price we got, and she lambasted me over it. I just let it roll off me, because I knew what she was going through. I didn't say anything, and the subject never came up again, and we've been fine ever since. It was a terrible, terrible emotional time. The fact they stayed together as long as they did was remarkable.

I would see Bobby, and he would force himself to keep going, all the while suffering from severe brain damage, the pain of the death of his sons, and the divorce. We didn't talk about any of this much. It's hard for men to talk about things like that. I just tried to be as supportive as I could. He and I had a mutual friend, Father Dale Grubba, who lived in Wisconsin. When Bobby was around, we'd go to Mass together. I knew Bobby talked to Dale a lot, and I was hoping that one day he and Judy would get back together again.

After being apart for two years, they met again at the wedding of Liz Allison, Davey's widow. Bobby and Judy began to talk. Then when Adam Petty died in an accident, they went to comfort the Pettys, and during that weekend they discovered there was still a spark, and they got married again—a storybook ending.

I'm so glad it happened. Not long afterward Davey's son (who was eleven) was driving a Bandolero (a small race car I had designed) at a little track outside of Nashville, and he crashed and was knocked out. It made all the papers. They took him to the hospital, and he was okay. But there was still that flash of, *Oh My God. This can't happen again.* Liz ended his racing then and there.

Last summer Bobby and I went up to Michigan together to the Michigan Motorsports Hall of Fame at Novi. Bobby seems to be taking life rather well, and he's got enough things going to keep him financially sound. He is quite stable and sharp mentally, so this saga has a decent, if not happy, ending.

CHAPTER 25

NASCAR and Bruton Go National

In the aftermath of the 1979 Daytona 500, we began to notice a lot more interest in our sport. We began to pick up sponsors who, before that race, had shown reluctance even to talk to us.

One of the things we did at the Speedway was put together a serious sales effort. I brought in my college roommate, Jim Duncan, an ex-teammate of mine from the West Coast. He had been head of variety for Reynolds Metals, a really good sales job. He was a great big square-jawed guy at about 6 feet 2 inches and 230 pounds. He was perfect for the kind of sales we needed. He was a jock, but he was a great salesman. He knew how to fit into the garage area, and he knew how to go to New York. He was perfect for the job. He sold everything we had at the Speedway—sponsorships, signage, program advertising—but he concentrated on the big boys. Over the years he started with $100,000 sponsorship deals and built them up into two million dollar deals. There was nobody in racing who could touch him.

Before I hired Jim, no one had done this. Tracks mostly sold program ads. Daytona had a few sponsorships, like Permatex, and money from a few companies. It didn't amount to much, but it was a start.

Racing was way ahead of the rest of the sports as far as sales were concerned, but we had to be because we didn't have any TV money like the other sports.

That revenue wasn't there for us, so we had to create it. One advantage the tracks had was that NASCAR didn't put many boundaries on what we could do. We couldn't sell liquor ads, or anything that conflicted with R. J. Reynolds, but that was about it.

And once R. J. Reynolds came in, the grocery and drug trade followed. For the first time we were able to sell to nontraditional automotive companies. This really opened the door.

For example, in the early 1980s we were trying to sell sponsorship to the 500, our fall race. We had a pretty good offer from GM Goodwrench, around $400,000. Because it was a good sum of money, I was involved, and I wanted half a million. We kept negotiating through October and then November. They went up to $410,000. I said, "No, we have to have $450,000."

Their offer of $410,000 was on Friday. I figured on Monday I'd call, and they'd give me what I wanted. But when I called, they said, "No, we're not going to give it to you. We bought a sponsorship somewhere else." They had gone to Rockingham and paid $400,000 to sponsor their GM Goodwrench 400.

I had screwed up when I turned down what turned out to be their final offer.

It was now November, and it was cold, and usually if you don't have a sponsor by December 1, you're not going to get one at a decent price.

We went into panic mode. I got our salespeople together. We had four people working for us, including Darlene Brigance, the daughter of Buck Brigance, a great motorcycle racer and later a Cup racer. She was a perky, cute girl who could sell the bark off a tree.

We got together, and I said, "We have three days to come up with a sponsor. If we don't do it in three days, we're out." I said, "Let's not go outside the Carolinas where we have to explain what stock car racing is." Not everyone back then was consumed with NASCAR.

We got a list of the top one hundred companies in the Carolinas. We eliminated the banks and textile companies. In those days banks didn't want to have much to do with racing. They hadn't yet figured out what a great marketing tool it was. And the textile people were just plain having a tough time.

I said, "Go through the book and look for an unusual angle." I didn't know what that angle was.

We came across Oakwood Mobile Homes. It was a New York Stock Exchange company located in Greensboro. We saw they were celebrating their twenty-fifth anniversary, and I figured a company celebrating its anniversary would have some extra money to spend. We dispatched Jim Duncan and Darlene Brigance to Greensboro, and within two days we had a deal. The idea hit them square between the eyes. They gave us $450,000 and signed a three-year contract that lasted several years beyond that. And Darlene ended up marrying the guy she sold the sponsorship to, Wayne Patterson. We lost her when she moved to Greensboro.

Ofttimes when we would make cold calls, we could see the blank stares in the eyes of the people we were pitching, and we knew it wasn't the place to be. But not all the time. I was in Winston-Salem visiting R. J. Reynolds, and I had some time to kill, so I decided I would call on Tom Chambers, the president of Goody's headache powders. What I knew about him was that he was a football referee in the Atlantic Coast Conference. Other than that, I didn't know him from a tree.

I showed up at his office on Salt Street in one of the old sections of Winston-Salem. The company was in an old warehouse. For me it was the ultimate challenge, because Goody's had spent zero dollars on advertising. They didn't even have distributors. Their salesmen drove around to country stores and small-town pharmacies and sold their powders out of the trunk of their cars.

Goody's was strictly a southern institution. I used it myself. In fact, later on I was promoting a world championship bout between Bernard Taylor, a Charlotte Olympian, and Eusebio Pedrosa for the featherweight title. Pedrosa was a Panamanian, and his people were very difficult to deal with. I was sitting there trying to hammer out a deal, getting nowhere, when I developed a hell of a headache. I pulled out the Goody's powder—I could take it dry. You learn to do it. I put the powder on my tongue and swallowed it.

Well, the Panamanians saw me swallowing this white powder, and they went crazy. They had to have some. I didn't know why. The obvious didn't occur to me. Then I understood. These guys thought it was something other than headache powder. So I let them try some. They were disappointed, but it helped me break the ice with them.

So I walked in to Tom Chambers' office, sat down, and after we exchanged pleasantries, I said, "Tom, you guys need to start advertising, and you can do it in an unusual way by sponsoring some lap leader awards at the Speedway."

Well, before I left I got $10,000 out of him. It was the first advertising money the company had ever spent. During the race on the radio we plugged Goody's several times, and on TV one of the drivers was caught taking a Goody's powder during the race.

After the telecast, people became curious about Goody's. One day Tom called me and said, "I want to spend some more money. I'm getting calls from all over the country. I want to put the Goody's name on a car."

I called Richard Petty and told him about it. Like me, Richard had grown up with Goody's and Stanback, the other headache powder. Richard agreed to work with them. That was back in the mid-1980s, and Richard to this day is still working with Goody's, even after he sold his race team. Goody's then did some advertising with the Atlanta Braves, and the product began to spread out of the Southeast until Goody's eventually got bought out by a much larger company.

Back then we had to make a lot of cold calls, because no one was knocking on our door. And when we were able to attract a sponsor, it was usually only for a year. To make the investment work, they really needed to sign multiyear deals. Once we were able to do that, the growth in sales became obvious and they extended their deals.

But it wasn't until the early 1990s that the money really began pouring in. We were selling tickets and sponsorships very fast, and now, with money in the bank, Bruton began talking seriously about growth and what we as a company needed to do.

Bill France Jr. became quite concerned about Bruton's intentions. In the 1980s they had clashed over their differences. France was an extremely conservative pragmatist, and on the other side you had Bruton, who got up in the morning eating nails and wanting to own and then devour the world. Bruton had the ability to make Bill France Jr. so mad the soles of his shoes would peel off.

In the 1980s Bruton tried to buy the Indianapolis Motor Speedway. That was the last thing Mary George wanted to do. Indy was her pet. But it didn't stop Bruton from trying. Once the Charlotte Motor Speedway began to have a good cash flow, there was no stopping Bruton's aspirations. I knew he wasn't going to stop until he either had it all or he ran into the biggest oak tree you've ever seen.

Bruton and I would travel to see Bill France Jr., and Bruton would say to him, "Bill, are you ready to sell me NASCAR?" Bruton was as serious as a heart attack. This went on constantly. Bill would gag and say, "I don't want to sell NASCAR."

Bruton was always wanting to buy speedways or to build speedways. Bill France was also buying what he could, but he wasn't pushing nearly as hard as

Bruton. Bill France was trying to maintain stability in the sport as best he could while pushing the sport to become less southern and more national.

Bill France bought Darlington after a battle with Bruton. Darlington was the first big track to come up for sale. Bob Colvin, the legendary owner, had died. Barney Wallace was running it, and the stockholders felt it was time for the track to be sold. Darlington had lost its place as the number-one track in NASCAR, a position it had held for a long, long time.

Bruton went down and met with Barney, and he came back and told me he had made a deal. And then a week later Barney called Bruton and told him he had sold the track to Bill France. Bruton went nuts. He made a counteroffer, but Wallace refused to entertain it. So the France family took over Darlington.

The world of stock car racing was beginning to change. Had Bruton been successful in buying Darlington, my idea was to shut it down and build a new track at Myrtle Beach. There were a lot of good hotels there, an important factor in attracting race fans. All we had to do was acquire the land but we didn't get to do that because France bought the Darlington track, which set up further tension between them. It almost became open warfare.

Bruton pushed Bill France Jr. hard to move the annual banquet from New York City to Atlanta or Charlotte. I thought the banquet needed to be in New York because it's the media center of the world, and I was pushing France to establish an office there.

They would argue the point endlessly. Bruton later argued the banquet should be moved to Las Vegas, where there's no media at all. It has been moved to Vegas, an awful idea.

FRANCE WAS WARY of Bruton's aggressiveness and, to a certain extent, mine as well. Bruton wanted to buy any track that was for sale. Bruton finally bought the Atlanta track in a bidding war with Roger Penske, so we had a second track, but we were still a long way from being able to compete with the International Speedway Corporation (ISC). He tried to buy Indianapolis, but to do it we needed a great deal of capital that we couldn't borrow.

The idea came up to take the company public. For a while we couldn't get anyone to underwrite us. Finally we found a small firm in Richmond called Wheat First. The founder, Jim Wheat, was a blind man who was a legendary investment banker. His people were mostly University of Virginia first family, and I was surprised when they embraced us, because stock car racing still had an image problem.

None of us—Bruton, Bill Brooks (our chief financial officer), or me—knew anything about going public. It was a new experience, and it meant going on the road, and it was brutal. Basically, what you do is hold a bunch of dice in your hand and get ready to roll them. You go to every major city as fast as you can in jet aircraft, call on as many money managers as possible, and give the same pitch over and over and over again on what your company is all about. It's like taking a Broadway play on the road. The script never changes.

In one day we started in Los Angeles, made a pitch at seven o'clock in the morning; flew to San Diego, made a pitch; flew to San Francisco, made another one; and spent the evening talking to a bunch of money managers in Seattle. As soon as that was over we got on a plane and flew to Minneapolis to spend the night.

While we were on the road, we discovered a lot of interesting things about Wall Street. I would be looking for older guys to talk to, but there weren't any. Everyone was a twenty-five-year-old MBA from Harvard or Stanford or somewhere like that. I kept thinking, *Are the 40-year-olds elephants? Do they go to a graveyard to die?*

I found out that on Wall Street there is basically no loyalty. It's all about money. They either make it big or they get tossed out. And when they make it, they leave. So the people who run Wall Street are very young. The people making the big decisions are very young. And you can see how screwed up things can become. That's just the nature of the beast.

During the trip, Bruton would get bored real fast because we were doing the same thing over and over. Usually he made the lead pitch, and then he'd get up and leave the room to make phone calls on the different deals he was working on.

We met with Warren Buffett at the airport in Boston, and then we hurried over to this rickety old building by the river in downtown Boston where we met two old ladies. I first thought they were matronly secretaries, but they ran the company. They came from very old Boston money that had been hot-housed, moss-grown, and stowed away for a couple hundred years, and they were part of the family that had a substantial family trust.

Bruton and I had our pinstriped suits on. One of the ladies said, "You boys want a drink?" Bruton doesn't drink, but I do. I said, "Yes, ma'am, I sure would like one." She poured me a shot of Bushmills, an Irish whiskey that's like scotch. That lit the room up. We went back and forth with the ladies telling jokes for an hour, and they were amused. They had read about our company, knew everything about it. They asked a few questions. I looked down at my chowder cup with a handle on it, and I was feeling pretty good, and it was completely empty. They wanted to fill it back up again, but I knew I'd never get back if I did. They said, "We don't know exactly what you do, but we like your company. Your terms are good." You never know if any of these money managers are going to buy the stock until it actually comes out, and it turned out these ladies did.

Usually, Wall Street people are as funny as scalded acorns. They probably laughed when they were kids, but then their mothers hit them in the mouth with something hard. Because Wall Street people don't laugh at jokes. Nothing to them is funny, so you have to be careful. I met with one woman money manager in L.A. who was the most uptight human being I have ever encountered in my life. She should have been a librarian at the Library of Congress. I was thinking, *Is there some way I can break through to her?* I pulled a can of Skoal from my back pocket. I uncorked it, put my fingers in it, and let the tobacco bits drop. All of a sudden she was fascinated by this strange product she had never seen before. When she asked what it was, I explained it was smokeless tobacco.

"Who would take it?" she asked.

"Race fans love it," I said. "Since people can't smoke in a lot of public places, this is big stuff. This is one of our big sponsors. The company is out of Connecticut. U.S. Tobacco."

That got her ever so slightly amused. It was probably the only time she smiled since she was seven. She later bought some stock too.

After we made our calls, the Wheat First people would call the money managers to get a feeling of how many shares they would want, if any. The idea was to tell them what your future plans were, but you had to do it under strict SEC guidelines. You have to be real careful, because later on you can get the heck sued out of you.

I EVEN WENT TO EUROPE to make my pitch. There was a lot of interest there because the Europeans saw that NASCAR racing was the coming thing, and that's what you want. People are investing in the future. When we got to Europe we were greeted with more enthusiasm than in the States. These people had massive dollars coming in from Mideast oil, and money from China also was pouring in, and they had to put it somewhere. Middle-Easterners don't buy bonds. They want equities.

I went to London, Edinburgh, Milan, Paris, and Zurich. In Glasgow I spoke to a bunch of Scotsmen in an ancient hotel overlooking a giant castle. I was talking in a Southern brogue they could barely understand, and it was noon, so the Scotch was not yet flowing, and I couldn't get any reaction from these guys. They were looking at me like I had shot their favorite dog.

We drove from Glasgow to Edinburgh and pulled in front of this building that had to be 400 years old. It said "The Scottish Railroad Pension Fund" on the front. If we thought the money was moldy in Boston, this was past mold. That railroad had been around forever. We were greeted by a dour Scots lady who said, "They will be with you in a minute. They've been up all night, and some of them have been drinking."

"Drinking?" I said.

"Yes, there was a big game last night."

I had seen it on TV. The night before we were in the hotel in Glasgow watching a rugby game on TV, when the Glasgow fullback was forearmed and had his eye split wide open. When the analysts finally came in that morning, all young guys, here was this great big guy with his eye all stitched up and a patch over it. Turns out he was the fullback who got forearmed on that rugby team, and he was also the manager of the stock company. He began talking about coming to North Carolina and investing in Lowe's and Bank of America and Wachovia. He knew all about our Speedway. We had a jolly good time, and he bought some of our stock.

The really funny meeting came in Paris. We met in a typical old Parisian bank, very fancy, everything in brass, and Louis XV furniture in the office. The head of the company wore a tight, brown tweed suit with a vest, and he looked like Adolph Menjou, a little guy with a twirly mustache. I sat down, and I was ready to make the pitch when he pulled out his pipe and lighted up. Everyone in Paris smokes, and the room began to fill with the smell of some kind of Turkish tobacco. Before I could speak, he proceeded to tell me how the French had won World War II, which interested me because, aside from the Resistance, I don't remember the French doing much more than getting in the way, but I wasn't going to tell the guy that. He kept going on and on, and he got to D-Day, and talked about how D-Day wouldn't have happened had it not been for the Resistance. Wine was poured, and we kept hearing more tales of French heroism. He totally rewrote the history of the war. I never said a word about our company. An hour later when he paused and I went to pull out a flip chart, he said,

"Not necessary." He knew all about the company, so he continued with his version of World War II, and we left.

A couple days before Wheat First was going to set the price of the stock, we were in Milan and staying at a fancy hotel when at two o'clock in the morning there was a knock at the door. I was asleep. I got up, and I noticed there was something slipped under the door. I opened it up, and it was a scathing article written by David Mildenberg, once a business writer at the *Charlotte Observer* now with the *Bloomberg News.* Bruton had had a run-in with the guy, and Mildenberg had waited patiently for some time sharpening his scalpel, and at the precise worst moment he unleashed a diatribe against Bruton.

We all were in a state of panic. We rushed back to New York City where we met with Wheat First. There was even talk of pulling the IPO after all this work. We had hoped to come out at twenty-five dollars a share, and subsequently we had to come out at eighteen, so the article probably cost us the difference because it scared off some people. But we got through it, and we raised $200 million, money that we used to expand the Charlotte Motor Speedway and to buy the Sears Point track.

I WASN'T A BIG FAN of his buying Sears Point because it's a road course well north of San Francisco in Sonoma County, a highly regulated place. The people there are not terribly enthused about racing. They thought it was going to wake the grapes up at the wrong time. And the track only held one race. Even though Bill France Jr. had fallen in love with San Francisco when he was stationed there during Korea, he wasn't terribly enthused about the track other than the fact that NASCAR needed the market. NASCAR's weakness in those days was that we weren't in the big markets. We were still a regional/national sport, though we were becoming more national.

But Bruton was going to buy anything that was standing, so when I got a call from the owner saying he wanted to sell, I called Bruton. He jumped all over it, and we bought it for $20 million. Bruton immediately went out there and tried to convert it to an oval track, because stock cars just don't put on a very good show on a road course. But Sonoma officials said no way.

I thought his investing so much money into Sears Point was a mistake because of the road situation. California race fans came from Bakersfield and Modesto and towns in the valley, and there were only two narrow main roads from Vallejo across twenty miles of marshland at the edge of San Francisco Bay. Knowing Californians, I knew they would never allow those roads to be widened because it would encroach on the bay. Jokingly I kidded that the only way that track was ever going to work was if everybody came in hovercrafts. To get there from San Francisco, you had to come up Highway 101, which is notorious on Sundays. It was four lanes, but it was a parking lot. And when fans got to the track, there were few hotel rooms for them to stay in. And staying in San Francisco was a little far. What was worse, when the race was over, the traffic jams were horrendous. There was no way to get out of the place.

Even though I didn't think too much of the place, Bruton ended up spending $45 million more. And we still had only one race.

Bruton then decided to build a track in Texas. He wanted Texas to be what Charlotte was supposed to be—only more perfect. Bruton and I went to Texas to take a look at land. I saw cedar trees and longhorn cattle. I knew the dirt was going to be damn hard to work with. A track is basically one big earth-moving job, and you want good dirt, and I knew it was going to be a problem, but Bruton had fallen in with Ross Perot Jr. and the Alliance Industrial Park. It's between Fort Worth and Dallas about twenty miles out of town. He bought the property and proceeded to build his dream track. At the same time he began to work on Bill France Jr. with a Chinese water torture on getting him another date on the Nextel Cup schedule. Every time Bill France Jr. was scheduled to be somewhere, Bruton also showed up.

The battle between Bill France Jr. and Bruton intensified after Bruton built the Texas Motor Speedway in 1996. He spent $250 million to build it, and I kept wondering, *Where is he going to get dates?* Because France wasn't going to give out any more dates. When they cut the schedule from fifty-four races to thirty-three, the schedule was set. Where were the dates going to come from?

France Jr. never did give him one, and after Bruton had spent $250 million to build his new track, he desperately needed a way to create two race dates.

What Bruton then did was interesting. He came up with the idea of buying two of the existing smaller tracks, closing them down, and moving the dates to his track in Texas.

A track in North Wilkesboro—The North Wilkesboro Speedway—in the heart of moonshine country was owned by Enoch Staley and Jack Coombs. Enoch, who had always been one of Bill France's right-hand men, ran the track, which started out as a dirt track and had a long and colorful history. Enoch was loyal to the bone to the France family. When Bill France Sr. wanted Bill Jr. to go off and learn the business, he sent him to learn the ropes under Enoch.

Even though Enoch had no trouble selling out the place on race days, Bruton kept after him, trying to buy the place. Bruton had already bought Atlanta, outmaneuvering Roger Penske to get it. Atlanta had been a track no one had been able to make work. He also was negotiating with Paul Sawyer to buy Richmond, with E. G. DeWitt to buy Rockingham, and with Enoch to buy Wilkesboro.

Enoch died, and his family continued to run the track. The Staleys refused to sell it to Bruton. They didn't like him and they weren't going to sell it to him, end of story. Or so they thought. Bruton then started working on Staley's partner, Jack Coombs. He made Coombs an incredible offer. When the Staleys found out Coombs was going to sell his share to Bruton, they sold their half interest to Bob Bahre, the owner of the New Hampshire Motor Speedway, which also had one date and needed another.

All of a sudden, Bruton owned half and Bob Bahre had the other half, and the sparks just flew. Bruton wasn't speaking to Bahre, and he was mad as a hornet at the Staleys. What they eventually did was agree to close the Wilkesboro track and each took a date.

The closing of the Wilkesboro track made the people in Wilkes County very angry. One day I filled up my tank at a filling station off Route 421 near the track. There's a restaurant attached to it where the good old boys eat, and after I went in there to have a bite, I really didn't know if I would get out of there alive. I could tell the denizens were really ticked about what we had done.

Meanwhile, the Wilkesboro track continues to sit there returning to earth.

With the demise of Wilkesboro, the closing of Rockingham, and Darlington having one of its dates taken away, it was like cutting the tongues out of the race fans in the South. It really cost us dearly to do that. I'd like to have thought that with Wilkesboro, Darlington, and Rockingham out of the picture that Charlotte would sell out more easily, but the exact opposite has happened. Those closings—along with the death of Dale Earnhardt, their hero—made many longtime race fans angry. Because that's where Dale's core audience was. It all took its toll on the South and the Southern race fans. They became very angry at Bruton and NASCAR.

THE TEXAS PUBLIC greeted the building of the Texas Motor Speedway with great enthusiasm. Texas and Oklahoma are two real race-crazy states. We sold thousands of tickets to the first race, which took place on April 6, 1997. But the Thursday before the race, it began to pour, raining as it can only in Texas.

On Friday it had rained so much I told Eddie Gossage, who was running the track, "The parking lots are unusable. The race is tomorrow, and there's no way anyone is going to be able to get in here." Eddie turned bluish-gray. I told Bruton, "We've got to do something." It was becoming a promoter's nightmare.

The powers of the local government called a meeting. I represented the Speedway. One guy stood up and said, "We should consider canceling the event."

"Did you say cancel the event?" I said.

He said, "Yes."

"Do you see that overpass over there?" I said. "The race fans will tear that down. They will tear this place up. They will tear up the interstate. They are coming from everywhere. You don't just call a race."

"What are we going to do?" he asked. "We can't park cars. We can't have them park on the interstate."

"We have to do something," I said.

Someone came up with the idea of using public transportation to take the fans to the speedway, a great idea considering that Dallas has a terrific bus system. I called the transit company and was told we could have all the buses we needed because they aren't used much on the weekend. It would cost the speedway $400,000.

We had no choice. I told Eddie Gossage, "You just added $400,000 to your budget. It's the only way people will be able to get in and out of here."

I got up bright and early Sunday morning. The weather was beautiful. I was staying at the Arlington Hotel in downtown Fort Worth, and as I went to get my car I saw this little, short guy in blue jeans and a cowboy shirt. He had missed his bus. I said, "I'm going to the track. Why don't you come with me?" He agreed.

I put on the country music station. "You don't have to play that," he said, as he pulled out his harmonica. I said, "You're going to play?" "Yeah," he said. "What's your favorite song?"

I said, "El Paso," and he played it drop-dead gorgeous. He then played "Blue Eyes Crying in the Rain" perfectly. When we arrived at the track I couldn't contain my curiosity any longer.

"Who are you?" I asked. He was Willie Nelson's brother, a professional musician who had been on the road with everybody from Ferlin Husky to Roy Clark. He said he and Willie grew up singing on their little farm in East Texas.

With the buses, we got everyone to the track just fine. There were a lot of wrecks, but the day was saved.

A YEAR LATER IT RAINED a whole lot the week before the race. When it came time to practice and qualify, even though it was sunny, we had a nightmare on our hands because the track began to weep like a wailing widow. Water was pouring out of the corners. Turns on high-banked tracks are actually giant dams cleaved on one side. When water gets built up in the clay behind the track, it's got to go somewhere. Even though there are drains in the track to take the water out the bottom, if there is too much water, it leaks onto the track's surface and makes racing very dangerous.

Earlier that week, the *Charlotte Observer*, which loved to taunt Bruton, came out with an editorial cartoon that said, "The Great Ship Texas." It showed the Titanic perpendicular in the water, inferring that the Texas Motor Speedway was Bruton's Titanic. Bruton was livid. We stayed in Eddie Gossage's office during qualifying, not knowing there was a problem because Bruton was calling everyone he could about the editorial. Meanwhile, drivers were crashing right and left. Our offices were about a third of a mile from the track, and by the time we got out there about seven cars had crashed because they kept hitting water spots. The drivers were screaming and hollering about the conditions, and it got really nasty—to the point that I began to wonder whether we had another Talladega on our hands.

We made and sold our own souvenirs, so we printed a T-shirt that said, "Shut up and race." Eddie Gossage got blamed for it. I would have done it had I thought of it, but I didn't. It didn't go over well in the garage area at all. Bill France Jr. went into the fourth stage of apoplexy over it. In fact, after the race he said to the press, "Bruton keeps wanting a second date. I'm not sure if we'll be back here for a single date next year."

We had to spend a million dollars redoing the track. It was supposed to duplicate the Charlotte track, but it's almost impossible to copy a track. The Texas track tended to pinch cars off in the second and fourth corners, so there were a lot of wrecks. Ricky Craven had his career ended there. A driver in the truck series was killed.

In the meantime, Bruton was wearing out Bill France Jr. demanding a second date. And taunting him by calling Texas "the world's greatest speedway." He spent about $350 million on the track and the facility, an enormous amount of money. He built palatial condominiums, put in tennis courts no one used, and a swimming pool no one swam in. As for the suites, he threw away the mold. We built 200 suites at the Texas Motor Speedway. Everything was over the top, and we were still sitting there with one date.

One day I learned that a guy by the name of Ferko had sued NASCAR because it didn't give Texas a second date. I had never met Ferko. He lived in Plano, Texas, and it was obvious Bruton was behind the suit. We had a board meeting over whether to continue the suit, which was an antitrust case. I knew Bill France Jr. was pulling his ears off because the lawsuit was costing him a lot of money. It was filed in federal court, and the future of racing depended on the result.

Bruton always had a battery of lawyers at his beck and call, particularly down in Texas. We were represented by John Connolly's firm. The suit had everyone up in arms. The issue was that second date, which Bill France Jr. refused to give us. He said he wasn't going to take a day away from any of the existing tracks. And he wasn't going to add a race. "We have enough races on the schedule," he said.

The suit had everyone tangled up and made life miserable. We had a board meeting, and the board told our attorney, Fred Lowrance, that it didn't want the suit to continue. I had asked a law professor at Yale his opinion as to whether we had any chance to win the suit, and he said it didn't look good hanging the case on antitrust and monopoly. I told Bruton that and, of course, he wouldn't listen. We had a phone conference of the board, and when he sensed hesitation he said, "Do I sense a smell of fear?"

"There's a chance we could win this thing," said Fred Lowrance.

"Well, in that case, everyone in favor say 'aye,'" said Bruton. And boom, that was it. The suit went on, and as the suit went on and got more and more expensive, and as Bill France Jr. got older, his son Brian France began to take a bigger and bigger role in NASCAR's decision making. Brian was much more compliant and much more amenable to solving problems than his father and certainly than his grandfather.

Someone—I presume it was Brian—came up with an idea to solve the second date problem. ISC, France's company that owns NASCAR, Daytona, and their other speedways, had bought Rockingham from Roger Penske when Penske sold his tracks to ISC. Brian offered to sell Bruton the Rockingham track for $100 million. At that time Rockingham had one race. France said, "Buy it, and you can have a second date in Texas."

The Rockingham track wasn't worth much of anything, and when I heard the price I almost fell over. Eventually we sold it for four million. But Bruton wanted his second date, and he paid a ridiculously high price to get it.

Bruton's empire didn't stop with the building of the Texas Motor Speedway. He immediately set his sights on Las Vegas, his favorite place on earth.

The Las Vegas track was built by Ralph Engelstad who owned the Imperial Palace, and Bill Bennett who owned a bunch of casinos and then sold them. The money for the track came out of their pockets. They didn't borrow a dime, and Richie Klein, Ralph's former son-in-law, ran it.

They had consulted me before they built the track. It was flat, and I told them I didn't like the design, but they said they wanted to run IndyCars. Even though I warned them that IndyCar racing didn't make any money, they built it that way anyway. A flat track produces terribly boring races, and eventually what I told them came true. They found out they couldn't make any money with it because they only had one race on the Nextel Cup schedule.

One good thing they did do was build every kind of racetrack on the property. There was a three-eighths-mile oval, and they built a half-mile dirt track, a drag strip, and a road course. As a result the track was rented nine months a year. You can't run races there in the summer because of the extreme desert heat.

Bruton agreed to pay two hundred and sixty-five million for it, a record for a speedway. I thought he was paying far too much, but it did include an industrial park, which at the time wasn't making any money. Effectively we ended up paying about $165 million for the racetrack complex, too much money for a track with one date. And it still has just one date.

By this time Bruton thought I was against everything he wanted to do. Which I wasn't. I just wanted us to be a little more conservative in what we were spending. We were a public company, and I was looking after the stockholders' money. As president, I had a fiscal responsibility to look after their interests. At the time Bruton had begun to invest the company's money in all sorts of crazy things, including zMax (a mystery oil) and oil wells in Russia. He also started something called Sold USA, which was going to be the next eBay. It lost a bunch of money and was finally dissolved. The investors were screaming at us for doing all this. They wanted us to run races, not get into the oil or merchandise business.

But Bruton was into empire building, so nothing was sacred.

CHAPTER 26

Joe Gibbs and Dale Jarrett

JOE GIBBS, THE COACH of the Washington Redskins football team, came to Charlotte in 1991 to talk about getting into Winston Cup racing. He had done some drag racing, and I could see his intense interest. I could also tell he was looking for a place to go after football. I had the sense that Joe saw that the people in NASCAR were similar to those he knew in football. It was a male-oriented sport populated by a bunch of rough, tough guys who actually welcomed leadership but didn't act like it. He displayed a confidence that told me he felt he could put a race team together and be successful.

He talked to a number of different people. He was like Rick Hendrick in that way. We were very excited about getting Joe into NASCAR because he was the sort of person you looked for—a celebrity from the outside who could raise the profile of the sport and someone who might put us in *Sports Illustrated* or even *The Sporting News*, which was a stick-and-ball-oriented magazine.

Joe did get a lot of publicity when he announced he was starting a race team. After all, he had won a Super Bowl, plus he was a hell of a nice guy. He spent time with people, and he began to assemble a talented group of racers. Joe was very good at getting and keeping sponsors. His first major sponsor was Interstate Batteries. He signed the deal with Norm Miller from down in Texas, and Norm continues to be one of Joe's sponsors today. It is one of the longest-running sponsorships in the sport.

He signed Dale Jarrett as his driver, and he named Dale's cousin, Jimmy Makar, as his crew chief. The Gibbs race team became known as the Newton Gang. Newton, North Carolina, is about thirty miles north of Charlotte, and it's where Ned Jarrett (Dale's dad) comes from. Dale and his crew had begun racing together at the Hickory Speedway. Ned begat Dale, who brought a lot of his buddies with him.

As a race driver, Dale is very even-keeled, and very consistent on the track. You don't see him make bold moves. He's a driver like David Pearson. All of a sudden with a hundred laps to go, he'll show up, and the next thing you know, he'll be running second, and then he'll lead the race.

If Ned hadn't been his father, it's quite possible Dale might have ended up as a professional golfer. No question he's the best golfer who ever drove a race car. He hits booming drives off the tee. He's 300 yards straight as an arrow down the fairway. In high school he was an excellent quarterback. But his father was a top driver, and Dale grew up in it, and it was something he wanted to do. Dale is very gentlemanly, a very good representative for any company.

Dale ran for Gibbs for three years and won a couple of races, not bad for a new team, but he really made his mark driving the UPS car for Robert Yates—switching teams only because he got a much better deal with Yates. I know it was hard for Dale to leave Joe Gibbs, but this was when salaries really started to go up for drivers. They were beginning to make some serious up-front money. It had to be a significant increase in order for him to have made the move. And it ended up being pivotal for Dale, who won thirty races driving the UPS car for the Yates team.

As a promoter, I dreamed of doing a stunt with that UPS truck, but I knew that if I did it, I would be going off a cliff. At the Speedway I would jump everything from school buses to garbage trucks in shows, and I had the idea of having an event that would measure how far that brown UPS truck could jump. I could have set a Guinness world record for UPS trucks, because no one had ever done it before. But I knew it would offend the UPS sponsors, who were nice guys. It would be like blowing up a Pepsi truck. It was something you just didn't do.

The departure of Dale allowed Joe Gibbs to sign Bobby Labonte and Tony Stewart. Bobby is a driver a lot like Dale, very even-tempered and quiet and not into controversy. Tony, of course, is another story.

I first met Tony Stewart about twenty years ago when he was still a teenager. I had a friend by the name of Charlie Patterson who made a living finding young drivers and helping them advance. Tony was an Indy driver. Charlie brought Tony to see me. He said, "This kid has really got it."

I had seen Tony run a little bit on *Thursday Night Thunder*, an ESPN show dedicated to the open-cockpit Sprint car races. At the time, Tony, a good-looking kid, was a fierce competitor. One time on a half-mile track in Indiana in a Sprint car, he ran off the edge of the backstretch—which sat up pretty high—and he went sailing into the woods. He literally landed in a tree. He didn't get hurt, but the experience had to be mind-numbing. I was very impressed when he returned to the track and didn't seem to be bothered by it at all.

After I met Tony, I kept up with him pretty closely. When he began racing at Indianapolis, he was certainly the best young driver on the circuit, and maybe the best driver period—though for a guy who led a significant number of races, he didn't win a race.

Tony had a horrific wreck in an IndyCar race. He broke his leg and had to stay out of racing for a while. The time between the sheets, however, didn't seem to deter him. He decided to bolt the IndyCar circuit and in 1998 he began driving in the Busch circuit for Harry Ranier.

It was a very difficult transition, but he made the move as smoothly as anyone I've seen. In 1999 he began driving for Joe Gibbs, and he began winning races right from the start. Things really took off for him. Joe signed Home Depot as a sponsor for Tony's car, and Home Depot spent a lot of money touting that Tony was the company's driver. Tony starred in their commercials, and he started winning Cup races.

But it wasn't too long before the hard side of Tony Stewart appeared. He had a terrible temper, and he had some ugly altercations on the racetrack. One time he struck a photographer, and he had other run-ins until the press began calling him Terrible Tony. NASCAR fined him, and Home Depot supposedly did, though I never did get to the bottom of that one. And I have to say Joe Gibbs may have been one of the few team owners who could have handled Tony Stewart.

Tony and I would talk a lot about how he had to control his temper. I told him I had had a similar problem. As we talked, I could tell that part of his problem was that he missed living back in small-town Indiana with his family and friends. In Charlotte, he was like a movie star in Hollywood.

He had no privacy. Eventually he sold his home in Charlotte and moved back home where he could walk around unmolested. And that seems to have settled him down.

Joe Gibbs, like Rick Hendrick, has been a successful car owner, even though mechanically he's no genius. What Joe knows how to do is put people together and keep them together. And he has a knack for keeping up morale. His sons, who are extremely nice, have come into the business, and they are quite helpful to him.

Over and over Joe swore to me that he would never go back into football again. I don't know how many times he told me that. But money talks, and the Redskins made him an offer he couldn't turn down, and that's what got him back in the game. But when he got there, he saw the same things that drove him away in the first place. After a couple years, he got back out again. He's happy now, and he's really enjoying working with his family on his race team.

CHAPTER 27

Jack Roush and Mark Martin

JACK ROUSH IS A MIDWESTERNER who first made his mark in road and drag racing. His company has been a big vendor to the Ford Motor Company for a long time. Jack is extremely well-organized, and devoted to racing. He's sixty years old, and he flies everywhere himself in a P-51 Mustang from World War II that he rebuilt from the bottom up.

One cold January night, Jack came to my house for dinner. My wife, Pat, cooked for him. We went into the living room and swapped stories for a couple hours, and then it got to be about nine thirty, and it was not a particularly good weather night, and Jack said to Pat, "I have to go now."

"Where are you going?" she wanted to know.

"I'm going back to Michigan."

"Tonight?" She didn't know Jack flew his own plane.

"Where is your pilot?" she asked.

"Well, I'm the pilot."

She was astonished. He got in his plane and flew off.

Jack is a short man who always wears a hat. Richard Petty calls him "the cat in the hat." Jack's favorite activity is to take a Holley carburetor back to the motel room and work on it during the night. That's his idea of a great evening. He's a mechanical genius, the opposite of Joe Gibbs or Rick Hendrick. He knows as much about the race car as anyone who works for him.

Jack doesn't hire drivers who will raise anybody's hackles. Tony Stewart and Kyle Busch would not have raced for Jack or wouldn't have raced long for Jack. Kurt Busch actually won a championship for Jack, then they parted ways.

Mark Martin is one driver who no other driver will ever say anything bad about. He gives the other drivers a tremendous amount of room on the racetrack. He won't block anyone out of the way. I would say Mark Martin is the most fair of any race driver we've ever had in NASCAR, and all the drivers have great respect for him. He gives them room, and they give him room. So he's never had any conflicts, and he always says the right thing.

Jack came onto the scene in 1988 with Mark Martin as his driver. Mark had come into NASCAR, didn't make it, returned to the ASA series and did well, and then came back to NASCAR as a new person. Jack saw that Mark had what it took to win races, and he was exactly the kind of driver that Jack likes—uncontroversial, nice to a fault. Mark drove for Jack for twenty years, winning thirty races, and they've been together until this year when Mark tried to retire until money lured him back.

Jack almost died flying a friend's experimental aircraft down at Talladega in 2007. The plane lost power, and when it got down to about 5,000 feet, Jack looked for a place to put it down. He was in the backwoods of Alabama, an area of rolling hills. It's hard to find a flat place to land over there, until he spotted a lake. It was his only hope.

He hit the water, and the plane flipped upside down. As fate would have it, an ex–Navy SEAL had a house on the lake and he was sitting on his porch looking out as he watched the plane crash. It was about six o'clock at night, and he jumped in his boat, went over to the plane, dove under the water, and opened the hatch. How many people would have known how to do that? He did because he was trained to do it. And he pulled out Jack, who was unconscious, and Jack survived, even though he was all busted up. Jack had a broken pelvis and a broken leg, and a concussion. Later, he brought the guy who pulled him out to a race, and I met him.

Jack was in critical condition, and it took him a long time to get well. He was taken to the same hospital in Birmingham that Bobby Allison had gone to after he had gotten out of the hospital in Allentown, Pennsylvania.

Jack recovered and is back flying full tilt. He doesn't remember anything about the crash. He can recall seeing the water, and then everything went black after that.

Jack is very good at training young race drivers. He knows how to bring them along and how to give them the confidence they need to win, and that may be his real forte as a car owner. He did this with Carl Edwards, Matt Kenseth, and Greg Biffle, and he is doing it now with David Ragan, who had never driven anything bigger than a Legends car. Jack literally moved him from there to trucks and then to Busch and then to Cup racing. David went through a year in which Tony Stewart criticized him unmercifully for being all over the racetrack, but then at the end of his sophomore year, Tony said David was the best young driver in racing and that he had seen more improvement in him than in any other driver.

Jack did the same thing with Carl Edwards, a handsome guy the kids love because he does a back flip after he wins a race. It's Carl's signature, and it's really neat. It also shows his athleticism. Carl does wonders with his ability to take a car so loose that it's about sideways and save it. Like Tim Richmond and Dale Earnhardt, he is a great loose race driver, which is one thing that makes the difference between a mediocre driver and a great one.

Something else Carl Edwards does: When he wins a race, he gives away the trophy. The winner of the Busch race in Nashville wins a very expensive guitar signed by singing stars like Loretta Lynn and others. David Ragan's older brother, Adam, has Down's syndrome and is about twenty-five years old. Adam's always around the track, and everybody loves him. When Carl won the race in 2008, he handed the guitar to Adam, and Adam has it in his room now. Giving away the trophy is a neat thing that Carl does.

In 2008 at Kansas, we had the best race of the season between three of the four Roush drivers on a mile-and-a-half track not known for terribly close racing. It came down to Carl, Matt Kenseth, and Greg Biffle, and they waged all-out war for the last twenty laps or so. People think a car owner will get on the radio and say, "Wait a minute. You guys calm down," but Jack let it go. The fourth-place finisher, who wasn't a Roush driver, could have just as easily have won the race. It was very similar to a race run at Charlotte back in 1965 between A. J. Foyt, Dick Hutcherson, Fred Lorenzen, and Curtis Turner—guys jockeying back and forth right to the end. Carl ended up winning.

Matt Kenseth, the second of the Jack Roush drivers, is a product of a state that has more races in a shorter period of time than any other state in the union: Wisconsin. The forte of Wisconsin racing is the short track, and it's a place where you can run literally seven days a week during the summer. Dick Trickle was one of a number of Wisconsin racers to come down to NASCAR and succeed.

Matt was a prolific winner up there. He came down here, and Jack put him in a Busch car, and he did well. Though he's a fierce competitor who will race you as hard as anyone, Matt is a nice guy who is not controversial.

Greg Biffle comes from an unusual place, Washington State, which, because of the weather and the more populated areas, does not have many tracks. Greg was a very good short-track racer—a driver who specialized in stock cars—and he made his way east, was picked up by Jack Roush, and did really well with him. He's particularly adept at the two-mile tracks like Michigan and California. When Greg's car gets hooked up, he's capable of running away from the show. He's not known for driving as deep into corners as Jeff Gordon or Jimmie Johnson, but he's very smooth and consistent. Although he does tend to get in slumps, usually you see him at the end of a race.

Greg is also a great lover of animals. He raises money for humane societies. He owns a 1,000-acre farm in Rutherfordton, North Carolina. He's a nice guy who has time for the fans. He isn't as popular as Carl Edwards, but again, he's a typical Roush driver.

The driver who may turn out to be Jack Roush's most popular driver is David Ragan, who is a breath of fresh air because he comes from a small Southern town. Just about every time we run short of Southern drivers, another one comes along, and David is the latest. He's from Unadilla, down in Georgia not too far from Albany, which is pronounced *Al-binny*.

David has a lot of Bill Elliott in him, though he doesn't talk like Bill because when he was ten years old he moved to Atlanta, where people don't speak "Southern." They speak "Midwestern."

David is totally unpretentious, yet he is a very good interview because he always seems to have something meaningful to say. He doesn't own a plane. He doesn't own a million-dollar motor home though he's made enough money to buy one. What he owns is Barney Fife's 1964 police car from *The Andy Griffith Show*. It's hilarious to see him driving around in it.

He has his pickup truck, and he has a roommate with whom he lives modestly. He's been a breath of fresh air, and he's beginning to show signs of being a serious contender. David had a number of top five finishes and led some races. He's the driver Jack Roush chose to replace Mark Martin with UPS. A raw-boned Georgia boy capable of winning a number of races, David is only twenty-three years old—twenty-three going on fifty. He's been racing since he was nine years old.

CHAPTER 28

The Death of Dale Earnhardt

IN MARCH 2000 IN TEXAS, Dale Earnhardt Jr. won his first race, and Dale Sr. was just ecstatic. That May, I told the press I was picking Dale Jr. to win the Winston All Star race at the Lowe's Motor Speedway. It really ticked Dale Sr. off. He was hot about it.

"You're putting too much pressure on him," he said.

"Maybe I am," I said, "but I'm not taking it back. I think he's going to win the race."

"Aah, that's too much heat on him," Dale said, and he kept gouging me about it.

When Junior won the Winston, it told me that I had a real race car driver on my hands now. The Winston is a great test because it isn't a points race. You can do whatever you want, and the only thing that counts is winning the race. And Junior did that.

Two weeks before the Daytona race of 2001, Dale called me. He and Junior were going to run a Corvette together, and he was very happy about that. Then he said, "I have 200 people working for me," and he started griping about all the problems he was having.

"I told you that you were going to have this," I said. "You're the dog that caught the Mack truck. Now you're going to have to live with it."

"Yeah, I know, but shit," Dale said. I could tell he wasn't really happy about it, but at the same time I knew he didn't have to fear what every driver in racing fears—having no place to go after the driving career ends. Dale now had a place to go—his mammoth DEI headquarters building—and he had a long-term deal with Budweiser for Junior. Dale was in high cotton even though he was complaining about all the people working for him.

We went to Daytona, and I talked to him a couple times that week. Before the race, I was over by the cars during the driver intros, and Dale pinched me, something he did a lot. I patted him on the back. Teresa was with him, and I said hello to her, and I didn't say a word to him. And we walked off.

Halfway through the race I flew home to Charlotte. I didn't want to get caught in the Daytona traffic. When I got home, I learned there had been a wreck on the last lap. Someone said, "Tony Stewart was in the wreck, and Michael Waltrip won the race." I thought that was neat.

When I arrived home, I told Pat, "I'm going out for a run."

About twenty minutes into my run, Pat drove the car to find me. She knew my route. I thought, *Oh shit, something has happened to my mother or something.*

Pat said, "You'd better get in."

"Why?"

"Just get in," she said. "Dale's dead."

That was a total shock. I watched them play the wreck on TV over and over, and I couldn't believe he died in such an innocuous accident. I don't know if anyone else pointed this out, but it was the exact kind of wreck that killed Neil Bonnett, Dale's best friend. There were two great friends, and they died in almost the same place.

This was the last in a litany of deaths—Neil Bonnett, Kenny Irwin, Adam Petty, Clifford Allison—that all involved twenty-five- to thirty-degree angle hits to the outer wall, and it's because the cars got to be too stiff. The drivers had to absorb the energy, where with the older cars you could have that kind of wreck, and the front ends would collapse. For a driver to survive, the G forces have to be less than forty. When Dale died, the G forces in that car were a hundred, and he died instantly from a basal skull fracture.

NASCAR got the car and took it up to Conover and put it in a compound where nobody could get to it, and they began to analyze what happened. They discovered that the left seat belt had rubbed raw underneath the seat, and when he hit the wall, the seat belt was so threadbare it broke, and by breaking it threw him over, and he hit his head on a bar in the right front of the car. Then it snapped back his head and neck, killing him. Death was instantaneous. Because of the snap, you can't recover from it, and before air bags it was how an awful lot of people died in roadway accidents. It just cracks that vertebra down in the ring at the bottom of the cervical area of the spine, and the driver is dead.

When I learned that Dale was dead, at first I didn't know what I was going to do, but then the next day I drove over to DEI to see how I could help out. I arrived there on Monday morning at about eight o'clock. I went and had coffee, and Dale Jr. showed up and Ty Norris, and they had a meeting, and they asked me to come along.

"I'm very sorry about this," I said, "but you guys have got to keep going." Then I said, "I don't need to stay in the meeting," and I left them. I stayed at DEI all day. At about ten o'clock Teresa called. She was still in Daytona Beach. She and Dale had their boat, *Sunday Money*, down there, and she was staying on it with their daughter, Nicole. Mike Helton saw her walking toward the boat Sunday night, and he said, "Teresa, you don't want to stay on the boat. You need to come and stay at our house." And that's where she spent the night.

It was chaos at DEI, and at the same time very somber. People were coming in droves to the front of the shop, dropping flowers and standing around not knowing what to do. I was walking around talking to the guys in the shop when Teresa called. She said she wanted to bury Dale in the Lutheran church where Ralph had been buried.

"Teresa, you can't do that," I said. "His fans will tear that place up. You need to bury him right here on the DEI property."

"I don't know if that's legal or not," she said.

"I know it's legal," I said, "but I'll make sure." I called Ken Poe who ran a funeral home in Charlotte.

"You can't do it in Charlotte," he said, "but you sure can do it in Iredell County" where DEI was located. Teresa made arrangements to do that, and then I called my daughter, Patti, and she called Teresa, and they agreed the service would be in the huge Calvary Church in Charlotte. Teresa said Patti, a TV producer, could film it live, which was fitting because all Dale's fans would not have been able to get into the church.

§

PEOPLE HAVE ASKED themselves a million times, "Why did Dale have to die?" Well, that's just what happens sometimes. There is never an answer for it. Looking back, I don't think Dale would have driven more than two more years. And the most amazing thing about that accident was how well Dale Jr. held up under it. Everyone waited for him to have a complete breakdown, but he never did and never has. It's just incredible how he was able to hold himself together through all this. A lot of kids would have gone off and done drugs or drank heavily, but Junior held up really well.

One result of Dale's death was the breakup between Teresa and Junior. She may have been the stepmother, but she also raised him, because he came to live with her and Dale when Junior was about ten years old. Brenda moved away from Charlotte—I don't know the details exactly—and by that time Dale was well enough off financially. He had married Teresa, so they had a home, and he took both Kelley and Dale Junior. Kelley is two years older than Junior, and Kelley really raised him. She was always very protective of him, and when she was thirteen she was going on twenty. She had it all together, and she still does, and she still runs his life today. She lives on Junior's farm with her husband and their kids, and she's his business manager.

About a year after they came to live with him, Dale called me and he said, "I have to do something with them. I want to put them in military school." He asked me about Oak Ridge, and I told him I thought it was a good school, and he did that. They didn't stay there long, but Junior talks very highly about the experience. He didn't like it at the time, but it helped straighten him out. It was like he was in the Marine Corps.

You could see the breakup between Junior and Teresa coming from four miles away. Junior didn't need Teresa anymore, and there also was friction when Dale's estate was divvied up. Who was going to get the airplane? Who would get the boat? Who would get this? Junior wasn't happy with how Teresa was dividing it up, and the relationship was headed for oblivion. Junior made a demand on her, moneywise, and she put her foot down and said no and wouldn't give in. And she brought in a smart businessman, Max Siegel—a nice guy, a Notre Dame graduate who had been around the record business, and he's still there. I thought from his reputation Max might be able to straighten out the bad feelings between Teresa and Junior, and I think if he had gotten there a year earlier he might have, because everyone respects him. But he was new to racing, and it was much too late.

The shocker came when Rick Hendrick signed Junior. At first when Dale Jr. left Teresa and said he was on the open market, Rick denied he was interested. Everybody thought the inevitable would happen, that he would end up with Richard Childress and that Richard would bring back the No. 3 black Chevrolet. As a promoter, it was something I wish had happened. The race fans love that car. It may come out again driven by Richard's grandson who is driving a black No. 3 in Late Model stock cars.

Rick told me, "No, I am not going after him," and he played it cool. One day I got a call saying that Rick Hendrick wanted to rent the Texas Speedway to have a press conference. I said, "I don't have a problem with that." As soon as I heard that, I knew that Rick and Junior had put a deal together.

I was quite surprised Junior did that, because he's going to be third man on a team that has two of the most successful racers who ever got behind the wheel of a stock car, Jeff Gordon and Jimmie Johnson. Rick's third car has never done a whole lot, even with decent drivers.

The real shockeroo, though, was Junior leaving Budweiser. He had become such an icon driving the red No. 8. In 2007, I became tremendously upset with Junior because before the World 600 it was announced that Junior was going to drive a camouflage car. It was a stupid idea.

I called the Budweiser people to complain. I called David Hill at Fox. I called Brian France. I said, "You've got to stop this. Nobody is going to know Junior's even in the car. Those fans have paid money, and they're going to walk in looking for that red No. 8, and they're not going to be able to find it. Why would you want to camouflage that race car?" I just blew my stack.

"This is really stupid," I told Junior, and I told Kelley the same thing. But I couldn't get anyone to do anything about it.

When Junior left Budweiser, he signed with three different sponsors, so he's going to drive three different cars, and I thought then it was another a big mistake. But I suspect Junior feels he can get more deals if he isn't tied to an adult beverage. He has never come out and said it, but that's what it is. And I'm still not sure it's going to be the best move in the end. Kasey Kahne is now in the red Budweiser No. 9.

For two years, Junior didn't win a race, and then he won at Kansas in a rain-shortened race. Junior is thirty-four now. Is he going to be the prolific driver everyone thought he would be? I don't know. He might go through a spell where he wins some races. Is he going to be a Kyle Petty? All Kyle had to do was win two races a year, and with the personality he had, that was enough to keep him going. Can Junior do the same thing? Absolutely. He's still extremely popular. He accounts for thirty percent of the souvenir sales.

But when his father died, the sport lost something it never regained. Quite frankly, attendance at stock car races has never been the same since. We have been going downhill at the gate, because we lost the last workingman driver we had. His fans were the shrimp boat operator, the mechanic, the backhoe guy, and the people in the Chevy ads with sweat dripping off their noses. And Junior is not that way.

When Dale died, we lost a tremendous number of fans. Some of Dale's fans went with Junior out of sympathy, but I'm not sure they stayed with him. Junior did bring in a whole new group of people. Usually, when a driver dies or retires, his fans transfer to someone else. When Richard Petty retired, a tremendous amount of his fans went to Bill Elliott, and Bill became the most popular driver for twelve years. Unfortunately, we haven't had anyone come along who's had that workingman ethic that Dale Earnhardt had. And I don't know that we ever will again.

CHAPTER 29

The Corporatization
of Racing

AFTER DALE DIED, ticket sales began to slow down. At first it was minimal, but it kept escalating until by 2006 I was noticing serious problems not only at our track but at other tracks. I had seen that corporatization of stock car racing had gotten completely out of control, and I began a campaign with Bill France Jr. to change it.

Everything at the speedways had a sign on it. I always thought Formula 1 courses were ridiculous, but we were just as bad. We had signage on the walls, signage on the grass, signage everywhere. The drivers looked like small billboards, and instead of a car having one sponsor on it, it had ten.

When Brian France took over from his dad, he started on a jet-powered marketing push. He hired consultants. He expanded the New York office. He began to commercialize NASCAR in massive ways. There was the official drink of NASCAR, the official bank of NASCAR, the official snack food of NASCAR, the official everything of NASCAR, and people were beginning to feel that NASCAR should be a sanctioning body, not a commercial entity—that it should let the drivers, the car owners, the tracks, and the TV companies do the selling.

The corporatization of the sport hit close to home when, without my knowledge, Bruton hired a company in New Jersey to sell naming rights to his tracks. He didn't tell any of his presidents or general managers he was doing this. I found out one day when he called me and said, "We need to have a press conference."

"What about?"

"We sold the naming rights to the Charlotte Motor Speedway."

"To whom?"

"To Lowe's."

I was in shock, because the Charlotte Motor Speedway meant something to me. And I thought this move was too commercial. The problem with changing the name of a speedway, particularly one like Charlotte, one of the epic speedways, is that the geographical destination is very important. People say, "I'm going to Charlotte," or, "I'm going to Indy." They continue to say that about Charlotte, but the other effect I feared would be on souvenir sales. They had bought T-shirts that said, "Charlotte." Would they buy one that said "Lowe's"? Lowe's is a wonderful company with a great reputation for outstanding management, but because of the way it was done, the sale wasn't well received.

Jim Duncan, who was vice president in charge of sales and the best in racing, never entered the picture at all. Bruton had put Marcus, his son, in charge of selling the naming rights.

Jim was incensed because he wasn't part of it—Marcus worked for him. I was also riled, and the track employees were in an absolute state of shock. They felt they had lost the Speedway. A lot of them mistakenly thought Bruton had sold it. They didn't know what to think. It had come out of the blue. I had to call a meeting of everyone at the Speedway, including the groundskeeper, to tell them we had only sold the name.

The original deal was for $1.5 million a year for 10 years.

We've lived with it. Unfortunately, during the first year of the deal we had an Indy race at the track in which three spectators were killed. Then a year later a pedestrian bridge collapsed, and a lot of people were hurt. Lowe's couldn't have been too happy about those incidents connected with its name. Looking back, I think we'd have been better off selling a race to Lowe's rather than the name itself. But Bruton wanted the money.

Money changes things, and not always for the better. The corporate people who now were spending huge dollars did not like the rough and tumble Southern image the sport had always projected. They didn't want anyone to know about the sport's roots in moonshining. They didn't want talk about Tim Flock, Curtis Turner, Bobby Allison, or anyone not currently competing. They didn't even want us playing country and western music at the tracks.

I wanted to play Flatt and Scruggs or Willie Nelson. They wanted the latest rock music. They began a campaign that, in my opinion, caused us great, great damage, including the sanitization of the drivers. They said: "Here's how you talk. Here's the way you look." The drivers started making huge sums of money, and now they began to isolate themselves in their dreaded motor homes instead of going around and shaking hands with their fans and signing autographs. It got to the point where I sarcastically said to somebody from NASCAR, "We need to change the garage area. Instead of putting the rock star busses in the rock star lots, let's back them up to the garage area fence. We need to install a submarine hatch and build a tunnel so the driver can climb down from his $2 million bus into the tunnel and come out in the garage area, and he won't have to see one fan."

I was frothing at the mouth over this. Here I'm trying to get the drivers to do things to promote the races, but what can you do with a guy who's making $10 million a year, $7 million of it guaranteed? Though I must say Jeff Gordon and a few others haven't been affected at all. What was getting me, though, was the sport was becoming so sanitized that, if there was the slightest misbehavior on the part of a driver, NASCAR came down very heavily on him. It's become like a schoolyard where at recess all the kids are allowed to do is jump up and down in one place and not move.

This all took place simultaneously, and it's had a devastating impact on ticket sales. And this was not caused by the tanking economy because in 2006 it hadn't tanked yet. Where was Jimmy Spencer carrying on when we needed him? Where was Bobby Allison going in reverse and slamming into Curtis Turner? Where was Dale Earnhardt taking someone's air and spinning him out? All of a sudden we had drivers with antiseptic voices, and Earnhardt's gone, and who's there to get his hands dirty? And all the while I kept thinking, *How am I going to sell this?*

That's not all. The most dreaded innovation of all—the aero push—which means that if you have the lead, nobody can pass you. I kept telling NASCAR officials, "Whatever we do, we have to get rid of the aero push. It's killing us." Because people buy tickets to see the leader get passed, and with the aero push, as soon as the leader gets some clean air, he's gone. This was part of the innovation for the Car of Tomorrow; its main attribute was safety.

And something else arose that should have been stopped immediately: coil binding. Coil binding makes a NASCAR race car into a go-kart. It forces the springs to come together in the corners. You keep putting softer springs into the car to make it go faster, and the springs literally rub together in the corners. To keep them from grinding off, they put these little rubber things in them called bump stops. But effectively you don't have any suspension in the corners. And this makes it very difficult for cars to pass. The Car of Tomorrow still has it, and it would have been quite easy to eliminate it, but NASCAR didn't do that.

I became very discouraged. I thought, *If the guys weren't so antiseptic, at least we could have some good racing.* But the racing began to really stink. We kept being told how great it was and how many passes there were, but the passes mainly were being made during the pit stops. Guys were winning in the worst way possible, by taking advantage of fuel mileage. Which is worse than kissing your sister.

I began to campaign to get rid of races that finished under yellow. I hated yellow flag finishes. It denied fans an ending to a race. And to NASCAR's credit, they did that and that was good, and so was new technology and new rules that brought an end to the driver fatalities that began in the late 1990s and culminated in Dale Earnhardt's death in 2001.

I was always a firm believer in the Hans device that prevents the instant death that results from a basal skull fracture. The head is thrown violently forward, and then it snaps back, and the cervical vertebrae and spinal cord snap, and that's it. It's what killed Kenny Irwin, Adam Petty, Clifford Allison, and Dale Earnhardt.

Even after Dale died, NASCAR wouldn't mandate the use of the Hans device. A lot of drivers complained that it was uncomfortable. They weren't used to it. At Charlotte we had an Automobile Racing Club of America (ARCA) race, and there was a tremendous battle between Blaise Alexander and Kerry Earnhardt. They fought coming off the fourth turn, and they both lost it, and Blaise went into the wall at that horrific thirty-degree angle full tilt, and he was killed instantly by a basal fracture. I went over to the hospital to talk with his parents, and in the press I let NASCAR have it.

"It's time that NASCAR mandated the Hans device," I said. "It is absolutely essential that it be mandated." The press jumped all over the issue, and a couple days later NASCAR mandated it, and since then we have not lost a single Cup driver. As a matter of fact, among Cup racing, the Nationwide series, and the trucks, we have only had a couple of drivers even go to the hospital. NASCAR did a great job with safety, though what was suffering was what was happening on the track.

I began to campaign about something called the "repass." I made up the term. I began keeping records of each race, adding up how many times a leader is run down, passed, and then re-passes within twenty laps.

We had races where that didn't even happen once. For most races it was a very low number, and seeing cars pass each other is why people buy tickets.

Another reason you don't see much passing for the lead at the end of a race is the points system. A racer who is running in second place at a tough track like Darlington or Charlotte may have a car that is slightly faster than the lead car, but does he want to risk losing his second-place points by challenging the leader and risking a crash? Most guys won't risk it, or else they make a half-assed attempt as if to say, "I tried but I didn't make it." Unlike Curtis Turner who would have quit before settling for points. Curtis preferred to try for the win and crash if it happened that way.

Today everyone wants to finish in the Top Ten. You see after a race the TV commentators interview the top five guys, starting with number five, and he'll gush, "I had a great points day. We finished fifth." Smokey Yunick would have beaten him to a pulp.

My critics say to me, "If you reward drivers for passing and re-passing, then drivers from the same race team will get together and make passes just to earn points." My answer is, "Great. At least the fans in the grandstands will see some action."

BUT WHAT'S HAPPENING with all this corporatization setting policy is we have a lot of young people who got into this business who weren't brought up in racing. A lot of this has come about because of a strange group of people with business degrees who are making decisions without knowing the essence of what we do. They never had an opportunity to work at a short track and they don't understand the essence of what brings people to the track. Plus a lot of them are highly educated, went to really good schools, and have led cloistered lives. They don't get to know the common person, and that's who's coming through the gates or turning on the TV. You can't just go into the RV lot for an hour.

To these people, winning isn't nearly as important as how many minutes a sponsor's car is seen on television. The sponsors have evolved into Joyce

Julius watchers. Joyce Julius is a company out of Chicago that issues a report every Tuesday on the time and exposure that the sponsors get at the racetrack that weekend. It's the most-read document in racing, and somebody at Lowe's or Home Depot is always poised to look at the report to see if they got their $600,000 of TV time during the race. It doesn't matter who's driving their cars. To them, drivers are helmet carriers. All they want is their car up front so their logos appear on TV.

"Why don't we eliminate sponsors from cars?" I asked. "Have nothing commercial on a car, like the other sports."

"How does a car owner afford to race?" is the reply.

"You triple and quadruple the purses, and instead of the track paying $8 million, it pays $20 million. Then the driver has to drive to win because how he finishes determines how he makes a living. We would put bonus money on passing, so if he has a good day and wrecks at the end, he still makes a lot of money."

I doubt NASCAR will ever do this, but racing's at the point where drastic moves have to be made to bring back the fans.

I kept pushing NASCAR for double file restarts. They finally did it. It has helped.

CHAPTER 30

Good-Bye

THE RELATIONSHIP BETWEEN Bruton and me deteriorated during our last five years together. Bruton became much more secretive, and he began doing things without bothering to talk to me first. I was the president of the company. I felt he owed me that. He had brought his son, Marcus, into the company, and it would not be too long before Marcus knew about the important decisions while I was being kept in the dark.

I had a decent office. It was perfectly acceptable. Behind it was an area I was going to use for the expansion of the Speedway Club, called the Roof Area. One day I encountered a strange man walking around up there, and I asked what he was doing. He said, "I'm working on plans. We're building offices out there."

"Who told you we were going to build offices out here?" I asked.

"Well, Bruton Smith did."

I immediately jumped in my car and drove over to Bruton's office at his car dealership at Town and Country. I wanted to know, "Why are we talking about building offices? What kind of offices? We have enough offices. We have office space we haven't even rented yet."

"Well, we need offices," he said. "We're not selling enough advertising."

"Wait a minute," I said. "We've gone from $500,000 in sales to $54 million in sales. We sell more advertising than any other speedway in the world."

"We need better sales offices," he said.

I said, "How can I run this place if you don't tell me what's going on? Who's going to be in these offices?"

He refused to tell me. But I still had the job of paying the bills. And I felt I owed it to the stockholders to keep costs down. The bills for the new offices kept coming in, until I finally learned that they were going to cost $5.5 million. One day, I got a bill for a television in the lobby that cost $38,000. I called Bruton.

"Why do we need a $38,000 TV?" I wanted to know.

"You don't have to let anybody know about it," he said.

"The floor where we work is twenty years old," I said. "This is where everybody works. The carpet is threadbare, and the walls need painting."

He didn't answer me. And then later I found out who these offices were for—his son Marcus, who was working for me but who eventually would take my job. It was Marcus—a very nice person who did a good job while working for me—who was making the decisions on this expansion.

One day the architect walked over to me and said, "Our firm has just broken a record. We have spent more per square foot for these offices than any office we have ever designed."

I looked at him and I said, "Do you know what that makes me want to do? I want to throw up on your shoes." He backed away. He didn't understand at all. He was so proud of all that marble he had put down. Those offices make the excesses of Wall Street look paltry.

BUT WHAT REALLY ENDED IT for me was the construction of the drag strip at the Speedway. In my early days I had worked part-time in drag racing. I was never interested in promoting drag tracks because it's very difficult to make any money in that you have to give the National Hot Rod Association (NHRA) fifty percent of your net profits. Plus they contract the events, so you are putting on an event you don't even control.

At the time I was putting in a much-needed campground for the race fans who were parked in the infield during race week. I was about halfway along its construction when I was told the plans had been canceled by Bruton.

Bruton was in the Speedway Club, and I ran over to find out what in the world was going on. He was sitting with Wes Harris, who worked in construction, and Wes said to me, "This campground is costing too much money."

"I've gotten the cost way down," I said.

Bruton said, "It's been canceled."

"You can't do that," I said. "I've already sold spaces."

"We canceled it," Bruton repeated.

I was really, really ticked off. I went back upstairs only to have somebody walk into my office and tell me, "The reason they canceled the campground is that they are going to build a drag strip over there." I hit the ceiling.

By this time Bruton had returned to his car dealership at Town and Country, and so I got in my car and drove over to confront him.

"How the hell can you build a drag strip at Lowe's Motor Speedway and not tell me."

"Well, this is going to be a great drag strip," he said.

"Bruton, you can't make any money with a drag strip," I said. I had done the research. Las Vegas made about $1.5 million, and Bristol made chump change. No one else made a dime. The return on investment was lousy.

"Aw, you can," Bruton said.

I told him what I knew. I said, "If you spend $50 million to build a drag strip, and we make $1.5 million a year, that's not even a 2 percent return on investment. That's just crazy."

"You have the wrong financial information," he said.

"I do not," I said. "It came straight from accounting."

What was going on was that the NHRA was in financial trouble, and they were coming to Bruton to be its savior. Bruton was eating up the attention they were giving him, wining and dining him, doing everything they could to get him to do what they wanted. They really showered him with compliments. And the reason he didn't tell me about the drag strip was that he knew I'd be against it.

I said, "Bruton, do you realize that this drag strip you want to put down is only 1,500 yards from a subdivision? It's right next to the biggest hotel in Concord. We have a school down the street. The noise alone is going to blow the lid off this thing." The Pomona drag strip is so noisy the town will only let it run once a year.

"Don't worry," Bruton said, "They can't do anything to us." Years earlier I had set the Speedway up as a sports district so we could sell alcohol at the Speedway Club. As a sports district, we could also do a number of other things you otherwise couldn't have done because of the zoning laws. Bruton was figuring the sports district designation would allow him to put his drag strip near a subdivision. I was equally certain he was wrong about that.

Bruton began building the drag strip without first informing the Concord City Council. This is typical of what he does, and as soon as the council heard about it, they called him in for a meeting.

These guys were friends of mine. One of the things I did as president of the Speedway was spend a lot of time making nice with the local politicians. I had a great relationship with them. Bruton didn't even ask me to come to the meeting. The council asked Bruton to do a sound survey, and when he didn't do it, they turned him down. He continued to build the drag strip anyway, so the council came down on him hard, and when they did, he threatened to abandon the Speedway and move to another location in another part of North Carolina. He told them, "I'm tired of this. I never get any cooperation from the city or county."

That wasn't true. We got *loads* of cooperation from them. This time they just didn't want to do what he wanted them to do. So he announced he was going to move, like he could get a great big trailer hitch and move a thousand acres of land somewhere else.

His announcement caused a panic. The area had just lost Philip Morris, and Cannon Mills had just gone down the tubes. Bruton did not inform me he was going to threaten the city with his moving the track. The next morning I read the huge headlines in the Charlotte paper. I called him and said, "What the hell are you doing?"

"I'm tired of fooling with these guys," he said.

"How could you do this?" I asked. "Where could you go? How much would it cost?"

After the initial report, one of the counties near Charlotte contacted Bruton and said they would donate the land to build a new speedway. That brought an immediate reaction from The Charlotte Regional Partnership, a quasi-governmental entity representing sixteen counties in the state of North Carolina. It's funded by a mix of government and private money. I happened to have been the vice chairman of the group and the incoming chairman, and without asking me, this organization issued an edict that ordered all sixteen counties not to get involved with a new track. As a result, the county that made the initial offer pulled back, so now where was Bruton going to go?

Bruton then announced he had an offer from South Carolina down in the Lancaster area to give him $80 million worth of assistance if he would leave the Speedway in Charlotte and move to Rock Hill, South Carolina.

The proposed spot was way south of the city, and we had talked many times about the mistake of ever building a track south of a major urban area because that means the race fans have to drive through the city to get to the track. I was livid.

After Bruton made his announcement about an offer from South Carolina, the state came back and denied that it was going to give him any money. Cabarrus County and the city of Concord came back and he said they would give him $80 million, but Bruton thought they were going to give it to him within three years. They since have said, "not three years, but only when you spend enough money at the Speedway to increase the property tax to the point where that increase in property tax will be reimbursed to you." If he builds a new grandstand, and it costs $20 million, his taxes will go up about $600,000 a year, and the state would forgive his tax obligation. What this means is that Bruton won't get his money back for 40 years. They turned the tables on him, and he's not happy about it. He sued them in county covet, which means the very people he sued will be on the jury. Smart?

While all this was going on, I went to Italy for two weeks, because I was sick and tired of hearing about it. While there, I decided it was time for me to leave the Speedway, especially after I found out that Bruton's son Marcus was making more money than I was.

I went to the board, which was controlled by Bruton, and I said, "If you want me to stay, you're going to have to do something about my salary." They refused.

In April 2008 I sat down with Bruton and told him I was going to leave. I said, "I'll be glad to do the honorable thing. The fiftieth anniversary is coming up in May, and I will stay through the race or you can kick me up to vice chairman and make it part time, and I'll stay around and help Marcus because I know you want to move him up. He'll have someone to talk to."

The week of the All Star race, I got a fax from Bruton saying he was going to announce I was retiring the Wednesday after the 600. I said to him, "You want me to just leave right after the race is over—to vacate my office and you're not going to give me any severance pay after I worked here for thirty-three years?"

"You got a retirement package," he said.

That had been something I had put together myself back in 1990. It had nothing to do with severance, I told him.

"We're too small a company for me to do that," he said.

The next day Bruton announced he was buying the Kentucky track. He did that without ever saying one word to me. It had gotten to the point where, even though this was a New York Stock Exchange company, and he was responsible to the stockholders, he was treating it like it was a private company.

He had me in a box, so I decided to hold my own press conference and announce my retirement. I tried to take the high road at the press conference, and I couldn't help but let someone know it wasn't all on my terms. That leaked out, but I've kept the rest quiet until now.

Working for him was a one-way street. It was not the money. It was a lack of respect he has for all people.

I had had enough. He only knows one way . . . his.

CHAPTER 31

Racing of the Future

WE ARE GOING TO SEE some massive changes in NASCAR in the next decade and beyond. Right now the two controlling companies are the International Speedway Corporation, owned by the France family, and Speedway Motor Sports, owned by Bruton Smith. Jim France recently announced his retirement, leaving the business to a third generation of Frances, and Bruton is eighty-two, and eventually he will be leaving his company to his son. The Indianapolis Racing League is itself in a third generation of ownership.

What I envision is a time in the not-too-distant future when major media companies or equity investors buy all the existing companies. When that happens, we will see majestic changes in racing, because it will then be fueled by the people who run entertainment companies who don't patiently wait around when ratings start to drop and attendance falls. They make changes. That's why Westerns went south and adventure/action films became popular. It's why sitcoms have lessened and reality TV has upstaged them. Once media companies take over, the executives won't abide boring races. They won't stand for drivers who are satisfied with finishing seventh in order to win points.

Instead, the entertainment czars will change the game so that the emphasis is placed on passing. Drivers will get a lot of points and prize money for passing and re-passing, so if a driver puts on a good show—even if he is knocked out at the halfway point—he will earn enough money to make his day worthwhile. No longer will he be thinking, "I have to be around at the finish so I can finish fourth" and not excite anybody.

Another thing the entertainment people will do is take the lid off the behavior of drivers. Fans love fiery drivers. They screamed and hollered when a Bobby Allison would get mad at a Curtis Turner and wipe out his car. They loved it when Dale Earnhardt would spin out a competitor, and then, when asked about it after the race, he'd grin and say, "That's just racin.'"

That sort of thing never happens anymore because the sponsors want their drivers to be squeaky clean and corporate. They have to be properly dressed, and they have to speak properly, and they have to behave themselves, and boy, that is so boring. We need a return of the Bobby Allison–Darrell Waltrip, Dale Earnhardt–Geoff Bodine feuds that we used to have.

One area where we have to get better in all motor sports in America is to take racing from its rural, small-town roots and bring it to the big markets. Will New York City ever embrace auto racing? That's going to be tomorrow's challenge, and that's why the entertainment gurus are going to go after it in a major way. That also means more diversity. People in New York City would pay a lot more attention to racing if there were a driver from New York City. Ideally a former Brooklyn cab driver whose father came from the Ukraine. Or if there were a black driver. That there hasn't been one in the sport since Wendell Scott is indefensible. And in Los Angeles, where the Fontana track is having a difficult time, how are you going to sell tickets in Southern California where fifty percent of the population is Hispanic if you don't have a Hispanic driver? As America's population continues to mix, to get to the next level, racing—which started out as a Scotch-Irish, mountain-based culture—is going to have to become much more diverse.

ANOTHER CHANGE THE NEW MONEY coming in will bring will be an emphasis on comfort at the track. Too many people stay home because the creative TV people, led by David Hill of Fox, have gotten so good at broadcasting races. We have to treat race fans who come to the track the way movie theater operators treat their customers. That means the tracks will reduce the number of seats, and each seat will be wider and more comfortable.

The track operators are also going to do something about the weather. It will no longer be acceptable to have a race called because of rain. The grand-stands and racing surfaces will be covered with hyperlon, a strong nylon-type fabric like what you see at the Denver Airport. It's used in Europe more than it is in the United States, and as the price continues to come down, we will see it used. And in places where covering the racing surface is impractical, we will just race out in the rain like Formula 1 does. The tire companies will provide the right tires, and the cars will have a film on the windshield to knock off the water.

In short, the fan of tomorrow will be in for a much more pleasant experience than today; the same way today is a hundred percent better than it was twenty-five years ago. Not only will the fan have a wider seat, but the fan will be totally involved in what's going on at the race because he'll have a little TV at his seat, and he'll be able to watch the replays the same as he does at home. There will also, of course, be huge screens at the track for views of replays.

Another dramatic change will be the way people get to the races. You'll see high-speed rail service and express bus lanes. Driving your car and sitting in traffic for hours is barbaric, and everyone in the racing business knows it. As good as TV is, race fans are not going to put up with it for much longer, so a lot of emphasis will be put on that.

It's also possible that the format may change. A 500-mile or 600-mile race is very long, and sometimes it runs without any interruptions. There is no seventh inning stretch or halftime.

Right now the people who run the sport don't want change, but I can foresee a time when racing moves toward shorter races, and that will be one change for the better. I remember when Rockingham went from 500 to 400 miles, and the entertainment value went up a 100 percent. Maybe some of the races will be run like the All Star race. As I said, once the entertainment people take over, they will stop at nothing to make the sport more interesting and more dramatic.

There's a new generation of young fans coming in whose childhoods are filled by playing video games. I remember the time I invited a man and his seven-year-old son to an Indy race at the Lowe's Motor Speedway. They had never been to a race, and when they finally arrived, they had missed the drivers' introductions and the start of the race. About twenty laps after they arrived, one of the cars hit the wall and slid down the front of the main grandstand. After a while the driver got out of the car, raised his hands, and everyone cheered. The little boy looked up at his daddy and said, "Hey, a man got out of that car." That's the world the seven-year-old kids live in. He's in a game world where there aren't any real people. Or, if there are people, they are automated. I suspect he thought there were people up on the roof operating those cars by remote control.

But the truth is, we really don't need drivers at all. I wanted to test a new bumper I was inventing to see if it would prevent the whiplash deaths suffered by Dale Earnhardt, Clifford Allison, Adam Petty, and so many others. To test it properly, the car had to reach a speed of 170 miles an hour before it slammed into the wall at a 25-degree angle—at the time that equaled a lethal hit. How do you find a driver to test the device? It's like asking someone to test an electric chair. Nobody would be crazy enough to do that, so I asked the mechanical expert, Paul Lew, who was conducting the test, if we could do it without a driver. He said, "Let's go down to Radio Shack," and for $3,000-worth of equipment, he was able to race the car at the applicable speed and force by remote control, and we were able to successfully complete the test.

So I discovered racing without drivers is certainly feasible, and afterward when I'd get upset with a driver, I'd jokingly say to him, "We can replace you for $3,000."

Yet another change I envision is that NASCAR will no longer be a purely American sport. We will be going to Europe, Malaysia, Beijing, Japan, Australia, and Dubai, because the next increase in revenue has got to come from global television. That's what makes World Cup Soccer so huge. Every country in the world embraces it. So we will have a schedule of twenty-five international super races, including the Daytona 500, the World 600, and a race at Talladega and at Indianapolis. But many of the races will be overseas. This also means a change in car companies as Mercedes, BMW, Honda, and a lot of other brands come into NASCAR. Drivers will be international as well, and that's when Formula 1 racing really will be challenged in a major way.

You will also see a second series, run on weekends, called the National series. It will be more like the current Sprint Cup racing. So Charlotte may have one international race and the second race may be a national race. Right now there are Formula 1 races in Beijing, Malaysia, and Japan, and this would give those tracks a second major moneymaker that would help them tremendously.

THE SINGLE BIGGEST CHANGE, though, will affect the race fan sitting on his couch at home. The fan of tomorrow watching from home will actually be able to participate in the race.

He will pay the entry fee of $29.95 for pay-per-view. He'll sit in his seat with his computerized steering wheel, brake, and clutch—equipment that is available today—and he will watch himself on the TV actually driving in the race.

All the race cars are equipped with GPS, and as a result it would be possible to transform the existing live telecast into a situation where the fan at home could drive his car on the track anywhere the real cars weren't. The fan's car would be animated. He couldn't put his car where Jeff Gordon Jr.'s car is, but he could put his car right behind him if there was a space. Come Saturday evening or Sunday afternoon, hundreds of thousands of race fans could pay their $29.95 entry fee and race against the real race cars. Once the computer geniuses figure out how to do determine the virtual winner, there would be two winners at the end of the race: the actual winner at the track and the virtual winner, and conceivably, the virtual winner would make as much prize money and earn the same trophy as the actual winner.

As I said, once the computer geniuses figure out the technology, this will come, and it will come because racing is one of the only sports where individuals compete against other individuals rather than teams competing against teams. Hundreds of thousands of race fans will do what many of them already do—practice driving on the real tracks with their computers. So conceivably Jeff Gordon Jr. might win the real Daytona 500 in 2025, and Joe Osborne from North Platte might be the virtual winner, and the next day Joe Osborne will be flown to Daytona to meet Jeff Gordon Jr. and be handed the same check and trophy as Gordon.

It's going to take a while, but change is inevitable in everything. The changes will be big. We'll have to go through tough times to get there, and there will be a great upheaval and a great gnashing of teeth. But that's what comes with change. There will be glamour and pizzazz like we have never seen before, and the racing will become more exciting. I look forward to seeing you at the track as those magic words are intoned, "Gentlemen, start your engines."

Index